The
Jekyll and Hyde
Syndrome

Also by Beverly Engel

Loving Him without Losing You: How to Stop
Disappearing and Start Being Yourself

The Power of Apology: Healing Steps to Transform
All Your Relationships

The Emotionally Abusive Relationship: How to Stop
Being Abused and How to Stop Abusing

Honor Your Anger: How Transforming Your Anger Style
Can Change Your Life

Breaking the Cycle of Abuse: How to Move beyond Your
Past to Create an Abuse-Free Future

Healing Your Emotional Self: A Powerful Program to Help
You Raise Your Self-Esteem, Quiet Your Inner Critic, and
Overcome Your Shame

The
Jekyll and Hyde
Syndrome

*What to Do If Someone in Your Life
Has a Dual Personality—or If You Do*

BEVERLY ENGEL

BICENTENNIAL
1807
⊕WILEY
2007
BICENTENNIAL

John Wiley & Sons, Inc.

Published by John Wiley & Sons, Inc., Hoboken, New Jersey
Published simultaneously in Canada

Wiley Bicentennial Logo: Richard J. Pacifico

Design and composition by Navta Associates, Inc.

Medical disclaimer: The information contained in this book is not intended to serve as a replacement for professional medical advice. Any use of the information in this book is at the reader's discretion. The author and the publisher specifically disclaim any and all liability arising directly or indirectly from the use or application of any information contained in this book. A health care professional should be consulted regarding your specific situation.

For general information about our other products and services, please contact our Customer Care Department within the United States at (800) 762-2974, outside the United States at (317) 572-3993 or fax (317) 572-4002.

Wiley also publishes its books in a variety of electronic formats. Some content that appears in print may not be available in electronic books. For more information about Wiley products, visit our web site at www.wiley.com.

Library of Congress Cataloging-in-Publication Data:

Engel, Beverly.
   The Jekyll and Hyde syndrome : what to do if someone in your life has a dual personality—or if you do / Beverly Engel.
        p. cm.
   Includes bibliographical references and index.
   ISBN 978-0-470-04224-3 (cloth)
   1.   Multiple personality—Popular works. 2.   Personality disorders—Popular works. 3.   Self-help, Health.   I. Title.
   RC569.5.M8.E54 2007
   616.85'236—dc22

                                                                        2006025165

Printed in the United States of America

10 9 8 7 6 5 4 3 2 1

This book is dedicated to all who care about someone who is a Jekyll and Hyde and all who suffer from the syndrome. May you find help and encouragement in the information and the stories shared here.

Contents

viii   Contents

Acknowledgments

My deepest gratitude goes to my wonderful agents, Stedman Mays and Mary Tahan. Thank you both for working so hard on my behalf. I am also grateful to Tom Miller, my editor at Wiley, for being excited about this project from the beginning.

I am deeply appreciative of the people who agreed to be interviewed for this book. I learned a great deal from your stories, and I realize that it took tremendous courage for you to share them with me.

My heartfelt gratitude goes to my psychotherapy clients. You teach me more each day.

I wish to thank Connie Zweig and Jeremiah Abrams for their wonderful book *Meeting the Shadow: The Hidden Power of the Dark Side of Human Nature*. It must have been no small feat to bring together so many experts on the Shadow and combine their articles to form such a remarkable book.

Of course, this book could not have been written without the short story by Robert Louis Stevenson or the work of Carl Jung. I am deeply indebted to both of them.

Introduction

More than a decade before Freud delved into the depths of the human psyche, Robert Louis Stevenson had an extremely revealing dream. In it, a man was being pursued for a crime. He swallowed a powder and underwent a drastic change of character, so drastic that he was unrecognizable. The man, a kind, hardworking scientist named Dr. Jekyll, was transformed into the violent and relentless Mr. Hyde, whose evil took on greater and greater proportions as the dream unfolded.

Stevenson developed the dream into the now famous tale *The Strange Case of Dr. Jekyll and Mr. Hyde* in 1886. Its theme has become so much a part of popular culture that we often refer to someone who is exhibiting erratic behavior as a "real Dr. Jekyll and Mr. Hyde." People have been fascinated with the Jekyll and Hyde phenomenon for more than a hundred years now, starting with the popularity of the Robert Louis Stevenson story. When a story like this touches so many people in such a profound way, it must speak to a place in us that is universal and instinctive.

We've all had the experience of being surprised by our mood shifts or shocked by the words that suddenly come out of our mouths. Many of us have been alarmed that we are capable of becoming angry, unreasonable people we barely recognize. The truth is, we all have the capacity to act in ways that are radically different from how we normally behave, some people more than others. No one is all good or all bad. The difference is that some of us are able to contain or keep down the so-called bad sides of ourselves and others are not.

While each of us does contain both a Dr. Jekyll and a Mr. Hyde personality—a more pleasant persona for everyday wear and a hiding, nighttime self that remains quiet most of the time—there are people who live out their lives in these extremes. Loving and kind one moment and angry and punishing the next, these people bewilder, hurt, and anger those who are close to them.

Although the phrase "Jekyll and Hyde" is commonly used in our culture, few people really understand much about the type of personality that changes so radically for no apparent reason. This is the first self-help book to explain in detail the various causes of this syndrome, how it is manifested, and the damage it can inflict on those who are close to such a person.

Who Will Be Interested in This Book

This book will interest many people for different reasons. We each have a dark side, a part of us that we keep hidden from others and often from ourselves. While some of us are better than others at managing our dark sides, there are far more people suffering from the Jekyll and Hyde syndrome than one might suspect. When we look at the causes of the syndrome, we can understand how the numbers can add up. For example, many people who suffer from the Jekyll and Hyde syndrome have a history of child abuse and neglect. More than 3 million cases of child abuse were reported in 1997, according to the National Committee to Prevent Child Abuse and the National Center on Child Abuse and Neglect. Add to this the fact that an estimated one in thirteen adults in the United States has grown up with overly controlling parents—another major factor in creating a Jekyll and Hyde personality—and the numbers increase tremendously. Many people with this syndrome suffer from either borderline personality disorder (BPD) or narcissistic personality disorder (NPD). When we add the numbers of people who suffer from BPD (between 10 and 20 million Americans) and NPD (an estimated 5 million Americans), we can see that the numbers are substantial.

Readers will learn how to deal with people in their lives (including lovers, family members, bosses, and friends) who behave in radically different ways. Others who are troubled by their own radical mood shifts, bizarre behavior, and conflicting personalities will learn why these things occur and how to begin to integrate their personalities.

There is another important aspect to this book. Oftentimes, the Jekyll and Hyde syndrome becomes a form of emotional abuse. In fact, most emotional abusers exhibit some form of the Jekyll and Hyde syndrome. Emotional abuse has taken the place of sexual abuse and domestic violence as the most talked about form of abuse, both in the media and in recovery circles. Perhaps this is because in many ways it is the last frontier in terms of facing how abuse permeates and shapes our culture. As I did in *The Emotionally Abusive Relationship*, in this book I provide concrete strategies for change, whether the reader is an emotional abuser or a victim of someone who is emotionally abusive.

Although this is primarily a self-help book, it also provides an in-depth exploration of the duality within us all. Important information about Carl Jung's concept of the human Shadow is provided for readers to gain a deeper understanding of their own Jekyll and Hyde tendencies, as well as guidance on how they can learn to embrace their dark sides instead of partitioning them off into separate parts of themselves.

In addition to appealing to those who are involved with a Jekyll and Hyde and those who suffer from the syndrome themselves, the book will interest those who are fascinated by people who exhibit the Jekyll and Hyde syndrome. For example, two years ago the nation became obsessed with the Scott Peterson case—the story of how a seemingly good husband and all-around nice guy was revealed to be an unfaithful playboy and, even worse, the murderer of his wife and unborn child. People who were close to Scott were shocked to discover that he had created a double life for himself. He was a doting husband, on the one hand, and a man who had numerous affairs, on the other; a man who was seemingly happy that his wife was having a baby and at the same time a man who shared with others that he did not want to have a child.

The truth is, there are many people like Scott Peterson who live double lives. Many seemingly exceptional human beings—people who are often kind, giving, and dedicated to helping others— also have dark sides, hidden from their families and friends. In 2006, we learned of two more cases of Jekyll and Hyde behavior: Congressman Mark Foley and Reverend Ted Haggard. Underneath the perfect public persona often lies someone who is the opposite— cruel, selfish, and hurtful to others. Now and then, one of these dual personalities gets exposed, and we are always shocked and fascinated to realize they live within our midst.

People want to know how a church leader, a boy scout leader, and an upstanding citizen could also be the BTK serial killer. They want to know whether Michael Jackson is really as sweet, innocent, and childlike as he appears or whether he is hiding a far more sinister dark side capable of manipulating and molesting children. This book will explain to the lay person why certain people are prime candidates for developing dual personalities and how these people are able to get away with atrocious acts of violence or betrayal because their good sides are so charming, lovable, or upstanding.

When cases like those of Scott Peterson, the BTK killer, and Michael Jackson emerge, we are plagued with questions:

- How do people like this fool so many people?

- Why is it that people such as ministers, doctors, and teachers who do so much good in the world are often the ones who shock us the most with their capacity to harm others?

- Is there such a thing as having a split personality that causes a person to behave in these radically opposite ways?

In *The Jekyll and Hyde Syndrome: What to Do If Someone in Your Life Has a Dual Personality—or If You Do*, readers will get answers to these questions.

In summary, this book explains in detail why certain people seem to have two strong sides to their personalities—so much so that they seem like two distinct people. I provide questionnaires to help readers determine whether they are in a relationship with a Jekyll and Hyde or whether they themselves suffer from this syndrome. I will help readers who suffer from this syndrome to integrate their personalities and those who are in a relationship with such a person to determine whether there is hope for the relationship, whether they and their children are safe with such a person, and whether they should continue the relationship or not.

PART I

Understanding the Jekyll and Hyde Syndrome

1

What Is the Jekyll and Hyde Syndrome?

When she was good
She was very, very good,
But when she was bad she was horrid.
    —Henry Wadsworth Longfellow

We all experience mood shifts from time to time. We are all multifaceted people who show different sides of ourselves depending on the circumstances and whom we associate with. And we are all sometimes shocked by our own actions or by the words that come out of our mouths. Yet there are some people whose mood shifts are far from normal, people who experience radical changes in their moods or violent outbursts for no apparent reason—people who become enraged, abusive, violent, depressed, or sullen at the drop of a hat. Some not only show different sides of themselves depending on the situation, but they are capable of creating double lives or entirely different personalities—personalities that would be unrecognizable to people who know them in other contexts.

These people suffer from what I call the Jekyll and Hyde syndrome. Someone with the Jekyll and Hyde syndrome seems at times to be two different people. Many people with this syndrome experience radical mood swings, often for no apparent reason. They can seem happy or normal one minute and the next become deeply depressed, angry, critical, or afraid. Often, this involves suddenly getting angry with those who are closest to them. They may fly into a rage and accuse their partners or children of doing something to hurt them when the other people are totally innocent. Or they may suddenly become critical, finding fault with their loved ones, their coworkers, or anyone who is in close proximity.

This is how my client Leslie described her husband's behavior: "You'll never meet a kinder man than my husband. He is so generous and loving. He has dozens of friends who adore him. And most of the time he is wonderful to me. But every once in a while something sets him off and he becomes this horrible man who says terribly cruel things to me. He'll berate me for the smallest things and insist that I don't love him, that I'm a terrible wife, that he deserves to be with someone who will treat him better. For years I took his complaints seriously and tried to change the things about myself that he didn't like. But no matter how much I changed, he just kept finding things to complain about. I'm beginning to think that I really have nothing to do with his moods."

Often, the people who experience these radical mood shifts don't seem to be aware that they have changed. Leslie continued: "The scary thing is that when he switches back to his normal self, he often can't even remember the cruel things he's said to me. When I tell him about how he has talked to me, he insists it can't be true. That's why I've come to realize that it really isn't me—it's him."

Instead of getting angry and lashing out at those closest to them, some Jekyll and Hydes suddenly become withdrawn, depressed, or sullen, as was the case with my client Andrew's wife. "You never know when Sheila's mood will change and she will become withdrawn," Andrew said. "Sometimes she wakes up that way; other times, she'll come home from work that way. I'll ask her what is wrong, and she insists that there is nothing going on. But you'd have to be blind not to see that something is bothering her. She barely talks to me or the kids, and she ends up going to bed and staying there for hours, even days sometimes. Then the mood just seems to pass and she's her old self again. She refuses to talk about what happened and gets angry with me if I try to push her. I've learned to just try to ignore it, but it's hard on us. I just never know when I'm going to lose my wife and the kids will lose their mother for several hours or even days. And I feel bad for her—there's no telling what kind of emotional torture she's going through."

Two Faces

Sometimes a Jekyll and Hyde's duality shows up in the fact that the person acts radically different depending on whom he or she is around or often on whether he or she is in a public place or some-place private. Many of them show one face to their friends and the public while showing another to their partners or families. For example, Carl is a mild-mannered project manager for a multi-million dollar corporation. His boss is a tyrant who insists on Carl always completing his projects perfectly and on time—even when Carl hasn't been given adequate lead time. If Carl's boss finds one mistake or isn't completely impressed with Carl's performance, he humiliates Carl in front of his coworkers. Carl is too intimidated by his boss to confront him and too afraid he'll get a bad review and not be able to find another job if he were to quit. So Carl takes his frustrations out on his wife and children. At home with his family, Carl is an entirely different person. At home he is the tyrant.

The moment Carl walks in the door, his children are supposed to drop whatever they are doing to come to greet him and report to him whether they have completed their chores. He then follows each child around the house or the yard, inspecting the area to make sure the job was done right. If a chore is not completed to his satisfaction, he insists that the child go back and work on it until the job is done just right. After finishing their chores, the children must sit down with Carl and show him their completed homework. Carl is a stickler for perfection and often browbeats a child for getting something wrong. Dinner will be held up for the entire family until all of the children have completed their homework to their father's satisfaction.

While many Jekyll and Hydes tend to be abusive when they switch over into another personality, others act out dark urges that are completely uncharacteristic of them. For example, Reverend Thomas Henderson is a highly respected minister in a conservative church that counsels against drinking alcohol, sex outside of marriage, dancing, and gambling. Although he fervently believes in the church and its teachings, Reverend Henderson experiences intense fantasies and desires that he cannot seem to control. He is such a charismatic speaker and is so highly regarded that he is asked to be the guest minister at various churches around the United States. Unfortunately, traveling to a strange city affords Reverend Henderson an opportunity to act out his darker urges. As much as he tries to resist, he is too weak to fight them.

While he is away, Reverend Henderson takes on another persona—that of a loud, boisterous man who goes to bars, drinks, dances, and flirts with women. If people in his congregation were to run into him, they would barely recognize him. Other than his physical features being the same, everything else about Reverend Henderson is different. Gone is his respectful, quiet demeanor and in its place is a vociferous, crude attitude. He even dresses differently. In the place of his conservative suit is a tight T-shirt and jeans. At the end of each evening, Reverend Henderson takes a new woman back to his hotel room for sex.

The Strange Case of Dr. Jekyll and Mr. Hyde

The Jekyll and Hyde syndrome is named after the classic Robert Louis Stevenson story *The Strange Case of Dr. Jekyll and Mr. Hyde*. The story is about a man not too different from Reverend Henderson—an upstanding, tee-totaling, philanthropic doctor who turns into a womanizing, drinking, murderous scoundrel, seemingly overnight. In addition to this being an engaging tale, it is also much more. It is a metaphor for a phenomenon that is all too common—the fact that so-called good people often have a dark side, a part of themselves they keep hidden from themselves and others. In some cases, this dark side actually forms a distinct personality radically different from the public persona, as was the case with Reverend Henderson. Ironically, it is often people who stand out as the most moral, the most kind, and the most magnanimous who are most likely to fall. It is, in fact, a rule of nature that the higher up on a pedestal we put ourselves or allow others to put us, the farther we have to fall.

For those of you who haven't read this story (and for anyone who read it a long time ago), here is the basic plot: Dr. Jekyll worried a little too much about how others perceived him. He had an investment in being viewed by others as a pillar of the community, but secretly he had the desire to act out some of his darker urges. And so he concocted a brew that would allow him to venture into the dark side of human nature, experience its forbidden pleasures, and then return to his more acceptable self, seemingly unscathed. Most important, he didn't have to take responsibility for what his darker self did during his excursions.

While many people with the Jekyll and Hyde syndrome are like the original Dr. Jekyll who completed his transformation in the darkness of night, with no one else witnessing his change, other Jekyll and Hydes change their personalities or experience their mood shifts in front of others. For example, a normally pleasant, amiable man can suddenly turn into an insulting, abusive monster, devastating his wife with his sharp criticism of her, going on a rampage and destroying property, or even becoming physically violent toward his family. A typically doting mother can suddenly burst into a rage, calling her children horrible names, throwing objects across the room, and even driving off without them to teach them a lesson.

Jennifer devotes her life to her husband and children. She is a stay-at-home mom who is usually patient and loving with her children, four-year-old Erin and six-year-old Josh. Yet sometimes, for no apparent reason, Jennifer becomes impatient and critical of her kids and husband. Nothing they do will please her. It's as if she is looking at them through different eyes. The qualities she complimented them on days earlier seem to have completely slipped her mind, and all she can see are their faults. "It's all or nothing with my wife," her husband, Bill, told me when, out of desperation, he came to me for help. "You're either the greatest person she ever met or the worst. When she puts you in the 'bad' box, there is nothing you can do to make her like you. I've learned to just lay low and wait for her to put me in the 'good' box soon. But I don't want my kids to have to grow up this way."

How the Jekyll and Hyde Syndrome Differs from Normal Mood Shifts

Those with the Jekyll and Hyde syndrome do not simply experience normal moods shifts and show different sides of themselves the way average people do. What sets people with a Jekyll and Hyde syndrome apart is:

- The fact that their mood shifts are far more frequent and severe than the average person's.

- In many cases, not only do their moods shift but their entire personalities change.

- Often, their sudden mood shifts include an element of abusiveness toward others.

- They seldom own up to or admit to their severe mood shifts or their dual personalities. In fact, some are not aware that they have such extreme mood shifts or that they have two distinctive personalities. Most will deny any change in their behavior and may even try to make their partners or others doubt their own perceptions regarding these mood shifts.

- Many Jekyll and Hydes are excellent liars who are extremely convincing and are experts in denial, distorting the truth, and shifting the blame.

- Their personality changes often represent deep conflicts within themselves (for example, the minister who is vehemently against adultery but has strong sexual urges he cannot control).

- Their personality shifts or dual personalities are often symptomatic of a personality disorder or are due to previous abuse experiences. (Many people who suffer from the Jekyll and Hyde syndrome were abused in childhood, and many suffer from personality disorders because of it).

- Some who suffer from the Jekyll and Hyde Syndrome actually live double lives. They may be highly respected elected officials, philanthropists, or even members of the clergy who hide a dark side to their personality that causes them to act in ways that would be shocking and hurtful to those who hold them in high regard, or they may create dual identities so they can participate in activities that are unacceptable in normal society.

The Seven Types of Jekyll and Hydes

From my many years of experience working as a psychotherapist specializing in abuse, I have determined that there are seven distinct types of Jekyll and Hydes:

1. *The super nice/abusive person.* For most of you reading this book, this is the type of Jekyll and Hyde you are probably concerned about. This person can be loving and charming one minute and abusive the next. Most often, the abuse takes the form of criticism, insults, and name calling, but at times it can include physical abuse. The person is often apologetic once some time has passed and goes back to his usual loving self. Yet no matter how apologetic he is or how many promises he makes to stop being critical, before long he has once again slipped back into his abusive behavior.

2. *The unpredictable person.* You never know when this person will become upset, blow up, go on a rampage, become withdrawn and sullen, or completely change her mind about something. Living with this person has been described as "walking on eggshells" because this type of person is exquisitely sensitive, and you never know whether something you say or do will upset her. Often, it is nothing you have done or said, but something that went on in this person's own mind that created the upset.

3. *The classic Jekyll and Hyde who truly lives a double life.* This person may be one type of person around his family and an entirely different one while away from them. For example, a hard working married man may appear in public to be the pinnacle of virtue, yet may be seeing other women or be involved with illegal activities. He may hold the position of a minister or a priest, or he may have been elected a mayor of a city or a senator of a state. He may be a philanthropist or a highly respected celebrity, and yet he has another life in which he goes against everything he stands for. Some people with this type of Jekyll and Hyde syndrome have set up separate identities, which includes going by different names or being married to more than one person.

4. *Someone whose personality radically changes when he or she drinks alcohol, takes drugs, or engages in other addictive activities.* Like Dr. Jekyll, whose transformation occurred after he took an elixir he created in his laboratory, this type of radical shift usually takes place only when the person is altered due to alcohol, drugs, gambling, and so on.

5. *The imposter.* This person deliberately tries to fool people into thinking he is something he is not. This can include pretending to be more concerned with the welfare of others or more successful than he is. He regularly lies, manipulates, and deceives others.

6. *Someone whose opinion of others fluctuates drastically.* This person tends to view people as either "all good" or "all bad." When she views someone as "all bad," she is unable to see any redeeming qualities in the person and feels justified in treating him poorly or rejecting him completely—even if he is her own child.

7. *Someone who changes dramatically when you challenge him or her in any way.* This person can be considerate and agreeable as long as things go his way or as long as he is in control. But if you don't do as he wants, if you challenge him in any way, or if you dare contradict him, you will see a completely different person. He will become defensive, insulting, and cruel.

QUESTIONNAIRE

Is Someone You Know a Jekyll and Hyde?

The following questions will help you decide whether someone you know is a Jekyll and Hyde:

1. Do certain situations tend to cause this person to change personality or have sudden mood shifts?

2. Does this person change radically depending on whom he is around?

3. Does she seem to have a public personality that is very different from how she behaves in the privacy of the home?

4. Does he frequently contradict himself? Does he state one point of view or belief one time and the opposite point of view another time?

5. Does this person appear to be hypocritical? Does she strongly disapprove of a certain behavior in others while often being guilty of the same behavior?

6. Does he have a radically different perception of himself from the one others have of him?

7. Is she often perplexed by how others view her behavior?

8. Does he often forget that certain events occurred?

9. Does she deny that she behaved in certain ways, even though you or others are certain she did? Does she accuse you of making it up or of being crazy?

10. Does he change personalities or become radically different once he has had a few drinks or has taken recreational drugs?

11. Does this person have an investment in being seen as the pillar of the community or as an extremely religious person yet sometimes exhibits behavior that is considered unacceptable, sinful, or even criminal?

12. Does she have an asymmetrical face—meaning that one side of the face is radically different from the other side of the face?

13. Does this person make reference to or joke about having "a bad side" to his personality, perhaps going as far as giving the bad side a name?

14. Does her wardrobe reflect extreme personality changes? For example, does she sometimes dress like a little girl and other times like a whore?

15. Does the person you care about tend to see you as either all good or all bad, with nothing in between?

16. Does he seem to start arguments soon after you have had some fun, intimate times?

17. Is this person's behavior so inconsistent that you feel you are always waiting for the other shoe to drop?

18. Are you the focus of intense, violent, and irrational rages, alternating with periods when the other person acts perfectly normal and loving?

19. Do you suspect this person is leading a double life?

20. Do you feel confused about who this person really is?

If you answered yes to even one or two of these questions in regard to someone you know, you have reason to be concerned. If you answered more than half in the affirmative, the person in question is definitely a Jekyll and Hyde.

How Jekyll and Hydes Affect Those around Them

People who are close to someone with this syndrome suffer from incredible distress, fear, confusion, and chaos. Many of them take on a hypervigilant stance, anticipating the next tirade or upheaval in their lives. This is how my client Jack described his situation: "I can't even tell you how terrible it is to live with my wife. We can be having a perfectly nice evening together, and suddenly she becomes upset about the smallest thing and everything changes. The atmosphere changes from friendly and light to this oppressive feeling. I find myself practically holding my breath, waiting to see if the situation will escalate or if she will calm down. You just never know. I hate living like this—never knowing when she'll get upset or over what. I'm nervous all the time, and I'm developing an ulcer. I just don't know how long I can go on living like this."

The damage caused by someone with a Jekyll and Hyde personality can be profound. Partners come to question or even to doubt their own perceptions, often thinking that they are crazy or that something is terribly wrong with them. This feeling is exacerbated by the fact that most Jekyll and Hydes don't recognize how upsetting their mood shifts can be. Instead of validating the fact that their behavior could be upsetting to others, they accuse people who are close to them of being too sensitive, of making a big deal out of nothing, or even of making up the fact that they act like two different people. Jekyll and Hydes who acknowledge that they do exhibit erratic behavior often blame their partners or other loved ones for their drastic mood shifts, and, consequently, many partners and loved ones of Jekyll and Hydes come to blame themselves as well.

The Jekyll and Hyde syndrome can be a form of emotional abuse, causing partners and children to suffer from severe confusion and disorientation. Celeste started therapy because she was confused about whether she should leave her husband. Married for one year, Celeste explained that her husband was what she called a real Dr. Jekyll and Mr. Hyde. "Before we married, James was the most loving, considerate man you'd ever want to meet. But now he is impatient and critical. He complains about everything—the way I dress, the way I cook, the way I clean the house. He seems to look for things to criticize—the other day he got on me because he found something old in the back of the refrigerator! Before we were married, we used to have long conversations, but now when I offer my opinion about something, he treats me like I'm a child or like I'm stupid and just dismisses what I say."

Celeste explained that if her husband acted this way all the time, she would know for certain that she should divorce him. But he keeps her off balance by sometimes reverting back to the way he was before they got married. "It's so confusing. Sometimes he can still be so sweet to me. He tells me he loves me, and he says he's sorry for being so critical of me. His father was critical of him, and he knows how much it hurts. He's been there for me with some problems I've had with my parents, and he's been really good to my daughter, who lives with us."

The harm done to children raised by a parent with the Jekyll and Hyde syndrome can be even more damaging. These children tend to develop chronic anxiety, suffer from a strong distrust in others, and take on a hypervigilant stance. Children with a Jekyll and Hyde for a parent often adjust to the chaos in their lives by learning to expect the unexpected. Craziness can begin to seem normal, and life without chaos may become boring. They can begin to associate love with fear and kindness with danger.

Consistency, continuity, and sameness of experience are essential to the development of trust and security for children. Since their parents' rules and expectations are so changeable, unreasonable, or unpredictably enforced, children with a Jekyll and Hyde for a parent seldom experience a sense of security and are often anxious and confused.

Christina Crawford, the daughter of the actress Joan Crawford, wrote in her autobiography, *Mommie Dearest*, about how her mother's moods fluctuated so dramatically that she was never certain of how she would be treated: "I never knew whether it would be a big hug of loving affection or a verbal slap in the face."

Often, children of Jekyll and Hydes learn to tune out by dissociating and disconnecting from their environment, their bodies, and their feelings. This is their way to protect themselves from feeling hurt, humiliated, and ridiculed. Children with such parents also have a tendency to blame themselves for their parents' mood shifts or blowups. And because their parents' rules or expectations are ever changing, they end up feeling like bad people.

When I was a child, I found it impossible to please my mother. I tried to be good and to stay out of her way. I knew she was tired from working and being a single mom, and I didn't want to make trouble for her. Of course, this was an impossible task for a small child. Even though I was expected to fend for myself at a very early age (about three years old), a child that young is incapable of taking care of all her own needs. I inevitably got myself into some kind of trouble, whether it was spilling milk as I tried to make myself breakfast or walking home all alone when I thought my mother had forgotten to pick me up from the babysitter's house. My mother, very good at presenting herself to the public as a warm, charming woman, suddenly became an angry, bitter witch whenever I caused her any trouble at all. I, of course, blamed myself for her change. After all, everyone loved my mother, so it must have been my fault that she changed into such a terrible person.

Interactions with their parents, even after they have become adults themselves, often leave adult children of Jekyll and Hydes feeling guilty and confused. When as an adult I visited my mother, she always made me feel guilty that I didn't visit her more often or that I didn't call her. Yet when I did call her, she always sounded annoyed, answering the phone impatiently and sounding disinterested.

Even close friends, siblings, and other relatives can be negatively affected by someone with the Jekyll and Hyde syndrome. I have a very close friend I will call Melanie. Melanie can be one of the most loving friends anyone would want to have. She is thoughtful and kind, and she is genuinely interested in what is going on in my life. When I talk to her, I get the sense that she is really listening; she's not thinking of what she will say next or interrupting me to tell me one of her stories. She's really there with me. She is very intelligent and is one of the few people I know who is as committed to personal growth as I am. We have had some very wonderful, deep conversations in which both of us have shared facets of our personalities that we would never share with anyone else. She also has a great sense of humor, which I appreciate very much. She genuinely cares about my well-being, and I know I can count on her in an emergency, especially a medical one.

Melanie has another side to her, though. As much as she can be loving and giving, she requires a great deal of special handling in order to keep her happy. She likes people to make a fuss over her, to buy her things, and to pay her way to social events. She has special dietary needs, and if you don't go out of your way to meet them, she feels highly insulted. In other words, she likes to be treated somewhat like a princess. At the same time, she is likely to blow up if she feels you are the slightest bit condescending. This ends up making you feel as if you can't win with her. If you go out of your way to meet her needs, you run the risk of crossing the line and treating her like a child, which enrages her.

The most difficult thing about Melanie is that you never know when she will shut down emotionally. She can be her loving, fun self for several hours and then shift into someone who is emotionally inaccessible. Her change comes completely without warning, and at first you may not even notice it. Suddenly, however, you feel an iciness coming from her. She still responds when you ask her something, but she is no longer forthcoming in the conversation, and there is usually a hint of impatience when she does speak. When you share something with her, you no longer get the feeling that she is really listening. Now you feel as if she is just putting up with you.

I mentioned earlier that Jekyll and Hydes can cause others to feel confused and disoriented. I can describe Melanie's Jekyll and Hyde behavior in detail now because I've observed her for many years. Early in our friendship, though, I didn't really know what was going on. I hadn't experienced this side of her when we first met—I saw only her charming side. This is the case with many people who befriend or become romantically involved with Jekyll and Hydes. As we became deeper friends, however, I began to notice that she became silent and withdrawn at times. When I asked her what was going on, she usually looked at me in surprise and said something like, "Why, nothing, why do you ask?" At first I just let it go, thinking that perhaps I was imagining a shift in her mood or that I was being too sensitive. Yet it became more and more clear that something indeed had occurred. She was different, whether she was willing to admit it or not. I felt very uncomfortable being with her when she was in her icy mood, and often I found a way to cut our visit short. The next time I saw her, she was usually her open, loving self, so I forgot all about her icy mood.

Over the years, though, I noticed that her radical mood shift occurred more often, particularly whenever we spent more time together. She had moved away to another city but occasionally came back to see me, often staying at my home. This is when her moods really began to bother me. We usually had a wonderful first day visiting and catching up, but often, by the next morning, Melanie woke up acting distant and stayed that way for several hours. This was very uncomfortable, especially since she refused to acknowledge that anything was wrong. At one point, I tried talking to her about her mood shifts, and she became furious, telling me that I was too demanding, that I didn't give her enough space. She accused me of needing constant attention and of being super-sensitive.

I was deeply hurt; not only did it feel as if she was shutting me out, but she was now making accusations that were very hurtful. Since my mother has always accused me of being too sensitive, part of me thought that perhaps the problem did lie with me. I tried telling myself that it was okay if Melanie didn't feel like talking or if she needed some space. If possible, I tried to go about my business and leave her alone, but if we already had plans to go out to do something together, it was almost unbearable to me. I was supposed to act as if nothing was wrong when there clearly was. There would be no friendly conversation, just silence as we drove to the movie or to dinner or, God forbid, went for a drive to the country. This was like ignoring the elephant in the room, and it made me extremely uncomfortable.

Just as suddenly as Melanie became her icy self, she then switched back to her normal, loving self, and this, too, was difficult because I was supposed to move on and act as if nothing had occurred. I was supposed to get over my hurt feelings at being ignored for hours and suppress any anger I felt because she wouldn't admit she had switched personalities. And always there was a lingering doubt in my mind that perhaps I really was too sensitive or too demanding.

How This Book Will Help

You may be reading this book because someone you care about (your partner, a parent, a sibling, a friend) behaves in radically different ways or experiences extreme mood swings. Or perhaps you're reading it because you're worried about your own tendency to have severe mood shifts or to behave in ways that seem very unlike you. Whichever your situation, this book will benefit you in many ways, starting with helping you to understand that you are not alone. Thousands of people suffer from the Jekyll and Hyde syndrome, and thousands more suffer because they are close to someone with this syndrome. This book will also help you gain a better understanding of yourself, whether you are close to someone who has this syndrome or you suffer from it yourself. Finally, the book will teach you strategies to help you cope with this syndrome, whether this means coping with someone you care about or coping with your own behavior.

For example, partners of people with the Jekyll and Hyde syndrome need to better understand what they are dealing with. If you are like Celeste, you need to understand that the person you are involved with may actually be emotionally abusing you and that often the longer you stay with such a person, the worse you will feel about yourself and the more confused and disoriented you will become. You need to understand how this kind of behavior damages your self-esteem and makes you question your perceptions and sometimes your very sanity. You may also need help to determine whether there is any hope for your relationship.

Joseph was in desperate need of help when he came to see me. Staying with his partner had caused him and his children serious emotional problems. Yet leaving a partner who can also be so caring is not an easy thing to do. What do you do when your partner acts like two entirely different people?

This is what Joseph told me about his situation: "My wife can be wonderful for two or three days, and then suddenly—poof! She turns into a monster. She's usually patient and caring, especially with the kids, but when she changes, she becomes cruel and heartless. She yells at them for no apparent reason, and she even tells them she hates them and wishes they had never been born! My kids are so wounded by this behavior that I am seriously considering leaving my wife and filing for sole custody. But she's such a loving mother most of the time that it breaks my heart to think of separating them from her. I really don't know what to do."

If you choose to stay in the relationship, you need strategies to help you confront this emotionally abusive behavior. On the other hand, if you end the relationship, you need to know the warning signs to avoid getting involved with this type of personality again and to understand that some people are more vulnerable than others when it comes to attracting Jekyll and Hydes.

To heal from the damage caused by a Jekyll and Hyde, you need to fully understand the phenomenon and its effects on victims. You need to realize that you are not to blame for the person's behavior. And you need permission to express your anger and other emotions since it is usually too frightening to do so in the presence of someone with this syndrome.

In addition to helping wives, husbands, lovers, children, friends, and family members of people who suffer from the Jekyll and Hyde syndrome, the book will also help those who suffer from this disturbance. Mark is a loving, warm, dedicated family man who loves his wife and children and works hard to provide them with everything they need. Even though Mark is frequently away from home on business, his wife, Carrie, trusts him implicitly. She knows her husband has very high morals and believes strongly in fidelity in a marriage. Mark calls Carrie every night just to tell her he loves her and to talk to the kids.

Yet as loyal and dedicated as Mark is, he also has another side to his personality—a side that he hides from everyone he knows. After his dutiful call every evening to his wife and kids, Mark became a different man. Instead of going to bed early, as he told his wife he was doing, he spent his evenings at strip clubs, where he squandered a great deal of money paying for lap dances—and often for sex. He justified his actions by saying that he worked hard and deserved to have some fun. Yet Mark knew he was just fooling himself. He had a serious problem—a problem he was absolutely helpless to overcome. As he shared with me on our first visit, "It's as if I am two people—the family man and the whoremonger. Each is an equally dominant force in my life."

After each incident, Mark suffered from horrible shame and guilt. Every time he vowed never to repeat this behavior again, but as much as he tried, he couldn't seem to control the side of himself that felt compelled to act out sexually when he was away from his wife and children. Mark was as baffled by his behavior as his wife will be once she discovers that the man she loves and trusts has been lying to her and is being unfaithful.

There are many people like Mark—people who have good intentions and good hearts, ethical people who, much to their shock and dismay, either break their own moral codes of behavior, betray everything they stand for, disappoint people who have trusted them, or hurt other human beings in deeply significant ways. These people need help to understand why they behave as they do.

Once Mark's wife discovers what he has been doing when he is away from her (which is inevitable), she will feel betrayed, hurt, and angry. She will also feel utterly confused and mystified. How could someone as kind and considerate as Mark do something so hurtful and selfish? Had she ever known Mark—the real Mark—or was it all a lie? Why hadn't she seen any of the signs that he was leading a double life? This book will help people like Mark and Carrie to cope with their situations. It will help those, like Mark, who suffer from this syndrome to understand the motivations for their behavior, and it will help victims like Carrie to realize that it's easy to be fooled by Jekyll and Hydes. Most important, it will provide steps for those with this syndrome to take in order to integrate their personalities, as well as advice for victims to help them handle the overwhelming emotions they feel.

Do You Suffer from the Jekyll and Hyde Syndrome?

Many people worry about themselves and fear that they might be Jekyll and Hydes, especially if they have been accused of it by others. The truth is, we all have a little Jekyll and Hyde in us. We all experience mood swings, and often we don't understand why. All of us are capable of committing selfish or cruel acts—acts that are totally uncharacteristic of us. Although we tend to feel more comfortable with the idea that someone is either good or bad, the reality is that we all have a combination of both good and bad characteristics; we all share the capacity to do both good and evil. In this book, you will come to understand the internal conflicts that can cause this duality.

In order to facilitate a deeper understanding of the duality of human nature, later in the book I offer a continuum that ranges from mild versions of the Jekyll and Hyde syndrome to more severe forms. This continuum will help you determine the seriousness of your own personal duality. For now, the following questionnaire will help you decide whether you suffer from the Jekyll and Hyde syndrome.

QUESTIONNAIRE

Are You a Jekyll and Hyde?

1. Do you often experience intense mood swings?

2. Are you often surprised and overwhelmed by your own behavior?

3. Do you often behave in ways that shock yourself and others—ways that seem uncharacteristic of you?

4. Do people tell you that your behavior seems radically different from time to time?

5. Does your behavior or mood undergo an extreme change whenever you've had a few drinks?

6. Do you often act in ways that you regret later?

7. Is there a significant discrepancy between what you say you believe and how you act?

8. Are you deeply conflicted regarding your values and beliefs and the way you lead your life?

9. Do you frequently feel like a hypocrite because you often end up doing things that you don't believe in?

10. Do you feel as if a battle is going on inside you between the part of you that wants to be good and the part of you that wants to be bad?

11. Do you often become upset or angry for no apparent reason?

12. Do you often have no memory of what you did the day or the night before?

13. Are you often surprised when people tell you what you did or said since you have no memory of it?

14. Are you often perplexed because people close to you report that you engaged in behavior—especially abusive behavior—that you not only have no memory of but can never imagine doing?

15. Is there often a significant discrepancy between how you perceived an event and the way others perceived it?

16. Do you often act very differently depending on whom you are around?

17. Do you frequently feel "triggered" by memories of previous painful experiences, and do these memories cause a severe mood shift in you?

18. Have you set up a separate life for yourself that people closest to you don't know about? For example, do you associate with people you would be ashamed to introduce to your family?

There are no hard and fast rules here, but if you answered yes to more than two of these questions, you have reason to be concerned, and I would encourage you to read this book. If you answered yes to more than half of these questions, I can safely say that you suffer from the Jekyll and Hyde syndrome, and you definitely need the help this book will offer.

The Causes of the Jekyll and Hyde Syndrome

Once you have determined that either you yourself suffer from the Jekyll and Hyde syndrome or that someone you are involved with has this syndrome, the next question that normally comes up is, What causes this syndrome? As you will discover in the next chapter, certain specific psychological conditions can cause this syndrome, but there are also some commonalties, no matter what the official psychological diagnosis.

People who suffer from this syndrome are often deeply conflicted human beings. The conflict may have to do with being raised by highly religious or controlling parents who punished them severely for misbehaving. A Jekyll and Hyde tends to develop a huge dark side or Shadow that holds all of his or her repressed emotions and desires. This dark side can literally take over an individual, causing the person to create a separate entity who is free to act out hidden desires.

A less extreme version is the person who cares too much what other people think and thus needs to be "all good." This person has an investment in being seen by others in an extremely positive way. Unfortunately, the more devout, respectable, and altruistic we seem to be in the eyes of others, the more likely it is that we have a dark side just waiting to get out.

In many cases, it's as if people with the Jekyll and Hyde syndrome suddenly have an "attack" that causes them to temporarily change their personalities. Those who were emotionally, physically, or sexually abused in childhood often suffer from radical mood shifts brought on by the fact that someone or something triggered memories of the abuse.

This sudden attack can also be brought on by alcohol or drugs, or it can be the result of an emotional disturbance, such as borderline personality disorder or narcissistic personality disorder. For example, borderline personality disorder is characterized by extreme shifts in mood and was, in the past, confused with schizophrenia. People who have borderline personality disorder tend to be intense, unpredictable, and sometimes volatile. Narcissistic individuals often experience radical shifts in their personalities whenever anyone doubts, challenges, or confronts them.

The Human Shadow

At the center of this book is the concept of the dark side, or what Carl Jung called the Shadow. As humans, we all contain within ourselves a whole spectrum of urges and potential behaviors, but society, religion, and our parents reinforce certain types of behavior and discourage others. These rejected qualities do not cease to exist simply because they have been denied direct expression. Instead, they live on within us and form the secondary personality that psychologists call the Shadow.

There is a beast within us all—a part of ourselves we hide away, not only from others but from ourselves. This dark side is made up of forbidden thoughts and feelings, undesirable and thus rejected personality traits, and all the violent and sexual tendencies we consider evil, dangerous, or forbidden. Each of us contains both a Dr. Jekyll and a Mr. Hyde—a more pleasant persona for everyday wear and a hiding, nighttime self that remains hushed up most of the time. Negative emotions and behaviors—rage, jealousy, shame, resentment, lust, greed, and suicidal and murderous tendencies—lie concealed just beneath the surface, masked by our more proper selves.

Sometimes we are aware of our dark sides, and, out of fear of being propelled into acting in ways that we will regret, we consciously work on pushing down and controlling our more prurient or unacceptable urges. More often, though, we are entirely unaware of our dark sides.

Later in the book, I will introduce you to what is commonly called "shadow-work." The goal of shadow-work is to integrate our dark sides. This is not accomplished with a simple method but by a deepening and widening of our consciousness. As Connie Zweig and Jeremiah Abrams so eloquently wrote in their classic book *Meeting the Shadow: The Hidden Power of the Dark Side of Human Nature*, "shadow-work forces us again and again to take another point of view, to respond to life with our undeveloped traits and our instinctual sides, and to live what Jung called the tension of the opposites—holding both good and evil, right and wrong, light and dark, in our own hearts."

No matter what particular version of the Jekyll and Hyde syndrome someone has, shadow-work can be a great benefit in helping the person overcome it. For example, those who suffer severe mood shifts due to borderline personality disorder can get help with their tendency to split things into black-and-white, all-or-nothing categories and to view others as all bad or all good. People with narcissistic personality disorder can get help with the repressed shame that often motivates their behavior.

Anyone who is involved with a Jekyll and Hyde can also benefit from learning more about the Shadow and from doing shadow-work. The first step of shadow-work—acknowledging that darkness lies inside every human heart—is often forced upon us. Sometimes it occurs when we come face-to-face with this darkness in the most unlikely place—in the actions and the words of a partner or a parent. Other times, it occurs because of the betrayal of a loved one. In either case, meeting the Shadow robs us of our innocence.

2

The Seven Types of Jekyll and Hydes

> Our shadow personality is often obvious to others, but
> unknown to us.
>
> —John A. Sanford, Jungian analyst and author

In this chapter we will delve more deeply into the distinctions among the seven types of Jekyll and Hydes. It is very important to note that there can be a great deal of crossover among the seven types. While they are different enough to warrant separate categories, there are often similarities between one category and another. This means that someone may fit into more than one category.

You'll find that most Jekyll and Hydes have the following behaviors and issues in common:

- Most Jekyll and Hydes are unpredictable.
- Many can be described as emotionally abusive.
- Most of them deny their erratic behavior or blame their partners or others for their mood shifts.
- Many Jekyll and Hydes lie to cover up their dual natures or dual lives.

- Many are overly concerned about their public images.
- Many were abused or neglected as children.
- Many suffer from personality disorders or post-traumatic stress disorder.

For example, abusive Jekyll and Hydes often experience their radical mood shifts as a result of issues related to personality disorders or alcohol or drug problems, and people who have personality disorders or alcohol or drug problems are often abusive—although that is not their primary identifying factor. Therefore, I have created each category based on the primary feature of the person's behavior (that is, abusiveness, addiction, personality disorder, and so on).

Type 1. The Abusive Jekyll and Hyde: "When I Become Unhappy, It Is Your Fault"

While the behavior of most types of Jekyll and Hydes can be defined as some form of emotional abuse, abusive Jekyll and Hydes are distinguished by personality changes that tend to manifest in abusive behavior toward others, usually toward people who are closest to them. In addition, unlike some other types of Jekyll and Hydes, their abusive behavior is often intentional.

The majority of abusive Jekyll and Hydes can be fairly reasonable and calm in most interactions with people outside the family or anyone not involved in their intimate relationships. Average abusive Jekyll and Hydes have an investment in looking good in public because they can rationalize their behavior and assuage any guilt feelings they may have, as well as justify their abusive actions. An abusive man's thinking often goes like this: "After all, why is it that I get along with everyone else but my wife? It must be her problem, not mine."

Abusive Jekyll and Hydes may also act pleasant and easygoing in public in a deliberate attempt to win people over. This makes it harder for their partners or children to gain support or assistance outside the relationship because people will have a hard time believing that such nice individuals could be so abusive. Even professional therapists can be fooled by the abusive Jekyll and Hyde's charming persona.

According to Lundy Bancroft in his classic book *Why Does He Do That? Inside the Minds of Angry and Controlling Men*, most abusive men put on charming faces for their communities, creating a significant split between their public images and their private treatment of women and children. As Lundy explains, an abusive man may be:

- Smiling and calm when he is outside the home, enraged when he is at home

- Generous and supportive with others, selfish and self-centered with you

- Willing to negotiate and compromise outside the home, domineering with you

- Nonviolent and nonthreatening with people outside the home, assaultive toward his partner or children or both

- A vocal supporter of equality for women in the public arena, highly negative about women and girls in his home

- Critical of men who disrespect or assault women but disrespectful and abusive at home

These contrasting behaviors can be overwhelming, painful, confusing, and insulting for a female partner. As her husband goes off to work, he may tell her she is a lazy cow who doesn't do anything all day long. That same evening, as they entertain his business associates, he may say something like, "I think the role of homemaker is one of the most important jobs that exist. I'm so happy that Marsha agreed to quit her job and stay home. She's doing a great job."

An abusive Jekyll and Hyde can go weeks and even months without an abusive episode, leading others to believe that he or she has some sort of personality split. In actuality, however, the abusive Jekyll and Hyde is merely repeating the same cycle of abuse that any abusive person goes through. The cycle goes like this: periods of relative calm are followed by a few days or weeks in which the abuser becomes increasingly irritable. As his or her tension builds, it takes less and less to set the abuser off on a tirade of criticism and insults. In the case of abusive men, their female partners often report that they have learned to read their partners' moods during this buildup and sense when they are about to erupt. One day the man finally reaches his limit and he blows up, often over the most trivial issues. He blasts his partner with hurtful and disgusting put-downs; he screams; and he throws objects, puts his fist through doors, or physically assaults his partner.

After he has purged himself of his rage, he typically acts ashamed or regretful about his cruelty or violence. He then may enter a period in which he seems like the man you fell in love with—charming, kind, and attentive.

So what causes this abusive cycle? Why can't the man stay in his "good" period instead of slipping into the abusive mode? First of all, we need to understand that the good side of an abusive man is not necessarily the real person, as many people assume. As I mentioned earlier, the good version of an abusive man is often an act—his attempt to protect himself from exposure should his abusiveness come out. It can also be his way of coping with the guilt that most abusers feel after they have had abusive episodes. "See what a good person I am, see how many people like me" can be a way to rationalize and minimize his abusive behavior. "I'm not all bad, after all—I do a lot of good things, too."

The other reason abusive Jekyll and Hydes cannot stay in their good personas is that even when they're being nice to their partners or children, they are thinking negative thoughts about them and looking at them critically, adding up their faults, mistakes, and shortcomings. Abusive Jekyll and Hydes tend to view their partners and children as extensions of themselves. Therefore, they tend to be highly critical of them.

Abusers tend to nurse their grievances and to view themselves as victims. Almost out of habit, they often walk around dwelling on their partners' purported faults. This is because they consider their partners responsible for making them happy, for fixing everything for them. Therefore, they logically choose their partners as their dumping ground whenever anything goes wrong in their lives.

Some abusers even stockpile their grievances as weapons against their partners should the partners attempt to express dissatisfaction with them.

The extreme mood shifts of abusive Jekyll and Hydes can be especially perplexing to their partners or children. They can be entirely different people from day to day or even from hour to hour. This is how Lundy Bancroft describes an abuser's radical mood shifts:

> At times he is aggressive and intimidating, his tone harsh, insults spewing from his mouth, ridicule dripping from his mouth like oil from a drum. When he's in this mode, nothing she [his partner] says seems to have any impact on him, except to make him even angrier. Her side of the argument counts for nothing in his eyes, and everything is her fault. He twists her words around so that she always ends up on the defensive.
>
> At other moments, he sounds wounded and lost, hungering for love and for someone to take care of him. When this side of him emerges, he appears open and ready to heal. He seems to let down his guard, his hard exterior softens, and he may take on the quality of a hurt child, difficult and frustrating but lovable. Looking at him in this deflated state, his partner has trouble imagining that the abuser inside of him will ever be back. The beast that takes over at other times looks completely unrelated to the tender person she now sees.

THE TWO SIDES OF MICHAEL

When I first met Michael, I was struck by how much pain he was in. "You've got to help me get my wife back. I can't live without her," he told me as he sat down on my couch. "I know I've treated her badly, but I've learned my lesson. I'll do anything to get her back." At this, he broke down and sobbed.

I wanted to believe Michael. He seemed genuinely sincere, and he had, after all, sought me out after reading my book *The*

Emotionally Abusive Relationship, which outlines a program for both those who are being abusive and those who are being abused. He had admitted to being emotionally abusive to his wife for many years. As he told me the story of how he would suddenly erupt in a rage, raving and ranting at his wife for hours, it seemed that he was indeed open to doing anything to get his wife back. I wondered if that meant he was willing to do the work that was necessary in order to change. Admitting you are an abusive Jekyll and Hyde is a first and significant step, but not many people have the strength and the courage to do the work that is required to discover the origins of their erratic behavior.

Unfortunately, it became clear fairly soon that Michael was interested only in getting his wife back, not in really changing. After meeting with Michael's wife individually to get her perspective, I once again met with Michael.

"Well, Michael, your wife tells me she may be willing to come home if she feels you have your anger under control. Are you willing to work with me to find out why you have these angry outbursts?"

"What do you mean she *may* be willing to come home—can't she be more definite? What if I do all this work and she still doesn't want to come home?"

"Well, you'll have to face that when you come to it. In the meantime, it seems to me that it is going to be important for you to get your anger under control no matter what."

"But you don't understand, *she's* the one who makes me angry. If she didn't act the way she does, I wouldn't blow up like I do."

"No, Michael, that isn't true. You blow up like you do because you have a problem with anger. Your wife may do things you don't like, but there are better ways of communicating your displeasure than yelling and screaming and throwing things."

"You don't understand. No one makes me angry like she does. I don't act this way at work or anywhere else for that matter."

"I do understand, Michael. Those who are closest to us can make us the most angry. But you are going to have to learn better ways of dealing with your anger. And I believe you will need to look into your history for the reasons why you are angry so often and why it is so intense and unpredictable."

As I had foreseen, Michael was not willing to do the work required. He continued to blame his wife for his problems and insisted that she make a definite promise to come home before he would commit to therapy.

Type 2. The Unpredictable Jekyll and Hyde: "You Never Know When I Will Change."

By definition, all Jekyll and Hydes can be unpredictable, but this type of Jekyll and Hyde is highly unpredictable on an hour-by-hour and even moment-to-moment basis. Things can be going along just fine. You are getting along; the other person is agreeable, even fun. But then, for no apparent reason, he or she gets very upset and may begin to argue with you, suddenly stop talking to you, or blow up in a rage.

The cause of this behavior is often grounded in the fact that this person has been triggered by something or someone. Being triggered means that something reminded the person of an unpleasant, painful, or even abusive incident in his or her life (most often, childhood abuse or trauma). This can catapult the person back in time, causing behavior that is typically unlike him or her.

This person may act perfectly normal in most situations, but when reminded of previous trauma he or she changes radically, often taking on a completely different personality and frequently reenacting the type of abuse that was experienced as a child. Often, the person is unaware of what set off this behavior, nor is anyone else who witnessed the metamorphosis.

Post-traumatic Stress Disorder

Unpredictable behavior like this is most common in people who suffer from post-traumatic stress disorder (PTSD), a psychiatric disorder that can occur following the experience or the witnessing of life-threatening events: violent personal assaults such as child abuse or rape, serious accidents, natural disasters, military combat, or terrorist incidents. People who suffer from PTSD often relive the experiences through nightmares and flashbacks, have difficulty sleeping, and feel detached and estranged. These symptoms can be severe enough and last long enough to significantly impair the person's daily life.

Recent studies have shown that childhood abuse (particularly sexual abuse) is a strong predictor of the lifetime likelihood of PTSD. Although many people still equate PTSD with combat trauma, the trauma most likely to produce PTSD was found to be rape, with 65 percent of men and 45.9 percent of women who had been raped developing PTSD (Kessler, et al., 1999). People who have experienced assaultive violence (interpersonal victimization) at home or in the community have also been shown to be at very high PTSD risk.

PTSD is marked by clear biological changes, as well as by psychological symptoms. PTSD is complicated by the fact that it frequently occurs in conjunction with related disorders such as depression, substance abuse, and problems of memory and cognition. The disorder is further associated with impairment of the person's ability to function in social and family life, which includes occupational inability, marital problems and divorces, family discord, and difficulties in parenting. These factors, in particular, play a significant role in making those with PTSD vulnerable to repeating the cycle of violence for the following reasons:

1. Many people with PTSD turn to alcohol or drugs in an attempt to escape their symptoms.

2. Some characteristics of PTSD can create abusive behavior, such as:

   • Irritability—extreme irritation and reaction to noise or minor stimulants.

   • Explosive behavior and/or trouble modulating and controlling anger. Rage must go somewhere, either to the self or to others.

Borderline Personality Disorder

In addition to or instead of PTSD, many individuals who fall into this category of the Jekyll and Hyde syndrome suffer from borderline personality disorder (BPD). People with this disorder are often extremely unpredictable, frequently "going off" (exploding in a rage or a tirade) or falling into despair and depression without any warning.

Those with BPD suffer from a sort of chronic anxiety. It's as if their insides are constantly churned up, sometimes mildly, other times more severely. They are seldom, if ever, at peace with themselves. You can imagine, then, that someone with this disorder can become easily upset.

Those with BPD also suffer from a debilitating form of low self-esteem. They don't just feel bad about themselves some of the time—deep inside, they feel bad about themselves *all* the time. In fact, they hate themselves. This combination of feeling chronically anxious and perpetually bad about themselves can make for a very tenuous situation. It doesn't take much for people with this disorder to flip into eruptive or depressed states.

This was the situation with my client Paul and his wife, Justine. "You know that book you recommended to me, *Stop Walking on Eggshells*?" Paul asked. "That's exactly how I feel with my wife. I never know what will set her off. It might be something I say or do, or it might be something someone else said or did. Sometimes it is a complete mystery. She just changes for no apparent reason. Most of the time she explodes in a rage, but even when she doesn't—even when she doesn't say a thing—you know that you better tread lightly because she could explode any minute. The energy around her becomes almost electric—you can just sense that something has shifted. She suddenly becomes more impatient; she closes off and doesn't want to talk. Her face even changes. You can actually see the tension in her features. If you ask her what is wrong—which I've learned to stop doing—she'll deny that anything is up, and she will probably get angry with you for asking. I don't think she even knows when she's changed, much less is able to explain the reasons for it. I've found it is best to just leave her alone and hope that it blows over."

People with BPD usually don't know what is going on inside them and seldom know what has caused their mood changes. Unfortunately, they tend to blame others for these changes, instead of being willing to admit that they simply don't know why they shifted. Blaming and criticizing others become defense mechanisms for many borderlines. Their reasoning goes like this: because they don't understand their own mood shifts, it must be something someone else has done to upset them.

What is it like to have a borderline parent? Children of border-line parents suffer tremendously from their parents' constant mood swings, conflicting feelings, rampages, and depressive episodes. "Now" is all that matters to borderlines. They can yell at you one minute and hug you the next.

My client Selena told me what it was like growing up with a borderline mother: "My mother constantly went on tirades. She'd suddenly storm through the house, yelling, crying, calling me names. Sometimes it was because my room wasn't clean enough, sometimes it was because she said I gave her a dirty look—you never knew what would set her off. In actuality, she was the one who gave the dirty looks—she sometimes glared at me with a look so full of hatred it scared me. That was often the only signal I had that a tirade was coming on. I felt that the only way I could survive was to try to stay out of her way until the storm blew over. Then she'd be fine again, even hugging me and telling me she loved me."

Type 3. The Classic Jekyll and Hyde: "You Only Think You Know Me."

This person has two distinct personalities and may have gone so far as to create two separate lives. This type can include super-good people who have denied their darker urges and impulses to the point that these urges burst out unexpectedly. Much like the classic story *The Strange Case of Dr. Jekyll and Mr. Hyde*, in which an upstanding man hides an equally dark side to his personality, this person creates a distinctively different personality in order to act out darker urges while keeping his or her "super-good" persona intact.

Like abusive Jekyll and Hydes, classic Jekyll and Hydes can be different depending on whom they are around. Often they have public personas while behaving very differently around their partners and children.

This is how my client Jessica described her Jekyll and Hyde mother: "I'll never forget the first time I went to one of my mother's charity events. I was eleven. When she introduced me to people, they all raved about what a wonderful mother I had—wasn't I a lucky girl to have such a loving woman for a mother? I stood dumbstruck, not understanding what they were talking about. They certainly weren't describing the woman I knew as my mother. The only mother I'd ever known was cruel and selfish—not at all generous or kind as they described."

This is typically the case with people who are overly invested in looking good to the outside world. Unfortunately, they can maintain their "good girl" or "good boy" act for only so long. Usually, their partners and children experience the real individuals, who are often domineering, cruel, and even sadistic.

This distinction between public self and private self can also characterize people who suffer from BPD. In her book *Cognitive-Behavioral Treatment of the Borderline Patient*, Marsha Linehan describes the facade of normalcy that borderlines present to others, particularly in work settings. While they may feel confident and in control at work, they often feel out of control and incompetent when it comes to personal relationships, especially intimate relationships. They are frequently gracious and engaging in social situations but unbearable at home with their partners and children. In her book *Mommie Dearest*, Christina Crawford described her frustration concerning the facade her mother presented when entertaining. She summarized how children of borderlines often feel about the dichotomy of the private versus public persona of the borderline mother when she wrote, "I just wanted to scream that it was all a fake."

I often complained to my friends about my mother's treatment of me, and yet when they came to visit me, they seldom saw the mother I had described. "But your mother seems so nice," they inevitably said. Because of this and because others always talked about how wonderful my mother was, I never had any validation for my feelings.

The impulsivity, the unpredictability, the emotional intensity, and the fear of abandonment that characterize BPD are observable primarily by those who have intimate relationships with the borderline. Casual acquaintances, coworkers, or neighbors are less likely to witness the borderline's sudden shifts in moods, self-destructive behavior, paranoid ideation, and obsessive ruminations.

Type 4: The "Addict" (Alcoholic, Drug Addict, Compulsive Gambler)

Addicted Jekyll and Hydes change radically whenever they drink alcohol, take drugs, or engage in other addictive behaviors, such as compulsive gambling. They often have little or no memory of the way they treated others while under the influence and can't understand why others are angry with them.

Most people change somewhat once they have one or two alcoholic drinks. Since alcohol relaxes us and lowers our inhibitions, many people become more open, friendly, and animated. After a few more drinks, they may even become the life of the party. But some people don't become more friendly. Instead, they become demanding or controlling and won't take no for an answer. Some of them become insulting, abusive, or even dangerous.

For certain people, alcohol acts like a truth serum, causing them to share feelings or information they have held in. Unfortunately, this truth telling often has an edge to it. For example, when Deborah has a few drinks, she becomes downright insulting to her friends. Under the guise of being honest, she tells them if she doesn't like what they are wearing or doesn't like their latest boyfriends. When her friends complain to her about how much she hurts their feelings, she just says, "I tell it like it is."

Because of this, many of Deborah's friends now avoid being around her when she drinks. One friend confided, "She's so cruel when she drinks. It seems to me that there must actually be a cruel side to her. I don't think the alcohol creates that in her; I think it just brings it out."

Deborah's friend was absolutely right. While alcohol can bring out the worst in us, it doesn't create the behavior that it brings out. The emotions fueling that behavior were already inside. This is what Margaret, a friend of a friend, told me when she heard I was writing this book: "My husband is like an entirely different person when he drinks. Normally, he's a really nice, polite guy who never says anything hurtful to anyone. But when he drinks too much, he becomes this cruel, sarcastic person. He says the most horrible things to me and to others. I just never know what will come out of his mouth. He's especially cruel to waitresses and waiters. I hate to go out to dinner with him if he's going to drink."

I have had firsthand experience of being on both ends of this kind of experience. My mother often got drunk and became very cruel to me. I got so that I hated to be around her when she was drinking, out of fear of what she would say to me. She normally didn't pay much attention to me, especially as I got older, but after a six-pack of beer she usually focused in on me. If I walked past her, she said, "What are you doing?" No matter what I answered, it was an opening for her to start in on me. If I said, "Nothing," she'd say, "That's all you ever do." If I said, "My homework," she would say something like, "Yeah, I'm sure." Then she'd start complaining that I never cleaned the house (I was the only one who did) or that I was ungrateful about how hard she worked to put food on the table or how I really thought I was something. By the time I got to high school, I started arguing back to her.

Unfortunately, as so often happens, I repeated my mother's behavior when I grew up. I started drinking in high school and drank too much from the very beginning. When I was drunk, I started arguments with my boyfriends, just as my mother had started fights with me. Later in my life, I remember friends telling me that I said hurtful things to them when I was drunk. Of course, I didn't know what they were talking about—I thought I was just being honest.

Becoming critical or starting fights is only the tip of the iceberg for some people who drink too much. Some Jekyll and Hydes engage in illicit or illegal activities when they drink that they would never do when they were sober. Others say things they regret later, as was the case with Mel Gibson. Many women and men become promiscuous after too many drinks, and some engage in dangerous sexual behaviors.

ABBY AND ALCOHOL

Abby, a longtime client of mine, came into her session one afternoon very upset. She started sobbing before she had a chance to sit down. "What is going on, Abby?" I asked, thinking that perhaps someone close to her had died. "I got drunk last night and ended up taking three guys home with me for a 'party.' I guess I had sex with all three of them—I don't know—I don't really remember. I came to while one of them was screwing me. I remember the three guys leaving my house, but nothing else. When I woke up in the morning, my house had been ransacked—they'd gone through all my stuff and ended up taking some jewelry, my CD player, a bunch of CDs, and I don't know what else. But the worst part about it was I don't think they used condoms. I didn't see any empty wrappers, and I keep condoms right by my bed. I remember asking the first guy to use one, and he said he didn't need it. My God, I may have contracted AIDS. I feel so dirty and so ashamed."

I was rather surprised to hear about Abby's behavior. I had no idea she had a problem with alcohol. She had told me she was a mild social drinker when I conducted my initial interview with her, and she never mentioned getting drunk when she talked about her issues. As it turned out, this was not the first time Abby acted out when she drank. In fact, it was a regular occurrence. Although she had never endangered her life quite as much as she had the previous night, she told me that when she drank too much, she became very sexual and almost always ended up having sex with someone she met that night.

"My friends say I act like a slut when I drink," she told me in between sobs. "But that's not who I am. It really isn't. I'm not even comfortable having sex with a guy until we have been going out for a long time. When I go on dates, I hardly even drink. I don't want the guy to get the wrong idea about me. But when I go out with my girlfriends, I always drink too much and end up acting like a whore. What's wrong with me?"

As we were both to learn, Abby's drinking was an excuse for her to act out some very dark urges—urges that had their genesis in her childhood. Abby had been sexually abused as a child and suffered from tremendous shame and extremely low self-esteem because of it. She also felt extremely uncomfortable becoming sexual with a man, even someone she had been dating for quite some time. When she drank too much, though, she suddenly felt confident and powerful—like another person entirely. The person she became liked being in charge sexually, which was a reversal of how she had felt as a child.

Alcohol and Sexual Acting Out

Sexual acting out is actually a very common form of Jekyll and Hyde behavior for those who have alcohol and drug problems. Some people cheat on their spouses when they drink and then conveniently blame the booze for their actions. Others get involved in kinky sexual practices when under the influence. My client Jeffrey shared with me that he first got into sadomasochism when he was under the influence of alcohol and cocaine. "This guy I was seeing was into it, and he was always trying to get me to try it. But it scared me. I wasn't interested in doing it either way—being the submissive partner or the aggressive one. But one night after I'd had a lot to drink and a lot of cocaine, he finally talked me into it. Now I'm hooked, even though it makes me feel so bad about myself afterward. I don't like who I become—this passive guy begging to be beaten, begging to be hurt. I've lost all respect for myself, but I can't seem to stop."

Still others engage in illegal and immoral sexual acts when under the influence of alcohol or drugs. My client Jim was arrested for indecent exposure and child endangerment after getting drunk on a business trip. He'd been out drinking with his colleagues, and by the time he got back to his hotel room, he was wasted. He started to get undressed and went to the window to close the blinds when he saw a young girl looking out the window of a room across from him. He waved at her, and she waved back. "I know it sounds crazy, but in my drunken state this felt like an invitation to me. I started rubbing myself, and she just stood there. So then I pulled out my penis for her to see. She suddenly walked away, and I knew I was in trouble. Sure enough, a little while later there was a knock on the door, and I was arrested. I told them I'd never done anything like this before, and that was the truth. I don't know what came over me. I know I wouldn't have done it if I hadn't been drunk."

Although Dr. Jekyll used an elixir in order to become Mr. Hyde, he didn't really need it—the dark side of him was already present. In the same way, alcohol or drugs can give us an avenue to act out our darker urges. That's what happened to Jim. The alcohol merely lowered his inhibitions and gave him permission to act out a sexual fantasy he had been having for a long time—that of exposing himself to a young girl.

Type 5: The Imposter

Unlike the other types of Jekyll and Hydes, whose different personalities are often unconscious manifestations of deeper conflicts, the Imposter actually sets out to fool people. Imposters may have discovered that their real selves are not acceptable to others or to society, so they create alternative personas to garner more acceptance and support from others. Or they may deliberately take on charming personas in order to fool others. This is clearly the type of person a romantic partner or a business associate needs to be careful of getting involved with because the Imposter is capable of doing almost anything to get his or her needs met.

Imposters have no compunction about cheating on their spouses or creating entire lives separate from the ones they share with their partners and children. Imposters have even been known to marry more than one woman at a time or to marry people they don't love to gain access to financial fortunes.

While not all Imposters are abusive, they do make up a large percentage of those who are guilty of domestic violence and malicious emotional abuse. Most sex offenders are also Imposters. They can be so charming, persuasive, and manipulative that experienced therapists are frequently taken in by them. They are often extremely articulate and are able to offer such plausible versions of events and can do such a good job of interpreting these events in their favor that even highly skilled therapists can be persuaded to believe them over the Imposters' partners. Confronted with a polished, self-controlled, and charming abuser and his or her often confused, hysterical, irritable, impatient, and sometimes abrasive victim, it is often far too easy for therapists to conclude that the real victim is the abuser or that both parties abuse each other. And since therapists rarely have a chance to witness an abusive exchange firsthand, the Imposter is often able to elicit the sympathy and support of the therapist by using the right vocabulary and expressing the appropriate emotions.

STEVE: THE LOVING HUSBAND

I experienced this phenomenon firsthand with a client I will call Steve. Steve appeared to be a caring, loving husband and father who was afraid he was going to lose his wife and daughter because of his wife's emotional problems. During our first session, he told me a sad tale of how his wife was emotionally unbalanced, how she was so paranoid that she accused him of doing and saying things he never did or said, and how she had turned his daughter against him.

When I met his wife, Danielle, I was struck by how angry she was and how emotionally fragile she appeared to be. When I asked for her version of what was going on between her and her husband, she had a very different story to tell. She had been unhappy for quite some time and, in fact, had tried to leave Steve several times. Each time, he managed to talk her into staying, but this time she said she was determined to get away from him, especially because their daughter seemed afraid of him. "When your own daughter tells you it is time to leave your husband, you need to listen," she told me.

She described a man who was incredibly manipulative. "No one believes me when I tell them about who Steve really is," she explained. "He is so nice and so charming to everyone. He really seems to listen to people and makes them feel like they're important. He knows just what people need to hear. He's a salesman, and he's actually studied how to manipulate people. I don't know who the real Steve is—I think it's all a game to him.

"He has to have his way—always. He'll ask me what I want to do—what restaurant I want to go to, what movie I want to see—but when I tell him, he'll say something like, 'Of course, we'll go if you really want to, but wouldn't you rather see . . . ' Or if I tell him I want Chinese food, he'll say, 'But wouldn't you just love some Mexican food tonight?' I've learned to just go along with what he wants because he'll stay on me until I do what he wants anyway."

Fortunately for Danielle, I believed her version over Steve's—although each time I was in his presence, it was difficult not to fall under his spell. He was such a good actor—producing tears at the appropriate time, talking in a gentle, loving voice when he spoke about his wife—that he was quite convincing.

Type 6: The "All-Good" and the "All-Bad" Person

Jekyll and Hydes in this category change dramatically depending on their opinion of you at any given time. They tend to see everyone as either "all good" or "all bad." If you make a mistake around them or say something that upsets them, they may suddenly put you in the "all bad" camp and treat you very poorly. Later on, they may act as if nothing happened and begin treating you nicely again.

This is especially characteristic of people who suffer from BPD. There is no middle ground as far as borderlines are concerned. When someone hurts their feelings, that person becomes "bad." When someone agrees with them or treats them especially nice, that person is "good."

Children with borderline mothers suffer from a particular kind of hell because of their mothers' tendencies to label them good or bad depending on the mothers' moods. For example, as Christine Ann Lawson wrote in her book *Understanding the Borderline Mother: Helping Her Children Transcend the Intense, Unpredictable, and Volatile Relationship*, "One day they [borderline mothers] may see their children as angelic; other days their rage or sarcasm can shatter their children's souls."

It's no surprise that children with borderline parents often develop two contrasting perceptions of themselves. Believing in her child's basic goodness is possible only if a mother believes in her own goodness. Unfortunately, some borderlines have an inner conviction of being evil.

Borderline mothers often make one child the "all-good" child and another the "all-bad" or "no-good" child. This is actually a way of splitting and projecting their own contradictory feelings about themselves into different children. Unable to grasp that something might be both good and bad, a person with BPD can see only the ends of the spectrum.

Many children of parents with BPD never know from one minute to the next how their parents feel about them. As Lawson wrote in *Understanding the Borderline Mother*, "Like the game 'she loves me, she loves me not,' the mother's moods can suddenly change from affection to rage, creating an uncertain and insecure emotional environment. Winnocott (1962) emphasized the importance of the child's need for 'the good enough mother' who provides enough consistency and calmness so that the child is not overwhelmed with anxiety. Without structure and predictability in their emotional world, children have no reality base upon which to build self-esteem and security."

The borderline's all-or-nothing thinking results in split perceptions of her children. Borderline parents of only children tend to alternate between perceiving them as all-good and all-bad. Male children are often viewed as all-bad by borderline mothers who were sexually abused. Borderlines raised in mysogynistic homes will often repeat the pattern and designate girl children as all-bad. In other cases, certain characteristics of the child may unconsciously remind the mother of a hated or a loved part of herself.

Type 7: "I'm Fine as Long as You Don't Cross Me."

If you do as these Jekyll and Hydes wish, they can be considerate and appreciative. But if you don't do as they ask or if you have the nerve to question them, you will see entirely different personalities. This is especially true if you challenge or contradict them. Then they can be insulting, degrading, and cruel.

I met Justine when she and I both volunteered to co-chair a committee for a charitable organization. Justine appeared to be a very sweet woman. She was soft-spoken and exuded an air of quiet confidence. I immediately felt comfortable with her. As we began to make some decisions about an upcoming event, I felt that we were working well together. She seemed to listen to my ideas with interest, as I did hers, and we apparently were able to compromise on a plan of action.

But I soon discovered that Justine was only pretending to be cooperative. She suddenly started to distance herself from me for no apparent reason, and when I asked her what was going on, she said, "I really don't think we can work together anymore. I really felt we needed more time to plan for the event, but you thought we should schedule it right away."

"So why didn't you say that?" I asked. "I would have been willing to consider scheduling it later on if you felt we needed more time." To this she merely shrugged and looked away. She suddenly seemed very different from the person I had originally met. She was now sullen and angry looking. She refused to work with me again and resigned as co-chair of the committee. As I found out later on, this was a pattern with Justine. If she couldn't have things exactly as she wanted, she became angry and distant and refused to cooperate further.

Often, Jekyll and Hydes of this type are merely controllers— people who insist on having everything go their way. Other times, they actually have a personality disorder called narcissism.

Narcissistic Personality Disorder

The term *narcissist* comes from the Greek myth of Narcissus. Narcissus was a man who stared endlessly at his own reflection mirrored in a lake. Unable to pull himself away from contemplating his own beauty, he eventually starved to death and fell into the water, never more to be seen.

People who suffer from narcissistic personality disorder have an inflated false self which creates tremendous problems in intimate relationships. According to Dr. James Masterson, a leading expert on narcissism, the narcissist is essentially unable to relate to other people except in terms of his own inflated self-image and his unrealistic projections of himself onto others. He requires adulation and perfect responsiveness from his partner or an idealization of the partner so that the narcissist can bask in the partner's glow.

The narcissist has no desire to develop his genuine self—he is in love with his false self—the self that wants to deal only with the pleasant, happy, beautiful side of life. He is reluctant to face the disturbing side of life, and this fixation cuts him off from a full range of life experiences and emotional responses such as anger, jealousy, and envy. As long as nothing infiltrates their cocoons, narcissists won't be aware of any serious personality problems. They think they have it all, and those who know them will agree, since they have carefully selected certain people to be part of their world and thereby bolster their view of themselves. If anyone crosses them, however, or challenges them in any way, narcissists are forced to come out of their cocoons. There will be hell to pay to whoever forces them to face themselves or face reality.

As long as their partners adore them, put them on pedestals, and meet their sense of overblown entitlement, narcissists can be charming, interesting, and even sensitive companions. Whenever these requirements are frustrated, however, or appear to be lacking from their point of view, narcissists become enraged. This rage is always externalized and projected onto their partners. Once narcissists become disappointed and enraged, they begin to devalue their partners because the partners are not living up to their wishes.

This cycle of behavior can be viewed by their partners or others as a shift in their moods or even as a personality change, causing narcissists to be seen as Jekyll and Hydes. In actuality, it isn't as if a narcissist is two people or has two personalities; rather, the real person is revealed when he or she becomes disappointed. Narcissists have a keen ability to appear charming and sensitive to others—that is, as long as their need for adulation and special treatment is fulfilled.

3

What Causes the Jekyll and Hyde Syndrome?

Everyone carries a shadow, and the less it is embodied in the individual's conscious life, the blacker and denser it is. At all counts, it forms an unconscious snag, thwarting our most well-meant intentions.

—C. G. Jung

In the previous chapter I revealed some causes of the Jekyll and Hyde syndrome. These include childhood abuse, post-traumatic stress disorder, and personality disorders. Overall, however, and notwithstanding other biological or psychological problems that may cause or mimic this syndrome, the Jekyll and Hyde syndrome is essentially caused by an *internal conflict*.

The most common conflict, experienced by most people at some time in their lives, is the conflict between the public self and the private self. The *public self* is the persona we show to the world—the social self. The social self is the side that is concerned with how others perceive us, what impression we make on others, what others think of us. The *private self* includes our innermost thoughts and feelings, our personal opinion of ourselves, our beliefs about ourselves, and our self-talk.

Oftentimes, our private and public selves are at odds with each other. We exhibit one set of behaviors when we are in public and another when we are in private. Or we may feel good about ourselves when we are alone with our own thoughts and feelings but feel insecure and even critical of ourselves when we are with other people. The reverse can also be true—we can appear self-confident when we are in public but privately agonize over our self-worth when we are alone with ourselves.

We all have a public self—which we portray to others in order to look good or to meet their expectations. Yet some people create a public self that is so radically different from their private or real self that those who know them only superficially would be shocked if they were to get to know the real (private) person. Jekyll and Hydes tend to have more of a discrepancy between their public and private selves than most people do. This is true for several reasons:

- Many Jekyll and Hydes are overly concerned about what others think about them. They have an investment in looking good in public, often because they hold positions of authority or because others have put them on pedestals of some kind (for example, a minister, a teacher, a psychologist, or someone involved in politics).

- Many Jekyll and Hydes feel very insecure and have extremely low self-esteem (often due to childhood abuse). To compensate for these feelings of insecurity or even worthlessness, the Jekyll and Hyde creates a false self—someone who appears to be confident—in order to feel more comfortable and to fit in with society.

- People who are controlling or abusive have an investment in hiding their unacceptable behavior from the outside world. At home they can be intimidating and suffocating, while in the outside world they are caring, giving, much-admired pillars of the community. Many abusers are adept at creating a veil of secrecy concerning their dysfunctional and abusive behavior.

- People with borderline personality disorder often behave quite normally in public environments, such as the workplace, since their disturbance doesn't get triggered unless they are in an intimate relationship.

- Some Jekyll and Hydes deliberately try to fool people by behaving normally in public because they know their real selves would not be acceptable to others. For example, sociopaths are very good at creating public personas that are likable and charming—this helps them get away with breaking the rules or even the law. How many times have you heard, "But he was such a nice man," when the neighbors of criminals are interviewed.

THE TWO FACES OF MATTHEW

Anna was referred to me by a colleague because she believed she was being emotionally abused by her husband. Anna described her husband as extremely controlling, possessive, and explosive. She was at her wit's end and said she needed space from her husband because he was smothering her. He called her several times a day and always needed to know where she was. When he came home, he demanded her complete attention and was even jealous of any time she spent with their son. He constantly pressured her for sex and never seemed to get enough.

"I'm getting so that I can't stand for him to touch me," she shared. "I can hardly breathe when I am around him." Whenever she tried to set some boundaries or get some space from him, he exploded in anger, accusing her of having a lover or of using him financially. She was afraid of what he would do if she told him she wanted a separation and felt that he was quite capable of becoming violent. She asked whether I would be willing to conduct couples counseling with her and her husband, and I agreed, stating that I would need to see her husband one time alone to get his side of the story.

When Matthew walked into my office, I was shocked to discover that I recognized him. We were members of the same organization, and I had heard him speak numerous times. He always spoke with humility and depth about his dedication to becoming as good a person as he could be. He seemed particularly devoted to his wife and son and appeared to be so genuinely kind that people were drawn to him.

He was his charming self and mentioned that he recognized me from the other setting. I asked whether this bothered him, and he said no, that he was happy to know that we had similar beliefs and convictions. Since it was a large organization, I didn't see any conflict of interest in seeing him.

Matthew then proceeded to tell me about his marriage. He said he adored his wife and son and believed he was an excellent husband and father. He assured me that he would do anything to save his marriage. He didn't understand why his wife was unhappy since she had everything any woman would want or need. She didn't work, and he spoiled her by showering her with money and gifts. "To tell you the truth, I honestly don't think Anna is capable of being happy. She's just the kind of person who always wants more—more material possessions, more space, more freedom. When she told me she didn't want to have sex as often, I backed off—but that wasn't enough. I love Anna, and she is a beautiful woman. Do you know how difficult it is for me to keep my hands off her? But I do it because I want to respect her needs."

At this point, I noted anger in his voice. When I mentioned this to Matthew, he immediately denied it. "I'm not angry; honestly, I'm not. But I do get frustrated. After all, I'm a man and I have needs. Is it so unreasonable to expect that my wife would want to have sex with me?"

Clearly, Matthew and Anna had very different perceptions of what was going on in their marriage. Anna felt smothered by what Matthew identified as his love feelings for her; Matthew felt hurt by what he experienced as Anna's rejection of him. I began to see Matthew and Anna together to try to get to the bottom of their issues and to resolve their differences.

At the beginning of each session Matthew always presented himself as a loving and patient husband. He always smiled adoringly at Anna. While Anna told me about the past week—how Matthew had called her several times a day, how he had blown up and accused her of having an affair when she didn't answer her cell phone because she was at the gym working out, how he had pressured her to have sex, how he wouldn't take no for an answer—Matthew's face was usually animated in disbelief. He consistently tried to break in to tell me that what Anna was saying was wrong.

When it finally became his turn to speak, Matthew explained away each of Anna's complaints—he had to call her because he needed to tell her something important, he hadn't done any such thing as accuse her of having an affair, she led him to believe she wanted to have sex with him. Matthew always came out smelling like a rose. When Anna tried to protest, he very sweetly accused her of exaggerating or insinuated that she had imagined something that hadn't really happened. I watched in amazement as Anna backed off from her original complaints and began to question herself.

Recognizing that this is a common reaction when someone is being emotionally abused, I supported Anna and encouraged her to stand her ground. I asked her more questions and told her that it was understandable that she would feel upset by Matthew's behavior. Then I tried to explain to Matthew that the behaviors Anna described were inappropriate and tended to come from people who were insecure. I explained that I was not trying to make him out to be a bad person, just someone who needed help in changing some of his behaviors so that his marriage could be saved. This made Matthew furious.

All of sudden I saw an entirely different side of Matthew. He became dismissive and insulting to me, insinuating that, of course, I would take Anna's side since I was a woman. He stood up and started pacing around the room. I asked him to sit down, but he shot me a vicious look that said, "Leave me alone." He then told Anna and me that the whole counseling thing was a waste of time because Anna was lying and I believed her. "You're not being objective. Why are you assuming that Anna is telling the truth instead of me? Why don't you assume that Anna is deliberately trying to turn you against me—that she's lying and exaggerating?"

I was seeing firsthand the side of Matthew that Anna had grown afraid of—his Mr. Hyde personality. As much as Matthew needed to look good to the outside world, as much as he wanted and needed to be seen as a highly spiritual, kind, and dedicated man, there was another side to Matthew that only his wife and son knew, a darker, more disturbing side that threatened to take away everything he held dear.

An Internal Conflict between Good and Bad

Another conflict experienced by many Jekyll and Hydes centers around the concepts of "good" and "bad." People with the Jekyll and Hyde syndrome tend to be preoccupied with good and bad, and they tend to see things in good or bad terms—someone is either good or bad, an activity is either good or bad. They also tend to see things in black-or-white, all-or-nothing categories.

Some Jekyll and Hydes are extremely moralistic, with strong opinions about what is right or wrong. They may be sticklers about rules, insisting that rules be followed to the letter, or they may focus a great deal on the concept of "sin." It is very common for them to be extremely religious or to hold to rigid values and beliefs.

While those with this syndrome are often deeply religious or moralistic, they tend to be conflicted because their impulses and their personal behavior don't always match their beliefs. In fact, there often seems to be a huge discrepancy between what they believe in and their own desires and actions. For example, a Jekyll and Hyde may strongly believe that sex outside of marriage is a sin against God, yet he may secretly lust after other women. In order to act on his lust, he must turn against his own beliefs, and to do this, he may have to create another persona, just as Dr. Jekyll did. A woman may pride herself on being a moral, ethical person and yet be tempted to embezzle money from the company she works for. To justify her actions, she may convince herself that the company owes her the money because she works so hard and the company doesn't pay her enough. Thus, the company becomes "all bad."

Charles Lindbergh was elevated to the highest echelon of international celebrity when in 1927, at the age of twenty-five, he became the first person to fly solo across the Atlantic Ocean. He is still considered one of the world's greatest heroes even today. His public identity also includes the status of tragic hero, following the kidnapping and murder of his three-year-old son, Charles Jr.

Yet Charles had another side to him, a side that was not revealed until well after his death. It seems that Charles had a secret life, one that was much different from his public image of someone who was disciplined, strict, and moral; a devoted father and a loving husband. Charles Lindbergh was an adulterer who fathered a total of seven children with three other women—a German woman named Brigitte Hesshaimer, Brigitte's sister Marietta, and his German secretary, Valeska.

Why would a man known for being uncompromisingly moral risk going against his own moral code in this way? What would cause him to jeopardize his relationship with his wife, Anne Morrow Lindbergh, his children, his friends, and his adoring public? Why would a man who was seen by even his closest family as stern and unemotional find himself in so many emotional entanglements? Several reasons have been presented, including the fact that he never experienced true intimacy with his mother, who carried herself with a formality that extended even to bedtime, when she would shake her son's hand goodnight. He may have spent his life searching for the experience of intimacy he missed in childhood, first with one woman, then with another. But we also know that his mother had a strict sense of right and wrong. Although such rigorous childhood discipline most certainly helped him to endure thirty-three straight hours alone in the cockpit of a plane, it also allowed him to compartmentalize his life to such an extent that he could have at least four distinct families.

Problems with Our Self-Concept

Another common internal conflict experienced by many involves problems with our self-concept. Our self-concept is our subjective perception of who we are and what we are like. The concept of self is learned from our interactions with others, most notably from our parents, other family members, peers, and authority figures such as teachers and coaches. For example, you may have learned that you are a good athlete by hearing your parents' and friends' telling you this or by seeing that you run faster than most other people.

Carl Rogers, one of the founders of humanistic psychology, distinguished between two self-concepts—the *self*, or the person I think I am—and the *ideal self*—the person I wish I were. Many people suffer from rather severe discrepancies between the self and the ideal self. It is fine for the ideal self to be slightly out of reach; in fact, this can stimulate us to improve ourselves. But if the ideal self is so unrealistically perfect that we know it can never be reached, we end up feeling like failures. This can also cause us to create a false self.

Children's reactions to society's rules go through a number of predictable stages. The first response is typically to hide forbidden behaviors from their parents. For example, if children have been taught that it's not okay to get angry, they may think angry thoughts but not speak them out loud. If they are taught that it's not acceptable to tease their younger siblings, they will do so when their parents are away. Eventually, however, children can come to the conclusion that some thoughts and feelings are so unacceptable that these should be eliminated. In order to accomplish this, children construct imaginary parents in their heads to police their thoughts and activities; this is a part of the mind psychologists call the "superego." Now, when children have forbidden thoughts or indulge in unacceptable behavior, they experience self-administered jolts of anxiety. These are so painful that children put to sleep some of the forbidden parts of themselves—in Freudian terms, they repress them. The ultimate price of their obedience is a loss of wholeness.

To fill the void, each child creates a "false self." This false self serves a double purpose: it camouflages the parts of the child's being that have been repressed and it protects the child from further injury. As Dr. James Masterson stated in his classic book *The Search for the Real Self*, "The purpose of the false self is not adaptive but defensive; it protects against painful feelings. In other words, the false self does not set out to master reality but to avoid painful feelings, a goal it achieves at the cost of mastering reality."

The Conflict between Our Ego and Our Shadow

Finally, we reach the most significant internal conflict of all: the conflict between our ego and our Shadow. In a broad sense, the Jekyll and Hyde syndrome is caused by a person trying to disown his or her dark side or Shadow. As mentioned earlier, our Shadow is the aspect of ourselves that we have repressed or rejected because we have come to believe that it is unacceptable to those around us. Here is another way of describing how the Shadow develops.

In order for us to adapt to and become part of society, we each must create an ego. Ego development depends on our repressing what is wrong or bad in us, while we identify with what is perceived and reinforced as good by our parents, siblings, caretakers, and other important sources of love and support. This helps us to eliminate the anxiety caused by our fear of our parents' rejection and to gain the approval of those we care most about. This process of growing an ego continues throughout the first half of life and is modified by external influences and experiences as each of us moves out into the world.

The Shadow, or dark side, is a natural by-product of the ego-building process. Because of the necessarily one-sided nature of ego development, the neglected, rejected, and unacceptable qualities in a person accumulate in the unconscious psyche and take form as an inferior personality—the personal Shadow. This disowned part of the self eventually becomes a mirror image of the ego. We disown that which does not fit into our developing picture of who we are, thus creating a Shadow.

What is disowned, however, does not go away. It lives on within each person—out of sight, out of mind, but nevertheless real—an unconscious alter ego hiding just below the threshold of awareness. Those who feel they had to disown or repress many aspects of themselves in order to be accepted by their parents or society in general will have very large Shadows.

Ego and Shadow are therefore in an age-old battle, well known in mythology and literature—opposing twins or brothers, one good, the other evil—symbolic representations of the ego and alter ego in psychological development. Taken together, these twins, or opposites, form a whole. In the same way, when the ego assimilates the disowned self, a person moves toward wholeness.

As a child's ego takes hold in awareness, a portion of it forms a mask—or a *persona*—the face we each exhibit to the world. These masks portray what we and others think we are. The persona meets the demands of relating to the environment and the culture, matching the ego-ideal to the expectations and the values of the world in which we grow up.

A Duplicity of Life

In the story *The Strange Case of Dr. Jekyll and Mr. Hyde*, we see all the internal conflicts listed previously: the conflict between self and ideal self, the conflict between good and bad, and the conflict between ego and Shadow. The reason Dr. Jekyll led such a double life was that he aimed too high. He wanted respect, honor, and distinction, and to be highly regarded in society. In order to gain (and maintain) this adulation, he believed that he needed to hide any less-than-perfect aspects of himself. The truth is, had Dr. Jekyll understood that no human being can be perfect, that everyone has a dark side, he might have been able to embrace his darker urges instead of disowning them. It was his shame at having his darker urges that intensified them and caused Dr. Hyde to be created. This was his evaluation of what happened to him:

> Many a man would have blazoned such irregularities as I was guilty of; but from the high views that I set before me, I regarded and hid them with an almost morbid sense of shame. It was thus rather the exacting nature of my aspirations than any particular degradation in my faults, that made me what I was . . . .
>
> Hence it came about that I concealed my pleasure; and that when I reached years of reflection, and began to look round me and take stock of my progress and position in the world, I stood already committed to a profound duplicity of life.

He goes on to explain how he was guilty of certain irregularities of life that he regarded with a "morbid sense of shame." He had what he called a "dual nature." "Both sides of me were in dead earnest; I was no more myself when I laid aside restraint and plunged in shame, than when I laboured, in the eye of day, at the furtherance of knowledge or the relief of sorrow and suffering." From this Jekyll concluded "that man is not truly one, but truly two."

Jekyll began to dwell "on the thought of the separation of these elements. If each . . . could be housed in separate identities, life would be relieved of all that was unbearable." He began to experiment and finally succeeded in producing a drug that could accomplish just such a separation of his two personalities. He then took the drug and began to undergo profound changes: "I felt younger, lighter, happier in body; within I was conscious of a heady recklessness, a current of disordered sensual images running like a mill race in my fancy, a solution of the bonds of obligation, an unknown but not an innocent freedom of the soul. I knew myself, at the first breath of this new life, to be more wicked, sold a slave to my original evil; and the thought, in that moment, braced and delighted me like wine." He then looked in the mirror and saw the small, young, and somewhat deformed body of Edward Hyde.

"This, too, was myself," Jekyll reasoned. And so Jekyll welcomed Hyde, and concluded, "All human beings . . . are commingled out of good and evil; and Edward Hyde, alone in the ranks of mankind, was pure evil." Jekyll found that all he had to do was drink the drug and he was transformed into Hyde and could then indulge in all the pleasures that in the past he had either forbade himself or had indulged in only with guilt and anxiety that he might be discovered.

In many ways, Dr. Jekyll was correct: humans are not one, but two. We are both good and evil. Efforts to hide one's darker side, however, while presenting to the public one's more acceptable side do not work in the long run. Ultimately, the answer is to merge the two—to own the dark side and allow it to be expressed in healthy ways. I will discuss this in detail later in the book.

A Continuum

In addition to there being different types of Jekyll and Hydes, there are also degrees of severity. The Jekyll and Hyde syndrome actually exists along a continuum, with all of us suffering from some degree of the syndrome by mere virtue of being human beings and experiencing the inevitable internal conflicts that come with being human.

←		→
Mildly conflicted	Moderately conflicted	Severely conflicted
Small dark side	Medium dark side	Massive dark side

At the beginning of the continuum is someone who suffers from a mild internal conflict (for example, public versus private self, good versus bad) and thus has a small dark side. In the middle of the continuum is a person with a moderate internal conflict and a medium dark side. And at the end of the continuum is the individual with a severe internal conflict and a massive dark side.

When the Jekyll and Hyde Syndrome Is Caused by Childhood Maltreatment

As mentioned earlier, childhood abuse or neglect is also a common experience among Jekyll and Hydes. Those who were abused or neglected actually make up the majority of Jekyll and Hydes because this category includes everyone who experiences post-traumatic stress disorder, those who have personality disorders, and those whose mood shifts cause them to be abusive to others. Again, this operates on a continuum with people who are only

←		→
Mildly abused	Moderately abused	Severely abused
Mild PTSD	Moderate PTSD	Severe PTSD
Borderline traits	Mild to moderate BPD	Severe BPD
Narcissistic traits	Mild to moderate NPD	Severe NPD

mildly abused or neglected at one end and those who are more severely abused at the other.

The experience of childhood abuse, neglect, or both helps to create the Jekyll and Hyde syndrome in several ways. First of all, as I explained earlier, those who have been traumatized often are triggered when something in their current environment reminds them of something from their past. This accounts for why some people unexpectedly become depressed and withdrawn or suddenly fly off the handle for no apparent reason. It can also explain why some actually become abusive themselves. Sometimes an individual does what I call "channeling" an abuser—suddenly becoming like the person who abused him or her as a child, even taking on that person's voice, facial features, and mannerisms.

There are also other reasons why people who have been abused or neglected develop the Jekyll and Hyde syndrome. Those who have been traumatized in this way carry a great deal of shame and guilt. For example, when a family dynamic is extremely negative, abusive, or dysfunctional, guilt and shame become a troublesome core of the Shadow. This core of shame and guilt can cause people to act out in ways that are not normally characteristic of them. We'll discuss this phenomenon in more detail later in the book.

When the Jekyll and Hyde Syndrome Is Caused by a Personality Disorder

A personality disorder is an exaggerated version of a personality trait. According to *The Diagnostic and Statistical Manual of Mental Disorders (DSM-IV)*, the manual used by clinicians to help determine psychological diagnoses, a personality disorder is an enduring pattern of inner experience and behavior that deviates markedly from the expectation of the individual's culture, is pervasive and inflexible (unlikely to change), is stable over time, and leads to distress or impairment in interpersonal relationships. In order to be classified as a personality disorder, the person's behavior must be so pervasive that it causes distress, both for the individual with the disorder and for those who interact with him or her.

A personality disorder differs from mental illnesses in that it can't simply be treated through medication management to address brain chemical imbalances. Unfortunately, the behaviors and the traits that define a personality disorder are engrained in the person's personality. Some of these behaviors have been learned at a very young age as protection against being hurt (known as defense mechanisms). As I will discuss later in detail, many people who were abused in childhood develop personality disorders, while others do not. Some people develop the traits due to genetic predisposition. Certain personality disorders occur due to a combination of genetic predisposition and environmental influences (lack of nurturing or abuse).

The three personality disorders that are most often associated with someone seeming to have a dual personality are borderline personality disorder, narcissistic personality disorder, and antisocial personality disorder (people with the latter are also referred to as sociopaths).

Borderline Personality Disorder

Borderline personality disorder (BPD) is the most common personality disorder (it affects approximately six million Americans). Although men can develop BPD, women outnumber men two to one (within clinical populations). Men with BPD are often diagnosed as antisocial due to aggressive and violent behavior and therefore tend to enter the justice system rather than the mental-health system.

Those who suffer from BPD are often deeply conflicted. Many have a constant battle going on inside their heads regarding how they feel about someone. One day they may love you and think you are the greatest thing that ever happened to them, and the very next day they may hate you and want you out of their lives. This is partly due to the fact that they tend to put people on pedestals, idealizing them and making them far more wonderful, loving, accomplished, beautiful, and so on, than they really are. Because the individual with BPD has idealized the other person so much, that person is bound to fall off his or her pedestal. As soon as the other person disappoints the borderline individual, he or she comes crashing down off the pedestal.

The primary reason for these vacillations, however, is that people with this disorder have twin fears—the fear of abandonment and the fear of engulfment. When their fear of engulfment is triggered, these people can become critical and angry, finding fault in everything you do. They convince themselves that you are selfish and unloving or that you are dishonest and conniving. They hate you and never want to see you again. In this way they have successfully pushed you away. They no longer have to deal with their fear of being engulfed in the relationship.

Unfortunately, though, they don't get much time to relax because their fear of abandonment sets in rather quickly. You may no sooner be out the door before they start begging you to come back. "I love you, don't leave me," they might cry. "I'm sorry, please, please, don't leave me." This pattern of pushing people away and then begging for them to come back is so prevalent among people with borderline personality disorder that there is a book about borderlines with the title *I Hate You, Don't Leave Me*.

As you can see, people with BPD can definitely behave like Jekyll and Hydes. Mothers with BPD have a particularly difficult time being consistent with their children. As Christine Ann Lawson, the author of *Understanding the Borderline Mother*, explained, "Although she can function extraordinarily well in other roles, mothering is the single most daunting task for the borderline female. Her fear of abandonment and her tendency to experience separation as rejection or betrayal lock the borderline mother and her children in a struggle for survival. The child is emotionally imprisoned. Children must separate to survive, but separation threatens their mother's survival."

Identifying BPD can be difficult because the disorder includes individuals with different symptom clusters. Although depression and suicidal feelings are common, they are not always present. What is common among most people who suffer from BPD is volatility, impulsiveness, self-destructiveness, and a fear of abandonment.

And many people with BPD exhibit Jekyll and Hyde tendencies. In fact, prior to 1980, many with BPD were misdiagnosed as manic-depressive or schizophrenic.

According to the *DSM-IV*, BPD is characterized by a pervasive pattern of instability of interpersonal relationships, self-image, and affects (moods), as well as by a marked impulsivity beginning by early adulthood and present in a variety of contexts, as indicated by five or more of the following criteria:

1. Frantic efforts to avoid real or imagined abandonment.

2. A pattern of unstable or intense interpersonal relationships characterized by alternating between extremes of idealization and devaluation.

3. Identity disturbance: markedly and persistently unstable self-image or sense of self.

4. Impulsivity in at least two areas that are potentially self-damaging (for example, spending, sex, substance abuse, shoplifting, reckless driving, binge eating).

5. Recurrent suicidal behavior, gestures, or threats, or self-mutilating behavior.

6. Affective instability due to a marked reactivity of mood (for example, intense episodic dysphoria, irritability, or anxiety usually lasting a few hours and only rarely more than a few days). Dysphoria is the opposite of euphoria and is a mixture of depression, anxiety, rage, and despair.

7. Chronic feelings of emptiness.

8. Inappropriate, intense anger or difficulty controlling anger (for example, frequent displays of temper, constant anger, recurrent physical fights).

9. Transient, stress-related paranoid ideation or severe dissociative symptoms.

What causes borderline personality disorder? According to Lawson, therapists find that borderline patients have had one or more of the following experiences:

1. Inadequate emotional support following parental abandonment through death or divorce

2. Parental abuse, emotional neglect, or chronic denigration

3. Being the no-good child of a borderline mother

The psychiatrist Bessel van der Kolk and his colleagues have found that early trauma and abuse are more frequent in the histories of adult borderlines than in other clinical groups. Moreover, excessive separations, losses, or disruptions were also more likely in the lives of borderline patients and federal prisoners convicted of crimes of violence. This was especially true for those convicted of family violence. Childhood trauma coupled with separations such as these almost always involve attachment disruptions for the child.

Even though we know what can cause BPD, it's impossible to predict who will develop BPD since experience alone does not cause a personality disorder. While the experiences mentioned previously place children at risk for BPD, other factors can increase or decrease the chances of developing serious personality disturbance. For example, studies indicate that the single most important factor affecting resiliency in children is the conviction of being loved (Werner 1988). The effects of parental abandonment, abuse, and neglect can be mitigated if a child has access to a relationship with a loving adult such as a relative, a teacher, or a minister who is empathetically attuned to the child's feelings.

One way of understanding how BPD develops in the aftermath of a given trauma is to consider the degree to which the child's emotional needs were met. When feelings regarding traumatic experiences are not worked through, emotional growth is stunted. Balint (1968) proposed that personality is influenced not only by traumatic events but by the degree of psychological support received from significant others. Therefore, parents must allow the child to express intense emotion in order to prevent repression of the feelings. Unfortunately, all too often the traumatic experience is never discussed, much less worked through.

Narcissistic Personality Disorder

Narcissism has not received as much attention as other psychological disorders, and yet it is often the cause of abusive and Jekyll and Hyde behavior and the core problem of many people who suffer from addictions. In fact, it has been called the most hidden disorder of our time. Most people think that narcissistic individuals are those who have extremely high self-esteem and who think too highly of themselves. Ironically, however, those suffering from narcissistic personality disorder (NPD) or those who have strong narcissistic tendencies have extremely low self-esteem. According to Dr. James Masterson, a leading expert on narcissism, on the surface the narcissistic individual is brash, exhibitionistic, self-assured, and single-minded, often exuding an aura of success in career and relationships. Narcissists seem to be the people who have everything—talent, wealth, beauty, health, and power, and a sense of knowing what they want and how to get it.

In its extreme, narcissism becomes a character disorder. Narcissistic personality disorder, as described in the *DSM-IV*, has the following characteristics:

1. An inflated sense of self-importance

2. Fantasies of unlimited success, fame, power, and perfect love (uncritical adoration)

3. Exhibitionism (a need to be looked at and admired)

4. A tendency to feel rage with little objective cause

5. A readiness to treat people with cool indifference as punishment for hurtful treatment or as an indication of the fact that they have no current use for the person

6. A tendency toward severe feelings of inferiority, shame, and emptiness

7. A sense of entitlement accompanied by the tendency to exploit

8. A tendency to overidealize or devalue people based largely on a narrow focus

9. An inability to empathize

In spite of their air of self-sufficiency, narcissistic individuals are actually more needy than most people. To admit that they are needy or to admit that a person or a relationship is important to them forces them to face feelings of deficiency. This, in turn, will create intolerable emptiness, jealousy, and rage inside them. To prevent this from occurring, narcissists must find ways to get their needs met without acknowledging their needs or the people who meet them. This they accomplish by viewing people as objects or as having need-fulfilling functions.

Narcissists remain aloof from other people and tend to have only transient social relationships. Because they cannot acknowledge that they need others, they are almost incapable of feeling true gratitude. Instead, they ward off this feeling by demeaning the gift or the giver. They can be charming when they wish to impress others, but with their spouses and families, narcissists do not even pretend to be grateful. They feel that their spouses and families belong to them and are supposed to meet their every need. Not only will their spouses' and children's efforts to please them not be appreciated, but their families can always count on their criticism when what is offered is beneath the standards of the narcissist.

What causes narcissistic personality disorder? As with BPD, no one can be absolutely sure what causes NPD. Yet most experts view NPD as the flip side of BPD—meaning that although it is likely caused by the very same conditions that create BPD, the child reacts in opposite ways. For example, while those with BPD tend to have thin, porous boundaries, those with NPD tend to have very thick boundaries. Those with NPD have usually been so shamed by childhood abuse or abandonment that they have built up huge walls in order to defend themselves from further shaming. It's as if they are saying, "No one can ever shame me again because no one can ever reach me." In actuality, they feel as vulnerable and as insecure as someone with BPD does—they simply hide it better.

Antisocial Personality Disorder

People with an antisocial personality disorder don't suffer from an internal conflict as most Jekyll and Hydes do. This is because someone with an antisocial personality disorder, or what is commonly referred to as a "sociopath," has a psychological makeup that is radically different from most people's. The concept of right or wrong is unknown to sociopaths. So is the concept of taking responsibility for their actions. A sociopath does not have a conscience. It's not that sociopaths fail to grasp the difference between good and bad, right from wrong, but the distinction doesn't limit their behavior. They simply don't care if something is considered bad or wrong by the majority of people in society. Because sociopaths have no guilt or remorse, they are free to do anything they want without suffering any internal, emotional consequences. They have created a personal set of values, but these do not match society's values.

Since sociopaths often appear to be two different people, they can easily be confused with a person who has the classic Jekyll and Hyde syndrome. Someone who is just getting to know a sociopath and is falling under that individual's charismatic charms will perceive the sociopath much differently than an intimate partner or a friend who knows the real person. Sociopaths are also good con artists and often create other personalities or entire identities in order to get away with their cons, their romantic indiscretions, or their illegal activities. For this reason, a sociopath is often labeled a "Dr. Jekyll and Mr. Hyde."

Although we usually think of sociopaths as being an anomaly— a small percentage of people—the fact is that approximately 4 percent of the population are sociopaths. This is actually a huge number of people—one in twenty-five individuals, to be exact. As Martha Stout, Ph.D., pointed out in her wonderful book *The Sociopath Next Door*, there are more sociopaths among us than people who suffer from the more publicized disorders of anorexia (3.43 percent of the population), four times as many sociopaths as schizophrenics (1 percent of the population), and one hundred times as many sociopaths as people diagnosed with colon cancer.

According to the *DSM IV* (considered the definitive text for determining psychiatric diagnoses), the clinical diagnosis of antisocial personality disorder should be considered when an individual possesses at least three of the following seven characteristics: (1) failure to conform to social norms; (2) deceitfulness, manipulativeness; (3) impulsivity or failure to plan ahead; (4) irritability or aggressiveness; (5) reckless disregard for the safety of self or others; (6) consistent irresponsibility; and (7) lack of remorse after having hurt, mistreated, or stolen from another person. The presence in an individual of any three of these symptoms, taken together, is enough to make many psychiatrists suspect the disorder.

Some researchers and clinicians have found that sociopaths also frequently exhibit the following traits:

- A superficial charm that allows the sociopath to seduce other people. This charisma can make a sociopath seem more charming or more interesting than most of the "normal" people around him. He is sexier, more entertaining, more spontaneous, or more intense than everyone else.

- In actuality, sociopaths are known for their shallowness of emotion—a callousness—and for the hollow and transient nature of any affectionate feelings they may claim to have for someone.

- They have no genuine interest in bonding emotionally with a mate. Once the surface charm wears away, their relationships are exposed as loveless, one-sided, and almost always short-term. Partners are typically viewed as possessions, and while a sociopath may feel angry at the loss of a partner, he or she will never feel sad or accountable.

- Sometimes the sociopathic charisma is accompanied by a grandiose sense of self-worth that can also be compelling at first but later, upon closer inspection, may seem inappropriate or even laughable.

- Sociopaths have no trace of empathy. They simply cannot put themselves in the place of another person, nor do they care to.

- Sociopaths are known for their pathological lying and conning and their parasitic relationships with friends.

- Sociopaths have a greater than normal need for stimulation. This causes them to take frequent risks (physical, social, financial, and legal). They can often charm others into attempting dangerous ventures with them.

- Many sociopaths have a history of early behavior problems, often including juvenile delinquency and drug use.

- They do not acknowledge responsibility for any problems that occur, whether it is talking a friend into a bad business deal or being arrested.

The first characteristic in the previous list—the sociopathic charisma—often allows sociopaths to fool other people, at least initially. Fortunately for people they have charmed or seduced, this false front tends to wear off rather quickly. For this reason, some people consider sociopaths to also be Jekyll and Hyde–like in their duality.

What causes antisocial personality disorder? Put very simply, the cause of antisocial personality disorder is unknown. Like many human characteristics, the answer is probably a combination of both nature and nurture—a predisposition for the characteristic is present at conception, but the environment regulates how it is expressed. Many experts through the years have theorized that sociopathy may be caused by an attachment disorder. Attachment disorder occurs when attachment in infancy is disrupted either because of parental incompetence or because the infant is left alone too much. Children and adults with severe attachment disorder (those for whom attachment was not possible during the first seven months of life) are unable to bond emotionally to others. Children with attachment disorder (such as the Romanian orphans adopted by Americans in the 1990s) are impulsive and emotionally cold and can sometimes become violent toward their parents, siblings, play-mates, or pets. They tend to steal, vandalize, and start fires, and they often spend time in detention centers when they are young and in jail when they become adults, just like sociopaths. On the other hand, unlike sociopaths, children and adults afflicted with attachment disorders are seldom charming or interpersonally clever. In fact, people with attachment disorders are typically somewhat off-putting, and they don't make much effort to fake being normal. Many become isolated from others, and their emotional affect is either flat and uninviting or directly hostile. They tend to swing between belligerent indifference and unmeetable neediness—a far cry from the sociopath's charming and seductive persona and his or her ability to manipulate others.

Although we don't know the cause of antisocial personality disorder, we do know what one of the underlying neurobiological deficits may be. According to Martha Stout, sociopaths who have been studied reveal a significant aberration in their ability to process emotional information at the level of the cerebral cortex. And from examining heritability studies, it is speculated that the neurobiological underpinnings of the core personality features of sociopathy are as much 50 percent heritable. The remaining causes, the other 50 percent, are much foggier. Neither childhood maltreatment nor attachment disorder seems to account for the environmental contribution to the loveless, manipulative, and guiltless existence of sociopaths.

SCOTT PETERSON—A SOCIOPATH OR A JEKYLL AND HYDE?

Scott Peterson, the man who received such media attention from being accused and eventually convicted of killing his wife, Lacey, and his unborn child, has been labeled a sociopath by the media and some media psychologists. But he has also been called a Jekyll and Hyde. It is my theory that Scott actually fits my criteria for a Jekyll and Hyde more than he fits the criteria for a sociopath. We don't find a history of any behavior on his part in childhood that is characteristic of a sociopath (no school problems, no difficulties with the law, and so on). It seems that all he was guilty of prior to the murder of his wife was creating a dual life so that he could have his cake (the security of a marriage) and eat it, too (have affairs with other women)—a typical Jekyll and Hyde move.

People often ask, "Why didn't he just get a divorce if he wanted out of the marriage?" If Scott is a true Jekyll and Hyde, however, he would have had a strong need to "look good," and divorcing Lacey—everyone's darling—would not have made him look very good at all, to his family or hers, to his friends or hers. In fact, Lacey was so well loved and seemed to love Scott so much that it would have made him look like a cad. In her recent book, Sharon

Roche, Lacey's mother, states that when Lacey was ready to have a child, Scott told her he didn't think he wanted children after all. Lacey became very upset because she had always wanted children and thought Scott did as well. Sharon said she heard no more about it until Lacey announced she was pregnant. "I assumed they had worked it out." Maybe, maybe not. Perhaps Scott merely gave in or appeared to, once faced with Lacey's persuasive arguments. (Lacey was known to be very persuasive when she really wanted something—she was used to getting what she wanted.) Maybe the "good" Scott couldn't disappoint Lacey, while his dark side may have felt manipulated and cornered.

If we go with this theory, we can see how Scott may have felt conflicted up to the very end. His good side and his dark side may have battled it out until finally the Shadow side won—and he decided to kill Lacey.

There are, in fact, many cases where husbands have killed their wives instead of simply divorcing them, and for the same reason Scott may have killed Lacey—they didn't want to look bad. Several convicted wife murderers have admitted that they didn't want to face the disappointment and the critical judgment of their families and friends if they had divorced their wives. Instead, they felt that they would elicit much more sympathy if their wives were dead. They would have been the grieving husbands and would have come out smelling like a rose.

Psychological and Physical Conditions That Can Mimic the Jekyll and Hyde Syndrome

Certain psychological and physical conditions can cause extreme behavior changes or even a so-called split in the personality, and these conditions can often mimic the Jekyll and Hyde syndrome. For example, those with dissociative identity disorder (DID), once called multiple personality disorder (MPD), can suffer from what looks like aspects of the Jekyll and Hyde syndrome. In addition, people with the Jekyll and Hyde syndrome are often accused of being schizophrenic or of having what is incorrectly called a split personality. Anyone with bipolar disorder (or what used to be called manic-depression) or with Asperger's syndrome can also manifest radical shifts in mood.

If the person you are close to has been diagnosed with any of these disorders or if, after reading the following descriptions, you think that this person may suffer from these disorders, they need special medical and/or psychological intervention, which may include medication. This does not mean that the information in this book may not be helpful to you. Much of it can still help you to cope with your reactions to his or her mood shifts; however, a person who suffers from bipolar disorder, schizophrenia, DID, or Asperger's syndrome does not technically meet the criteria for Jekyll and Hyde syndrome.

Bipolar Disorder

Like those who suffer from the Jekyll and Hyde syndrome, people who have bipolar disorder experience mood episodes. These mood episodes can include depressive episodes, manic episodes, and mixed episodes. During depressive episodes, people usually experience a sad mood, feelings of hopelessness or worthlessness, diminished energy and interest in usual activities, and disturbances in sleep, appetite, energy, and concentration. Manic episodes typically involve either an extremely happy or irritable mood accompanied by other changes in behavior, such as increased activity, decreased need for sleep, grandiose thinking, poor judgment, racing thoughts, and provocative, intrusive, or aggressive behavior. Mixed episodes involve the simultaneous occurrence of depressive and manic symptoms. Sometimes people with bipolar disorder experience psychotic symptoms (such as delusions and hallucinations) during the mood episode, but these psychotic symptoms go away when their mood returns to normal.

The mood episodes of someone with bipolar disorder typically last from a couple of hours to many months. Between episodes, people with this disorder often return to their usual functioning and personality. Some can enjoy healthy, stable moods for many years between episodes, while others rapidly go in and out of mood episodes almost continually. Still others experience mood episodes at frequencies between these two extremes.

In the current *DSM-IV*, a distinction is made between bipolar I disorder and bipolar II disorder. People with bipolar II have so-called hypomanic episodes, as opposed to the full-blown manic episodes experienced by those with bipolar I disorder. Both hypomanic and manic episodes involve the same symptoms (for example, elevated mood, increased activity, decreased need for sleep, grandiosity, racing thoughts, excessive involvement in pleasurable activities, and so on), but there are several important differences, the most crucial being severity. That is, hypomanic episodes themselves do not cause significant distress or greatly impair one's work, family, or social life, but manic episodes do disrupt these things.

Some evidence indicates that there might be certain common genetic causes of schizophrenia and bipolar disorder. This is not too surprising, since there is symptom overlap between the two disorders. Specifically, some people with bipolar disorder experience hallucinations and delusional ideas during mood episodes, while those with schizophrenia can also have these psychotic symptoms. In addition, many people with schizophrenia experience episodes of manic or depressive symptoms. It is the timing and the overlap of mood and psychotic symptoms that differentiate these two diagnostic categories.

Treatment for bipolar disorder often involves a mood-stabilizing medication, such as Lithium, Neurontin, Depakote, or Tegretol. People with bipolar disorder who experience psychotic symptoms might also be treated with an antipsychotic medication, such as Haldol or Zyprexa. Therapy, support, and education about the illness are also important elements of a good treatment plan.

Schizophrenia

Jekyll and Hydes are often accused of being schizophrenic, because people with schizophrenia are often thought to have "split personalities." But those with schizophrenia do not actually have split personalities. Instead they suffer from a chronic, severe, and disabling brain disorder involving problems with their thought processes. These problems lead to hallucinations, delusions, disordered thinking, and unusual speech or behavior. Other symptoms include movement disorders, flat affect, social withdrawal, and cognitive deficits.

Schizophrenics often hear voices others don't hear, believe that others are broadcasting their thoughts to the world, or become convinced that others are plotting to harm them. These experiences can make them fearful and withdrawn and cause difficulties when they try to have relationships with others.

Schizophrenia affects about one percent of people. Symptoms usually develop in men in their late teens or early twenties and in women in their twenties or thirties, but in rare cases, they can appear in childhood. Schizophrenia is a lifelong illness, and most patients will need treatment for the rest of their lives. Despite the availability of new medication with less severe and fewer side effects, only one person in five recovers from the illness, and one in ten people with schizophrenia commits suicide.

Many people still believe that schizophrenia is caused by poor parenting, but this is not true. Schizophrenia is a complex illness; scientists believe it is caused by a number of different factors that act together. These factors included genetic influences, trauma (injury) to the brain occurring during or around the time of birth, as well as the effects of social isolation or stress. In some cases, the use of drugs, such as cannabis, can also be a contributing factor.

Dissociative Identity Disorder (DID)

Partners and family members of Jekyll and Hydes sometimes ask me whether their loved one could have multiple personality disorder (MPD). The answer is typically no, although Jekyll and Hydes often dissociate. To understand why this is true, you must first understand what MPD actually is and what it is not. The psychiatric community has changed the name multiple personality disorder to dissociative identity disorder because *multiple personalities* is a somewhat misleading term. A person diagnosed with DID feels as if she has within her two or more entities, or personality states, each with its own independent way of relating, perceiving, thinking, and remembering about herself and her life. If two or more of these entities take control of the person's behavior at a given time, a diagnosis of DID can be made. In the past, these entities were often called "personalities," even though the term did not accurately reflect the common definitions of the word as the total aspect of our psychological makeup. Other terms often used by therapists and survivors to describe these entities are *alternate personalities*, *alters*, *parts*, *states of consciousness*, *ego states*, and *identities*. It is important to keep in mind that although these alternate states may appear to be very different, they are all manifestations of a single person.

Unlike Jekyll and Hydes, those who suffer from DID have more than one alternate personality, and they often suffer from severe memory loss. In extreme cases, some people with DID dissociate to such an extreme that they "lose time" and cannot remember what they did the day or night before.

DID is a fairly common effect of severe trauma in early childhood, most typically the result of extreme, repeated physical, sexual, and/or emotional abuse. The vast majority of people who develop DID have documented histories of repetitive, overwhelming, and often life-threatening trauma at a sensitive developmental stage of childhood (usually before the age of nine), and they may possess an inherited biological predisposition for dissociation.

What is dissociation? When faced with overwhelmingly traumatic situations from which there is no physical escape, a child who is being abused may resort to "going away" in his or her head. For example, many survivors of sexual abuse describe the sensation of leaving their body and floating up into the ceiling while the abuse is taking place. This dissociative process enables thoughts, feelings, memories, and perceptions of traumatic experiences to be separated off psychologically, allowing the child to function as if the trauma had not occurred.

Dissociative disorders are often referred to as highly creative survival techniques because they allow individuals enduring hopeless circumstances to preserve some areas of healthy functioning. For children who have been repeatedly physically and sexually assaulted, the dissociative escape may become so effective that they use it automatically whenever they feel threatened or anxious—even if the anxiety-producing situation is not extremely abusive.

Repeated dissociation may result in a series of separate entities, or mental states, which may eventually take on identities of their own. These entities may become the internal "personality states" of a DID system. Changing between these states of consciousness is often described as "switching."

People with dissociative disorders may experience any of the following symptoms: depression, mood swings, suicidal tendencies, sleep disorders (insomnia, night terrors, and sleep walking), panic attacks and phobias (flashbacks, reactions to stimuli or triggers), alcohol or drug abuse, compulsions and rituals, psychoticlike symptoms (including auditory and visual hallucinations), and eating disorders. They can also experience headaches, amnesia, time loss, trances, and out-of-body experiences. Some people with dissociative disorders have a tendency toward self-sabotage, self-persecution, and even violence (both self-inflicted and outwardly directed).

Research shows that, on average, people with dissociative disorders have spent seven years in the mental health system prior to receiving an accurate diagnosis. This is partly due to the fact that their symptoms are similar to those of many other psychiatric diagnoses. Many diagnosed with dissociative disorders also have secondary diagnoses of depression, anxiety, or panic disorders and 80 to 100 percent also have a secondary diagnosis of post-traumatic stress disorder. If the Jekyll and Hyde syndrome was an official psychiatric disorder, someone with DID might be considered to have it as a secondary diagnosis.

People with dissociative disorders are highly responsive to individual psychotherapy, as well as a range of other treatment modalities, including medications, hypnotherapy, and adjunctive therapies such as art or movement therapy. Treatment is long-term, intensive, and painful, as it generally involves remembering and reclaiming the dissociated traumatic experiences.

Asperger's Syndrome in Adults

Adults with Asperger's syndrome can also exhibit Jekyll and Hyde behavior, but they are not true Jekyll and Hydes. Asperger's syndrome (AS) is one of the autism spectrum disorders and is classified as a developmental disorder that affects how the brain processes information. People with AS show a wide range of behaviors, but common characteristics include difficulty in forming friendships, communication problems (such as an inability to listen or a tendency to take whatever is said to them literally), and an inability to understand social rules and body language.

More males than females have Asperger's syndrome. While every person who has the syndrome will experience different symptoms and severity of symptoms, some of the more common characteristics include average or above average intelligence; inability to think in abstract ways; difficulties in empathizing with others; problems understanding another person's point of view; hampered conversational ability; difficulty controlling feelings such as anger, depression, and anxiety; adherence to routines and schedules, and stress if an expected routine is disrupted; inability to manage appropriate social conduct; and specialized fields of interest or hobbies.

A person with Asperger's syndrome may have trouble understanding the emotions of other people, and the subtle messages that are sent by facial expression, eye contact, and body language are often missed. Because of this, a person with the syndrome may be seen as egotistical, selfish, and uncaring. These are unfair labels, because the affected people are neurologically unable to understand other people's emotional states. They are usually shocked, upset, and remorseful when told their actions were hurtful or inappropriate.

There is no cure or specific treatment for Asperger's syndrome. Those with this syndrome can be given social training, which teaches them to behave in different social situations.

PART II

If You Have a Jekyll and Hyde
in Your Life

4

How to Cope with a Jekyll and Hyde

My husband is two people. There is the person I married, a kind and considerate man. Then there is the person I call Marcus, which is my husband's father's name. I can always tell when Marcus is with us because Van begins to act like his abusive father. It is scary. His face and voice change. He really is a different person.

—Claire, age forty-three

Now that you know what type of Jekyll and Hyde you are deal-ing with and understand what causes the Jekyll and Hyde syndrome, the next issue is how you will handle the problem.

Those who are involved with someone who has the Jekyll and Hyde syndrome usually feel a great deal of confusion, anger, dis-tress, and embarrassment due to the behavior of their loved one. Many people experience emotional abuse on a regular basis when the person they care about suddenly becomes insulting, blows up unexpectedly, or frightens them with bizarre behavior. Others are traumatized when they discover that the person they thought they knew is actually someone else entirely.

In this chapter I offer specific information and techniques that will help you to cope with someone who has the Jekyll and Hyde syndrome. This begins with a step-by-step process for coming out of denial about the fact that your loved one is a Jekyll and Hyde. For partners and children of someone with this syndrome, it includes learning not to take their partners' or parents' behavior personally and learning how to shield themselves from emotionally abusive statements and behavior.

Come Out of Denial

The first and perhaps most important step in coping with someone who has the Jekyll and Hyde syndrome is to come out of denial. You must face the fact that this person in your life who is so changeable actually has a serious problem and that because of it, you have suffered. All too often we simply endure situations, no matter how uncomfortable or even destructive, instead of acknowledging how damaging the situation is and determining that we need to do something about it. It is part of human nature to acclimate ourselves to discomfort and pain, and this tendency can sometimes act as a positive survival mechanism. On the other hand, simply putting up with unacceptable, unreasonable, or destructive behavior is not a healthy coping strategy.

Coming out of denial is not a simple task. It actually involves several important shifts in your thinking. In other words, coming out of denial means that you literally have to change your mind about what is going on, about the other person, and perhaps about yourself. There are five steps to the process of coming out of denial about the Jekyll and Hyde in your life:

1. Face the fact that this person is not behaving normally.

2. Admit to yourself that you are being emotionally abused and are therefore being damaged by the situation.

3. Stop isolating yourself, and get feedback from others.

4. Face the fact that the Mr. Hyde part of his or her personality is a real aspect of this person that will not go away just because the person promises never to act this way again.

5. Don't fool yourself into thinking this person will change without extensive outside help.

Step One: Face the Fact That This Person Is Not Behaving Normally

As I have discussed previously, we all experience moods shifts and we all have different sides to our personalities. But there needs to be an overarching sameness to a person, a consistency that identifies who this person really is. This kind of consistency helps other people to feel comfortable and at ease. When someone is not consistent overall—meaning that at any given moment we cannot identify familiar personality characteristics, behavior, and beliefs—we become confused, emotionally threatened, or even emotionally damaged.

Imagine how a child feels when someone he or she has come to love and trust suddenly begins to look or behave very differently. We see this all the time in very young children who don't recognize a parent who has a mask on. The child's initial confusion often turns into panic if the parent doesn't take off the mask quickly and show the child that it was just a game. Oftentimes, people with the Jekyll and Hyde syndrome can seem to us as if they are wearing masks, and we often react with the same feelings of confusion and panic that a young child would. If the person is behaving somewhat differently from what we are used to but there are enough familiar aspects to his or her personality, we may only become confused and shocked by the change. But if someone is behaving so radically differently that we cannot recognize him or her, we will begin to panic. There is a sort of cognitive dissonance that occurs. We can visually see that this is the same person, but we cannot match up the face with the behavior.

If one or both of your parents or another significant caretaker had the Jekyll and Hyde syndrome, you may actually have come to feel that radical mood swings and personality changes are normal. After all, it is what you experienced all your life. It is not normal, however, for a person to suddenly turn into someone you barely recognize, to treat you one way one time and a completely different way another time. It is not normal for someone's expectations to change depending on his or her mood. And it certainly is not normal for someone to suddenly demonize you, reject you, or perceive you as the cause of all his or her problems. It is important that you face this.

Step Two: Admit to Yourself That You Are Being Emotionally Abused

If a significant person in your life is behaving in the ways that have been described in this book, you are being emotionally abused. I realize that abuse is a strong word, but I have never known anyone who was involved with a Jekyll and Hyde who was not being emotionally abused on some level. In fact, chaotic abuse is actually a form of emotional abuse.

Emotional abuse can be defined as any *nonphysical* behavior that is designed to control, intimidate, subjugate, demean, punish, or isolate another person through the use of degradation, humiliation, or fear. Emotionally abusive behavior ranges from verbal abuse (belittling, berating, insulting, constant criticism) to more subtle tactics like intimidation, manipulation, and refusal to be pleased. It can also include any and all of the following:

- Humiliation and degradation
- Discounting and negating
- Domination and control
- Judging and criticizing
- Accusing and blaming
- Trivial and unreasonable demands or expectations
- Emotional distancing and the "silent treatment"
- "Crazy-making" behavior
- Isolation or cutting off support systems

In addition, there are types of emotional abuse most often experienced by those involved with a Jekyll and Hyde. These include:

- Unpredictable responses—includes drastic mood swings, sudden emotional outbursts for no apparent reason, and inconsistent responses such as reacting very differently at various times to the same behavior, saying one thing one day and the opposite the next, or frequently changing one's mind.

- Constant chaos—continual upheaval and discord (constant conflict with others, "addicted to drama").

- Gaslighting—the use of insidious techniques to make someone doubt his or her perceptions, memory, and sanity. A partner who does this may continually deny that certain events occurred or that he or she said something you both knew was said, or he or she may insinuate that you are imagining things or that you are exaggerating or lying. This is often done to discredit a partner, in order to turn others against him or her, or as a way to justify inappropriate, cruel, or abusive behavior. The term *gaslighting* is taken from the 1944 film *Gaslight* starring Charles Boyer as a husband who psychologically tortures his wife (played by Ingrid Bergman) until she doubts her own sanity.

- Abusive expectations—includes a person placing unreasonable demands on loved ones such as expecting you to meet his or her every need and believing it is perfectly okay to chastise, criticize, or humiliate you or to treat you in disrespectful or cruel ways. It can also include expecting you to ignore or accept his or her radical mood swings, or to forgive and forget after every unexpected emotional blow-up.

All these forms of emotional abuse cause a person to feel constantly unsettled and off balance. Other effects of emotional abuse include depression; a lack of motivation; confusion; difficulty concentrating or making decisions; low self-esteem; feelings of failure, worthlessness, and hopelessness; self blame; and self-destructiveness. Emotional abuse is like brainwashing in that it systematically wears away at the victim's self-confidence, sense of self-worth, trust in his or her perceptions, and self-concept. Emotional abuse cuts to the very core of a person, creating scars that may be longer lasting than physical ones.

Jekyll and Hydes with personality disorders are particularly guilty of emotionally abusing their partners, children, or other family members. Although it is not necessarily their intent, their behavior is experienced by their loved ones as abusive. Some personality-disordered Jekyll and Hydes actually do intend to abuse their loved ones as a way to keep their loved ones off balance and confused.

Emotional abuse is also a powerful tool that is used to maintain power and control over another person. It is designed to instill negative feelings such as shame, embarrassment, guilt, and fear. For more information on emotional abuse, read my book *The Emotionally Abusive Relationship*.

QUESTIONNAIRE

Are You a Victim of Domestic Abuse?

Your partner doesn't have to hit you for you to be a victim of domestic abuse. Answer the following questions as honestly as possible.

1.   Has your partner ever threatened to hurt you?

2.   Are you afraid of your partner?

3.   When your partner drinks, does he or she get rough or violent?

4.   Does your partner always blame others for his or her problems?

5.   Does your partner frequently explode in a rage?

6.   Does your partner throw objects or break things when he or she is angry?

7.   Has your partner ever deliberately hurt a pet?

8.   Does your partner have a Jekyll and Hyde personality?

9.   Do you usually give in when you argue because you are afraid of your partner?

10.   Are your children afraid when your partner is angry?

11. Are you afraid to have friends and family come over for fear of your partner exploding?

12. Does your partner listen in on your phone calls?

13. Does your partner constantly accuse you of doing things behind his or her back?

14. Does your partner insist on going everywhere with you?

15. Is your partner suspicious of your every move?

16. Has your partner ever forced you to have sex even though you did not want to?

17. Have you ever called, or thought of calling, the police because an argument was getting out of control?

18. Does your partner ever threaten to take the kids away if you leave her or him?

These are all warning signs of potential physical violence, and they should be taken seriously. If these things take place regularly, you are already being emotionally abused, even if the physical violence has not started.

Sometimes people don't realize they are being emotionally abused by Jekyll and Hyde behavior because it's what they are used to. Anyone who experienced a childhood in which one or both parents had radical mood shifts can react one of two ways to another relationship with a Jekyll and Hyde. Some people react as if living with a person who changes radically were completely normal because, in essence, it is normal for them. After all, it's what they grew up with. They became so numbed to the trauma of having to adjust to the shock of someone changing before their eyes that they carried this numbness into their adult lives. This is often the case with adult children of alcoholics and people who were raised by parents with serious emotional or psychological problems.

Others panic at the first signs of change in another person. They are what is called "hypervigilant," constantly scrutinizing the other person for any sign of impending change and reacting very power-fully when a change occurs. As children, these people may have closely watched a parent, waiting anxiously for a change, and may have run away and hid every time this parent experienced a mood shift or a personality change.

You will need to decide just how damaging it is for you to be involved with someone who has the Jekyll and Hyde syndrome. If one or both of your parents or another significant caretaker was also a Jekyll and Hyde, you need to face the fact that you are being retraumatized every time you reexperience this form of emotional abuse. If you react with numbness, don't fool yourself into thinking it doesn't affect you. If you panic at any sign of change, your nervous system is being overloaded with stress.

Step Three: Stop Isolating Yourself, and Get Feedback from Others

The danger of isolation cannot be stressed enough. Many abusive people isolate their partners and their children from others in order to gain control of them. In isolation, these partners and children lose touch with what is normal.

For you to completely face the fact that you are involved with a Jekyll and Hyde and that you are being emotionally abused, you need to stop isolating yourself. This may be difficult, especially if your partner is jealous and possessive and doesn't want you to associate with others. Yet this is exactly what you need to do, even if it means sneaking behind your partner's back to do it. Start calling your old friends again, and make arrangements to get together with them. Ask your friends what they think of your partner and whether they think you've changed since you've been with him or her. Make some new friends, join organizations, or get involved with physical activities that will allow you to get out more.

You also need to tell someone about how your partner, parent, or other loved one has been acting. In other words, you need to get a reality check. You may be in such denial about his or her behavior that you've lost touch with reality. Getting feedback from someone who is more objective may help you come out of denial and may act as a safeguard if the Jekyll and Hyde in your life ever becomes violent. For your own protection, you may need to have someone else know about what is happening to you.

Telling another person will not only provide you with a different perspective but can also be therapeutic and help you feel less alone. We all need to have a compassionate witness to what is happening to us, especially if we are in a lot of pain.

Step Four: Face the Fact That the Mr. Hyde Aspect of Your Loved One Is a Definite Part of His or Her Personality

Abusive Jekyll and Hydes almost always have a good side, no matter how critical and difficult to please they are. The fact that the person has this good side creates a lot of confusion in the people who know him or her. Very few of us are able to write off a person as abusive and therefore someone to get away from. Most people who are close to a Jekyll and Hyde tend to buy into the idea that the *real* person is the kind, charming version, while the abusive version is an aberration caused by too much stress or pressure at work, an unloving partner, career disappointments, childhood abuse, or any number of reasons. But don't fool yourself. The nice side of this person is simply not the complete picture of who he or she is. This person has two sides—as we all do—but in this case, the two sides are drastically different, and there is no connection between the two. It's as if the two sides of this person exist independently of each other. Unless and until this person is able to integrate the dark side with the light side, he or she will continue to behave like two different people. He or she will continue to let the dark side—with all its dark impulses, urges, and behavior—take over and consequently will continue to hurt you with abusive words and behavior.

As mentioned earlier, the real cause of the Jekyll and Hyde syndrome is usually an internal conflict between two sides of someone's personality. Both sides are equally real and equally powerful. The so-called good part is no more real than is the so-called bad part of this person. Without professional therapy, the bad side of this person is likely to actually grow larger over time.

*Step Five: Don't Fool Yourself into Thinking This
Person Will Change without Extensive Outside Help*

No matter what type of Jekyll and Hyde you are dealing with (with the exception of someone who has been diagnosed with bipolar disorder, Asperger's syndrome, or another biologically, chemically based disease), you must realize that this person has an exceptionally potent dark side—a dark side that has grown so powerful that it bursts out uncontrollably and unexpectedly. This dark side won't go away without a great deal of work on that individual's part. This means that no matter how apologetic the person is after an episode, no matter how much he or she promises never to do it again, you must not buy into this fantasy. While Jekyll and Hydes may have every intention of stopping the inappropriate behavior, they simply cannot change this behavior on their own. They need extensive professional help in order to make these changes. The same is true of Jekyll and Hydes who suffer from personality disorders.

As difficult as it is to live your life anticipating another painful episode, you must be realistic. You must prepare yourself for just such a contingency. It is far more damaging to you to continually be caught off-guard than it is to live in a hypervigilant state. Although it's extremely stressful to live your life "waiting for the other shoe to drop," at least you won't be blind-sided when the next episode occurs. At least you will be living in reality.

If you are romantically involved with a Jekyll and Hyde, facing the truth about your situation—that, in fact, another episode will occur—will help you decide whether you wish to continue the relationship. In the event that a parent or another family member is the Jekyll and Hyde in your life, facing the truth about the situation will help you to set limits and take care of yourself with this person.

Learning How to Cope with the
Jekyll and Hyde in Your Life

Coming out of denial can be difficult, but once you've done it, your world will open up. You will begin to see things as they really are, and this is a prerequisite to creating change in your life. Once you are out of denial, you can face the true task at hand—learning how to cope with the Jekyll and Hyde in your life. The following suggestions will help.

Stop Blaming Yourself for the Jekyll and Hyde's Behavior

Jekyll and Hydes tend to blame other people for their behavior. You are probably so used to the Jekyll and Hyde in your life blaming you, accusing you, and telling you that his or her mood swings, bad temper, or other inappropriate behavior is your fault that you have actually begun to believe it. You may think that if only you had done something differently, said something different, or adjusted your behavior in some way, the person you care about would not react as he or she does. The truth, however, is that Jekyll and Hydes respond as they do because of their own problems. They react to you in anger not because you were bad but because they feel so bad about themselves. Most often, their hostile reactions have nothing to do with you, even though the typical Jekyll and Hyde (especially those who have borderline personality disorder) is able to point to some obscure incident or behavior on your part that supposedly caused his or her mood shift or violent outburst.

Remind yourself repeatedly that you did not cause the behavior of the Jekyll and Hyde in your life. Jekyll and Hydes are confused people who are looking for someone else to blame for their circumstances. They don't understand why they have such erratic moods or behavior. They feel out of control of their own emotions (especially their anger). Since you are the person who is right in front of the Jekyll and Hyde, you are the most convenient person to blame. You must refuse to take responsibility for the Jekyll and Hyde's anger or behavior. Instead, place the responsibility back where it belongs—on the Jekyll and Hyde.

Believe That You Don't Deserve to Be Treated This Way

You don't deserve to be treated poorly by anyone, much less by your intimate partner or another family member. You deserve to be treated with respect and consideration no matter how bad a day someone else is having, no matter how much stress your partner is under, no matter how difficult a life your parent has had. No one has a right to take out his or her anger and frustration on you. For you to gain the strength necessary to stand up to an abusive Jekyll and Hyde, you must begin to believe these things. The following suggestions will help you do this:

1. When someone treats you poorly, tell the person to stop it. I realize this is easier said than done, but start out with someone who isn't threatening and work your way up to the Jekyll and Hyde in your life. Tell the person that his or her behavior is unacceptable and that you don't deserve to be treated poorly. Even if you don't believe it yet, the more often you say it, the more you will believe it. (If the person continues to treat you poorly, however, don't keep telling him or her over and over that you don't deserve to be treated that way. This is like begging; it makes you look weak in his or her eyes, and makes you feel weak and lose respect for yourself.)

2. When the Jekyll and Hyde in your life treats you poorly or insults you, make sure you don't absorb it. People who really care about you won't insult you if they don't like something about you; they will kindly take you aside and have a talk with you. Even then, you are not obligated to take in everything everyone says. People often have hidden agendas in pointing out your faults. The important thing is that you don't allow someone else to make you feel bad about yourself or make you feel as if you are not a valuable human being. Most especially, don't allow yourself to replay negative feedback or messages over and over in your mind.

3. Spend more time with people who know you and accept you for who you are. Choose your relationships based on how you are treated, as opposed to whether the person makes you feel comfortable. We are often most comfortable with the kind of people we are used to being around, including those who treat us poorly and remind us of people from our childhood who treated us badly.

4. Open up more with people who already accept you as you are. The fewer secrets you have, the less shame you will experience and the more you will begin to believe that you deserve to be treated well.

5. When people treat you well, make sure you absorb it. When they do something nice for you, take it in for a few minutes and feel the good feelings. Don't doubt their sincerity or tell yourself they are being nice because they want something. Trust that they are being nice because they simply want to be and because they like you. If someone gives you a compliment, take a deep breath and really absorb it. Don't negate the compliment or talk yourself out of believing it. Most people don't give compliments unless they really mean them.

6. When you are treated well, make sure you give yourself time to enjoy it. When you are alone, remember the positive things people said or the kind things they did. Replay the positive experiences in your mind so you can really take them in.

Understanding Your Reactions

The way you react to a Jekyll and Hyde's mood shifts or behavior changes can tell you a lot about yourself. Begin by closely observing how you react when a sudden change occurs. This won't be an easy task because your responses are probably automatic and unconscious. The following questions will help you focus.

QUESTIONNAIRE

What Do You Do When Your Jekyll and Hyde Changes?

1. Do you try to ignore it and pretend that nothing happened?
2. Do you become numb and almost paralyzed, unable to say or do anything?
3. Do you try to placate the Jekyll and Hyde, doing everything the person wants just so he or she will calm down?
4. Do you panic and become almost hysterical?

5. Do you run away and hide, trying to get as far away from the person as possible?

6. Do you start an argument?

7. Do you doubt your perceptions and wonder whether the Jekyll and Hyde really did what you think he or she did?

8. Do you confront the Jekyll and Hyde and criticize him or her for changing?

Once you are more clear about how you respond, ask yourself why it is that you react this way. The chances are high that you react as you do because your behavior is an automatic response based on childhood experiences. For example, if you were traumatized by your mother's sudden, violent outbursts as a child, you may become triggered every time your Jekyll and Hyde partner has a sudden mood shift. Being triggered like this can cause you to feel paralyzed or to feel as if your legs are stuck to the floor. If this is the case, you need to know that you are being retraumatized every time your partner has a mood shift. This is a very unhealthy and psychologically wounding situation, meaning that you need to get away from it as soon as possible.

Do you panic because you are so afraid of what this person is capable of doing or because it reminds you of how your father's personality would change just before he blew up and beat your mother? Do you try to get away because you just don't want to face it, or is it because you are afraid of being hurt as you were by your older brother? These, too, are typical reactions of people who have previously been traumatized.

Understanding your reactions can help you to be less critical of yourself and instead be more compassionate toward yourself. Although understanding why you react as you do won't change the Jekyll and Hyde's behavior, it might change yours. If you are passive because the Jekyll and Hyde in your life reminds you of your violent father, try to make a distinction in your mind between your father and your current partner. Tell yourself that you are no longer a helpless child but an adult who can stand up for yourself. In the next chapter we will discuss *learned helplessness* and other reasons why some people tend to be passive in the face of abuse.

Begin to Take Back Control

When you were a child, you were powerless whenever you experienced a Jekyll and Hyde going through one of his or her dramatic changes. Today, however, you have more power when it comes to affecting a Jekyll and Hyde's behavior. The first thing you need to do is take back control of your life. You have more than likely given your power to the Jekyll and Hyde just to avoid his or her temper tantrums or to avoid conflict. Here are some suggestions for how to take back control:

1. Stop agreeing to things you don't want to do just to avoid a huge tantrum.

2. Stop agreeing to everything your partner says just to avoid conflict. If you don't agree, say so. Yes, you risk making him or her angry, but so what? Your partner will probably get angry about something anyway.

3. When the Jekyll and Hyde in your life blames you for something you didn't do, tell him or her that you aren't willing to take on the responsibility for something that isn't your fault.

4. When the Jekyll and Hyde starts criticizing you or goes into a tirade over something, simply walk away. You don't have to stay and listen to criticism or tirades, and you don't want to encourage such behavior by paying attention to it. If the person follows you into another room, you may have to leave the house. If the Jekyll and Hyde tries to pin you down or block you from leaving, say that you will call the police if he or she doesn't let you go.

5. Ask yourself if the way you react to Jekyll and Hyde behavior is getting the results you want. In other words, is it effective? If it isn't, you may want to think about responding differently. For example, if you normally try to ignore a Jekyll and Hyde's erratic, explosive, or abusive behavior, try instead to bring his attention to it with a comment such as, "What just happened? Why did you become so withdrawn?" If you normally confront the Jekyll and Hyde in your life with comments such as, "What's wrong with you? Why are you shutting me out?" only to have the person withdraw even more, try saying something

like, "It seems like you need space right now. I'm here if you want to talk about it later."

6. Perhaps most important, stop taking things personally. Recognize that the Jekyll and Hyde in your life has a problem and that problem includes mood swings and other erratic behavior. His or her erratic behavior is not your fault; you did not cause it, and it has little or nothing to do with you.

None of these things will be easy, and you can rest assured that the Jekyll and Hyde in your life will fight to maintain control. For many Jekyll and Hydes, maintaining control is their source of power in relationships.

Sometimes taking control of your life can be as simple as learning how to say no. The following suggestions will help.

EXERCISE

Learning How to Say No

1. Start by simply saying the word *no* out loud. Try it again, and this time make it sound like you mean it. Try it one more time with feeling. Notice how uncomfortable you are with saying this word.

2. Continue to practice saying no out loud until you become more comfortable with it. Walk around your house when no one is there and say the word *no*, over and over. Say it with different inflections and at various volumes. Continue to say it until you become more comfortable with it. Notice how empowered saying no can make you feel.

3. Pretend you are talking to the Jekyll and Hyde in your life. Imagine that this person is asking you to do something you don't want to do. Say "No," firmly and with feeling. Imagine that your Jekyll and Hyde is blaming you for his or her problems, and say "No!" to being willing to take the blame anymore.

I offer further suggestions for taking back control in the upcoming chapters on coping with a Jekyll and Hyde who is abusive or who has a personality disorder.

Confronting the Jekyll and Hyde
in Your Life

Once you have grown stronger in your conviction that you don't deserve to be treated as you have been, you will need to decide whether you are willing and able to confront the Jekyll and Hyde in your life. Up until now, this person may have been able to convince you that the problem was yours or that you were exaggerating and making a big deal out of nothing. Now that you know you are being emotionally abused or lied to (in the case of the illusive Jekyll and Hyde), you may feel like confronting the Jekyll and Hyde about his or her behavior. This can be risky, however. Certainly, you must be prepared for denial. Most Jekyll and Hydes won't admit they have a problem. In some cases, be prepared for a very dramatic or even violent denial, especially if the person has shown signs of violence in the past. The following suggestions will help to make the confrontation process as safe and productive as possible:

1. Don't confront a Jekyll and Hyde in the middle of an argument. Try to pick a quiet time when he or she will be more likely to hear you.

2. Never confront a Jekyll and Hyde when he or she is drinking or using drugs. Wait until the person is sober.

3. Open the conversation with something like, "I need to talk to you about something. I think I understand you better than I ever have before, and I'd like to share with you what I've learned."

4. You may want to refer to this book specifically: "I've been reading a book that has helped me understand you better. I'd love it if you could read it, too."

5. It will be most productive if Jekyll and Hydes actually read this book themselves. That way, they can draw their own conclusions and feel that they still have a sense of control over their own lives (as opposed to someone telling them who they are). If your Jekyll and Hyde agrees to read the book, say that you'd like to discuss his or her thoughts on it afterward.

6. If you feel that your partner has a personality disorder, hold off on telling him or her this. Instead, ask your partner to read this book. Ideally, your partner will recognize himself or herself in the book.

7. If your partner or a family member actually reads the book, tell this person that you want to work together to make your relationship better and that you want to support him or her in any way you can. Say that you have your own issues to work on so that he or she doesn't feel completely to blame for all the problems in the relationship.

8. If you are afraid of your Jekyll and Hyde's reactions to your confrontation, consider having someone else present. This decision needs to be made very carefully. Only you know whether this will cause your Jekyll and Hyde to react more violently or whether it will encourage this person to keep a lid on his or her emotions out of a desire to "look good."

9. Be aware that confronting an illusive Jekyll and Hyde (one who has been leading a double life) can be especially dangerous. Refer to the next chapter for information on how to handle this situation.

So what exactly do you say in your confrontation? It's always best to start by telling Jekyll and Hydes how their behavior makes you feel. They may try to tell you that, in fact, this is not how you feel, but the truth is, you are the only one who knows how you feel. Don't allow them to sidetrack you or confuse you. Remind yourself of how their behavior makes you feel and hold on to that truth even if they don't listen. Don't get into an argument about it. Just speak your mind, and hold on to your truth.

The next step is to ask the Jekyll and Hyde to get some help. Have some materials, names, and phone numbers handy. For example, if you think your Jekyll and Hyde is an alcoholic, give him or her the local number of Alcoholics Anonymous. If you feel that your Jekyll and Hyde has a personality disorder, give him or her the number of a local therapist or a clinic that specializes in working with personality-disordered people.

Specific Strategies to Help You Cope with a Jekyll and Hyde

The following strategies and advice are probably the most important aspects of this book. I suggest you read and reread this list to remind yourself of what you should be focusing on.

1. Don't expect a Jekyll and Hyde to own up to his or her dual nature. Many of them are not even aware of their mood shifts, and those who are aware won't admit they have these shifts because it makes them feel far too vulnerable and shamed. Jekyll and Hydes who are aware of their mood shifts feel embarrassed by them. They also feel out of control. Admitting that they are out of control would only add to their shame.

2. Don't allow a Jekyll and Hyde to avoid responsibility for his or her mood shifts by blaming you. Jekyll and Hydes are excellent at deflecting and blaming. You are not responsible for the fact that they have radical mood shifts or that they are out of control of their emotions. You didn't cause them to suddenly become angry, withdrawn, or depressed. It is *not* your fault.

3. Jekyll and Hydes may justify that the reason they are not honest with you is because you react so strongly or because you become so angry when they are honest. Don't buy into it. Jekyll and Hydes tend to lie. They are very good at it. They lie in order to get away with their secret lives; they lie in order to save face when they are out of control or when they have radical mood swings. You do not make them lie. You have a right to react to their mood swings or their attempts to conceal things from you.

4. Don't allow a Jekyll and Hyde to make you doubt your perceptions or make you feel crazy. One of the strongest tools Jekyll and Hydes have in leading double lives or in excusing their dual natures is to make you doubt that you saw what you saw or heard what you heard. They are masters at denial, putting up smokescreens, distorting the truth, twisting your own words against you, and making you doubt yourself. Don't let your Jekyll and Hyde get away with it. If you need to, write down your

experiences and your truths so that you can refer to these later. Tell a friend about the Jekyll and Hyde's behavior so you can get a reality check. Most important, trust your own perceptions.

5. Don't allow a Jekyll and Hyde to make you feel as if you are overreacting or exaggerating. The sudden mood shifts and emotional outbursts that some Jekyll and Hydes exhibit are truly shocking and overwhelming. They may not think that it's such a big deal if they erupt in anger and start screaming at the top of their lungs at you over a minor incident, but it is. Jekyll and Hydes can be emotionally, verbally, or physically abusive when they are upset and yet still turn around and expect you to just "get over it" when their moods have changed again.

6. If your Jekyll and Hyde tends to become sullen or depressed or gives you the silent treatment without explanation, don't continue to ask him or her to tell you what is wrong. Ask once, then leave it alone. Remind yourself that it isn't your problem and isn't your fault. Busy yourself with something else, and try not to obsess about why he or she has withdrawn.

7. Allow yourself time to bounce back after each episode of anger, withdrawal, or the discovery of another lie. It's understandable that you will feel leery or afraid of someone who suddenly erupts in anger, and it's normal that you would feel hurt by someone who lashes out at you for no apparent reason or withdraws from you without warning. Don't allow yourself to be bullied into feeling as if you are punishing or unforgiving or that you are feeling sorry for yourself. You have a right to your feelings and a right to take some time to lick your wounds.

8. Give yourself permission to leave the company of a person who has suddenly switched into a different personality or erupted in anger. You don't have to stay around someone who is behaving in unacceptable ways or who is acting so differently that it scares or disturbs you. If this person is unwilling to admit that he or she has switched or is blaming the mood shift on you, just walk away. You have absolutely no obligation to try to work with someone who is being completely unreasonable, and you have every right to take care of your own needs.

9. Above all, don't allow yourself to become isolated. You need friends and family to validate your feelings. You need their input to help you stay in touch with reality when the Jekyll and Hyde tries to gaslight you.

Earlier, I told you of my experiences with my friend Melanie. Through my relationship with her, I learned firsthand many of these coping strategies—strategies I then passed on to my clients who had similar experiences with Jekyll and Hydes. For example, I learned that Jekyll and Hydes are often completely oblivious to the fact that they have experienced a mood shift and even more oblivious to how their behavior affects people close to them. I also learned that confronting Jekyll and Hydes and expecting them to own up to their behavior can be a waste of time, and many of them become angry and even violent when confronted.

One of the most important lessons I learned from my experiences with Melanie was to trust my perceptions more. You'd think that as a therapist I would have learned to trust my perceptions long ago, especially since I receive so much positive validation from clients that my perceptions and intuition are "right on" most of the time. But Melanie was so adamant about making it my problem instead of hers that I initially doubted myself, especially when coupled with Melanie's accusation that I was being too sensitive, which echoed my mother's messages to me.

The longer I knew Melanie, the more I learned to take care of myself with her. When she went into one of her icy moods, I learned to disconnect from her emotionally until she came back. If she was visiting me, I busied myself with chores around the house or made phone calls to friends. If we had plans to go to dinner, I often told her I'd rather eat at home and then served our meals in front of the television so I wasn't forced to make idle chatter with someone who really wasn't there. I found that I could almost predict when she would shift her mood (as I mentioned earlier, usually on the second day of a visit), and I emotionally prepared myself for this. Although she always came back as if nothing had occurred, I knew something had. I allowed myself time to become emotionally invested in her again, and I stopped feeling guilty about it.

Quite recently, I received validation regarding my perceptions of Melanie. I had gone to visit her and another friend of hers was there, someone she had also known for a long time. Her friend, whom I will call Joan, asked me what I was working on, and I said a book about people who are like Dr. Jekyll and Mr. Hyde—people who had radical mood shifts. Joan immediately laughed and said to me, "Well, we both know someone like that, don't we?" I looked at her and knew exactly who she was referring to—Melanie. We laughed. Melanie overheard our conversation, and for a moment I thought she realized we were talking about her. Instead, though, she started telling us about her sister and how she acted this way. "You never know when she's going to blow up," Melanie said. "It's just terrible. It makes it really hard to be around her." Once again, Joan looked at me knowingly and said, "Yes, we understand; we know someone like that, too. We know what it's like to never know who you're going to get."

Melanie looked at her, but it seemed as if she didn't understand what Joan was implying. But I certainly did. I felt so validated. So relieved. Even though I already knew it intellectually, emotionally there was still a part of me—the child part—who doubted myself. A part who felt as if maybe my mother and Melanie were right: I was too sensitive. Yet, here was someone else who knew Melanie almost as well as I did, who understood what it was like to be around her. I realized that I'd never met anyone else who knew Melanie, so I had been operating in a vacuum. That's why it's so important not to isolate yourself and, if at all possible, to get to know a Jekyll and Hyde's other friends and family members.

5

Abusive or Illusive?

Specific Strategies Depending on What Type of Jekyll and Hyde You Are Dealing With

There are people on the earth who eat the earth and all the people on it like in the Bible with the locusts. And other people who stand around and watch them eat it.

—Lillian Hellman, *The Little Foxes*

Oh what a tangled web we weave
When first we practice to deceive!

—Sir Walter Scott

To some extent, your way of coping with a Jekyll and Hyde will depend on whether he or she falls under the broad category of *abusive or illusive.* As mentioned earlier in the book, many Jekyll and Hydes hurt the people around them when they change into their alternate personalities because they become verbally, emotionally, or physically abusive. Most illusive Jekyll and Hydes, on the other hand, don't hurt people around them by becoming abusive. In fact, because they hide their duality so well, their loved ones often don't know they are being hurt—that is, until they discover the level of deceit they have been subjected to. Illusive Jekyll and Hydes are the ones who have multiple affairs behind their partners' backs, who may even have more than one wife. Illusive Jekyll and Hydes often live double lives, being pillars of the community while at the same time involving themselves with activities such as gambling, drugs, kinky sex, or shoplifting or other crimes. In this chapter we will focus on how to cope with both the *abusive* and the *illusive* Jekyll and Hyde.

Coping with an Abusive Jekyll and Hyde: Continue to Come out of Denial

Denial is a powerful defense mechanism. It can help us to tolerate unbearable situations. But denial can also keep us from facing the truth about our loved ones and about our situation. I addressed the importance of coming out of denial in the previous chapter, but people who are dealing with abusive Jekyll and Hydes tend to suffer from even more denial than do others who have a Jekyll and Hyde in their lives.

Just as we cannot continue to deny and repress our darker thoughts, feelings, and impulses without creating a tremendous dark side and without risking acting out these impulses, we cannot deny and ignore the darkness in others. By doing so, we actually allow the darkness in others to thrive and grow. By being ostrichlike and keeping our heads in the sand, we not only refuse to face the truth but leave ourselves vulnerable to being attacked.

If you are with an abusive Jekyll and Hyde, you absolutely must face the fact that you are being harmed by his or her behavior. You must face the fact that every day that you allow your partner or other family member to emotionally abuse you, you lose more of your self-confidence, self-esteem, sense of self, and trust in your perceptions.

Learn about the Cycle of Abuse and Your Role in It

Discovering your role in the abuse doesn't mean that you blame yourself for how the Jekyll and Hyde in your life behaves. As we've discussed, someone with the Jekyll and Hyde syndrome has serious emotional problems that were more than likely caused by his or her upbringing. In other words, this person was this way when you met him or her. What it does mean is that if you are in a close personal relationship with such a person, you need to look carefully at why you brought this person into your life. For example, did you fall in love with a Jekyll and Hyde because your father suffered from this syndrome? Did you choose a Jekyll and Hyde to be your close friend because your older, abusive brother was one? Or were you attracted to someone with this syndrome because you suffer from it yourself? Take some time to really think through these questions. Remember, although none of these decisions are made consciously, they are decisions nevertheless. You had a reason for being attracted to your Jekyll and Hyde, and it's important to understand what that reason was.

If you have been putting up with abusive behavior, it's also important to carefully examine your reasons for doing so. The following information, taken from my book *Breaking the Cycle of Abuse*, will help you discover your reasons for staying so long and your reasons for choosing a Jekyll and Hyde in the first place.

EXERCISE

Your Reasons for Choosing a Jekyll and Hyde
and for Staying in the Relationship

Put a checkmark next to each of the following items that you relate to.

1. *Familiar territory.* One of the most common reasons people put up with Jekyll and Hyde behavior in others is simply that they are used to such behavior. Children who grow up with parents who are Jekyll and Hydes are far more likely to become involved with Jekyll and Hyde partners as adults than are people who don't grow up with such parents. This may be because they simply have never known anything else and thus view erratic behavior as normal. People often choose negative situations that are familiar over positive

situations that are unfamiliar. If what is familiar in an intimate relationship is abuse, you may unwittingly get involved with someone who mistreats or abuses you. Remaining unaware of this repetitive cycle, you maintain the childhood victimization into your adulthood.

2. *The repetition compulsion.* The main reason people are attracted to Jekyll and Hydes is that they are unconsciously attempting to redo the past in order to get another outcome. In other words, you marry someone like your father and work at getting him to love you in an attempt to work past the painful truth that you were unloved as a child. Originally defined by Freud as the repetitive reenactment of earlier emotional experiences, this type of behavior is often seen in the lives of trauma survivors. Essentially, the repetition compulsion is an unconscious drive that compels us to "return to the scene of the crime," so to speak, in order to accomplish a new outcome or to gain understanding of why something occurred. For example, a survivor of traumatic abuse may put herself in a situation where there is a risk of additional abuse, in an attempt to psychologically master the previous traumatic experience.

3. *Learned helplessness.* Learned helplessness may also explain why you have put up with Jekyll and Hyde behavior, especially if you are with an abusive Jekyll and Hyde. *Learned helplessness* is a term developed by Martin Seligman, a pioneering researcher in animal psychology, to describe what occurs when animals or human beings learn that their behavior has no effect on the environment. The impact of this experience leaves an individual apathetic, depressed, and unwilling to try previous or new behavior. Certain survivors of childhood trauma show some degree of learned helplessness due to repeated exposure to traumatic events that they could not change or avoid by their behavior. Studies have found that a true inability to control the environment is not necessary for learned helplessness to occur. Those who have been unable to escape violent situations in their homes are

much more likely to refuse help and to accept future violence as inescapable.

4. *Post-traumatic stress disorder.* Earlier I wrote that one cause of Jekyll and Hyde behavior is post-traumatic stress disorder (PTSD). It's important to note that some characteristics of PTSD can also create victimlike behavior, including:

- Helplessness and passivity—an inability to look for and find problem-solving solutions.

- Self-blame and a sense of being tainted or evil.

- Attachment to trauma. Relationships that resemble the original trauma are sought. Involvement with helping figures may end in an attempt to become one with the helper or in total rejection of the helper. A person with PTSD may vacillate between the two reactions.

5. *Self-blame.* Self-blame can lead to a lifetime pattern of victimization. Children blame themselves when they are abused by their parents because children need to hold on to an image of the parent as good in order to deal with the intensity of fear and rage that is the effect of the tormenting experiences. Victims may also blame themselves for their own victimization because it allows the locus of control to remain internal and thus prevents helplessness.

6. *Clinging behavior.* Small children, unable to anticipate the future, experience separation anxiety as soon as they lose sight of their mothers. As we mature, we develop more coping responses, but adults are still intensely dependent on social support to prevent and overcome traumatization. When exposed to extreme terror, even mature people will have protest and despair responses (anger and grief, intrusion, and numbing) that make them turn to the nearest available source of comfort to return to a state of both psychological and physical calm. Thus, severe external threat may result in renewed clinging in adults.

When there is no access to ordinary sources of comfort, people may turn toward their tormentors. Adults, as well as children, may develop strong emotional ties with people who intermittently threaten, harass, or beat them. Abused children often cling to their parents and resist being removed from the home. In what has become known as the Stockholm syndrome, hostages have been known to put up bail for their captors, express a wish to marry them, or have sexual relations with them.

7. *Shame.* Shame is often responsible for causing people to stay in abusive relationships. The inner experience of shame is to feel seen in a painfully diminished way. The self feels exposed, and it is this sudden, unexpected feeling of exposure and the accompanying self-consciousness that characterizes the essential nature of shame. Within this experience of shame is the piercing, overwhelming awareness of ourselves as fundamentally deficient in some vital way as human beings.

In addition to feeling deficient when we feel shame, we also tend to feel impotent because it seems as if there is no way to relieve the situation. Therefore, those who were heavily shamed in childhood can easily come to believe that they are powerless to change things. This leads to a victim mentality. To live with shame is to feel alienated and defeated. It is to believe you are never quite good enough. This can set the stage for getting involved with emotionally or even physically abusive partners who are demanding and hard to please. If you already feel like a failure, you will be more likely to put up with unreasonable demands and put-downs and be less likely to leave a relationship, no matter how abusive.

Realize That the Jekyll and Hyde's Behavior Is Not Your Fault

Sometimes children who grow up in a blaming family will learn to blame themselves—to internalize, rather than externalize, blame—as a way of avoiding blame from significant others. These children learn that if they are quick enough to blame themselves, their parents' blaming will subside or be altogether avoided. It is as though the child makes an implicit contract with the parent: I will do the blaming so you will not have to. In this way, the intolerable blaming, which induces shame in the child, is placed under the child's own internal control. It becomes internalized such that the child's inner life is forever subject to spontaneous self-blame.

Self-blame and shame are closely related. Children tend to blame themselves for their parents' behavior, no matter how inappropriate or abusive. Self-blame is also consistent with the thought processes of traumatized people of all ages, who search for faults in their own behavior in an effort to make sense out of what happened to them. In the environment of chronic abuse, neither time nor experience provide any corrective for this tendency toward self-blame; instead, it is continually reinforced. The abused child's sense of inner badness may be directly confirmed by parental scapegoating. Survivors frequently describe being blamed, not only for their parents' abusiveness or violence, but also for other family misfortunes.

EXERCISE

Turn Your Shame to Anger

If you have a tendency toward self-blame, turning your shame to anger can be a positive and powerful way to rid yourself of shame. Instead of taking the negative energy in, against yourself, the energy is directed outward, toward the person who is doing the shaming or causing the shame.

1. Make a list of all the reasons you are angry with the Jekyll and Hyde in your life. For example, "I'm angry because he blows up at me for no apparent reason." "I'm angry because she refuses to admit that she has a problem." "I'm angry about the way he treats our daughter."

2. Think of what you would like to tell the Jekyll and Hyde in your life if you weren't so afraid of his or her reaction.

When no one is around, walk through your house and say these words out loud. Don't censor yourself. Tell the person everything you wish you could say to him or her in person.

3. If saying the words out loud is not your style, try writing a letter telling the Jekyll and Hyde everything that you feel. Again, don't hold back and don't censor yourself. Use swear words if you feel like it. Really get your anger out. Then you can burn the letter or tear it up into little pieces, which in itself can be a release.

The important thing is that you take the shame that is inside you and turn it into righteous anger. Anger is a motivating force; it can empower you to stop blaming yourself, stop believing the Jekyll and Hyde's excuses and lies, and start believing that you don't deserve to be treated like this. It can empower you to begin to stand up for yourself once and for all.

Strategies to Help You Rid Yourself of Shame from the Past

Oftentimes, the reason you have put up with unacceptable behavior is that you were so shamed in the past (by childhood abuse, by blaming parents) that you have come to believe that you deserve to be treated poorly. If this is the case, you will also need to work on ridding yourself of this old shame. The following strategies will help.

1. *Accept the fact that you didn't deserve the abuse or the neglect.* Tell yourself that nothing you did as a child warranted any kind of abuse or neglect that you experienced. If you continue to blame yourself for your parents' inappropriate or inadequate behavior, you may need to get in touch with how vulnerable and innocent children are. Spend some time around children who are the age you were when you were neglected or emotionally abused. Notice how fragile and innocent children really are, no matter how mature they try to act.

2. *Tell significant others about the abuse and the neglect you experienced.* As the saying goes, "We are only as sick as our secrets."

By keeping the fact that you were abused or neglected as a child away from your close friends and family, you perpetuate the idea that you are keeping it secret because you did something wrong. By sharing your experience with someone you love and trust (your partner, a close friend, a therapist, members of a support group), you will get rid of the secret and get help getting rid of your shame.

3. *Give back your parents' shame.* When a parent abuses a child, it's often because the parent is in the middle of a shame attack. The parent is, in essence, projecting his or her shame onto the child. And while any form of abuse is taking place, the child often feels the shame of the abuser and is overwhelmed by it, causing the child to actually take on the shame of the abuser. You may have been told many times by your therapist or by your friends and loved ones that the abuse or the neglect you endured was not your fault. Now is the time to start believing it. Releasing your anger toward your parents or other abusers will help you to stop blaming yourself, since they are the appropriate targets for your anger. Getting angry at your abusers will affirm your innocence. While you may not feel safe in doing this directly, writing letters you don't send or other indirect ways of releasing anger can be just as effective.

4. *Trade self-criticism for compassion and self-acceptance.* Compassion is the antidote to shame. In order to heal your shame, it is very important that you trade your tendency to be impatient or self-critical for compassion for yourself. Remember the way you felt when your parents talked to you in an impatient or critical way. Take out pictures of yourself when you were a child, and remind yourself that you were innocent and vulnerable and didn't deserve to be insulted, humiliated, criticized, or shamed for just being who you were. Work on replacing the critical or demanding voice inside your head with a more nurturing, compassionate inner voice. Having compassion for yourself will give you the strength and the motivation to change, whereas self-criticism will only continue to tear you down.

5. *Expect others to accept you as you are.* In order to heal your shame, you also need to consciously work on believing that it is okay to be who you are. Surround yourself with people who like and accept you just as you are, as opposed to people who are critical, judgmental, perfectionistic, or otherwise shaming.

Coping with an Illusive Jekyll and Hyde

We haven't discussed the illusive Jekyll and Hyde much so far. An illusive Jekyll and Hyde includes anyone who has lied to and deceived his or her family and friends in order to live a double life. This can include people who are having affairs outside their marriages or committed relationships and those who hide from their partners or their families the fact that they gamble, drink, take drugs, or frequent sex establishments. It can also include people who are involved in illegal or criminal activities.

As it is with partners and family members of abusive Jekyll and Hydes, people who are close to an illusive Jekyll and Hyde are often stuck in denial. Many of them refuse to believe that someone they love could possibly do anything dishonest or deceitful.

My client Reese is a prime example. When I first met Reese, I was struck by how angelic she appeared. It actually seemed as if she was surrounded by a white light. She spoke in a very soft tone and smiled often.

Reese had come to me because she had recently discovered that her husband had been unfaithful to her not once, but many times during their marriage. She also discovered that he had been gambling and had lost nearly all their savings.

"I just can't believe that the man I have loved for so long could do this to me. I've been a good wife. I do everything I can to please him. He has two beautiful children who adore him."

When Reese said that she couldn't believe it, she meant it. The only reason she had come to me was she had been forced to face the truth about her husband when he lost all their money and had to confess to her. "If he hadn't told me in his own words, I would have refused to believe it," Reese explained. Shortly after her husband's confession about his gambling, a woman he had been involved with told Reese about his affairs. Her husband was in such shock about losing all their money that he admitted the affairs as well. Even so, Reese had an investment in not facing the truth about her husband. She simply did not want to admit that people did the kind of things he had done. She continued to make excuses for him and to slip back into denial.

Reese was what is considered "blissfully ignorant" since she preferred to remain in her fantasy world rather than face the fact that there is indeed evil in the world. If you are like Reese, you are putting yourself in great danger. Just as we cannot afford to reject aspects of ourselves and expect to be whole people, we cannot stick our heads in the sand and refuse to believe that evil exists. To do so is to risk learning the lesson the hard way—by being forced to face evil head-on. Those who choose to stay blissfully ignorant are easy prey to those who have huge Shadows. They attract Jekyll and Hydes like magnets.

If you have discovered that your partner has been lying to you, having affairs, or engaging in addictive or illegal behaviors behind your back, you will undoubtedly feel betrayed. In fact, *betrayal* is the word most people use when they discover that their partners are illusive Jekyll and Hydes. This is what my client Toby expressed after discovering that his wife of fifteen years had been having an affair with a married man for more than three years. "I feel so betrayed. I never imagined in a million years that my wife would have been the kind of woman to have an affair outside her marriage. She is such a religious woman and believes so strongly in the importance of the family. How could she expose her children to this kind of thing, much less jeopardize our marriage this way?"

Feeling betrayed is healthy. It shows that you are facing the truth about what happened, that you are facing the fact that your partner was capable of such dishonesty. Unfortunately, many people don't allow themselves to feel betrayed because they are still in denial. Don't do this to yourself. Don't continue to be naive. Admit that your partner did indeed betray you. Admit that your

Jekyll and Hyde lied to you and that you cannot trust him or her.

Accepting that you were betrayed by a loved one can be very painful, but unless you face this truth and allow yourself to grieve the loss of the person you thought you knew, you won't be able to recover from the pain. Instead, you will harden your heart and refuse to trust anyone again, or you will continue to be naive and set yourself up for further betrayal.

In order to heal from this betrayal and at the same time smarten up and come out of denial about people in general, you probably also need to face these truths:

1. We never really know anyone completely. Everyone has secrets he or she hides from even close family members and friends.

2. No one is all good or all bad. We are all a combination of good characteristics and bad ones.

3. We are all capable of lying and deceiving others, even people we are close to.

4. In fact, we are all capable of every act of unkindness, betrayal, and violence.

Confronting Your Jekyll and Hyde with His Secrets

Although we all keep secrets from one another, for some people secret keeping is a way of life. For example, sociopaths are experts at secrecy. They are not the people they present to the world, and they know it. They will do anything to keep their secret identities—including murder. A recent example of this was Mark Hacking, the man who killed his wife, Lori, in Salt Lake City after she learned that he wasn't the aspiring doctor he said he was and that, in fact, he'd never even graduated from college. Because people can become desperate when their secrets are revealed, you need to tread lightly when you find out that your partner is an illusive Jekyll and Hyde.

Even though you may become furious when you discover what your Jekyll and Hyde has been up to, it's probably not a good idea to confront him or her in an angry or threatening way. For example, don't threaten to tell everyone about his indiscretions or expose her shoplifting to the whole family. This may only cause him or her to become enraged with you and possibly become violent. People can do radical things when they feel cornered or when they feel threatened with the destruction of their public personas.

Instead of confronting your Jekyll and Hyde in an angry manner, be smart. You probably don't have a Mark Hacking on your hands, but you need to protect yourself nevertheless. The following suggestions will safeguard you from an illusive Jekyll and Hyde:

1. Tell at least one friend or family member about what you have discovered. The time for secrets is over. Whether you decide to stay with an illusive Jekyll and Hyde or not, the secrets need to come out, and telling someone else about your discovery can also help to protect you.

2. Make copies of any evidence you may have discovered, and put them in a safe place, such as a safety deposit box or at a friend's home. For example, if you have found love letters, make photocopies and then put the letters back until you decide it is time to confront the person. If you have seen something suspicious or incriminating on the computer, print it out or make a copy on a disc. It's amazing how good illusive Jekyll and Hydes are at lying. Unless you have hard evidence, your partner will continue to deny what he or she is being accused of. You may also need this hard evidence for divorce or child custody proceedings or to protect your interests in other ways.

3. If at all possible, confront your partner in a public place or in the presence of someone you trust. This will likely prevent your partner from becoming abusive or violent toward you in the moment, and if he or she does become abusive or violent, you will be in a situation where you can easily escape.

4. If you are afraid that the person you have confronted will retaliate later when you are alone or when you least expect it, get away from this person. You don't have to live one more minute under the roof of someone you don't trust or someone you are afraid of.

5. If you are afraid that the illusive Jekyll and Hyde in your life
    will hurt you, tell someone else about your fears and stay away
    from this person until you have proof that you no longer need
    to be afraid (for example, your partner has agreed to enter ther-
    apy or he or she comes clean in front of the family so that there
    are no more secrets).

6

If the Jekyll and Hyde in Your Life Has a Personality Disorder

One minute he was kind and loving, and the next minute he treated me like a stranger.

—Kylie, age twenty-four

If, by reading the earlier descriptions of personality disorders and taking the quizzes, you have come to believe that your partner, a family member, or someone else in your life has a personality disorder, this chapter will provide you with special assistance in learning how to deal with the person's behavior. As mentioned earlier, a personality disorder is an enduring pattern of behavior that usually begins in early childhood. This means that unlike other behaviors that can be modified, the behaviors of someone with a personality disorder cannot be easily changed. They are part of the fabric of the person's very character or personality. It normally takes long-term or ongoing professional therapy for people with personality disorders to begin making any changes in their behavior. This means that if you decide to continue the relationship with this person, you will be the one who will need to make changes to your behavior in order to take better care of yourself, versus expecting the other person to be able to immediately extinguish his or her negative behavior.

Coping if Your Partner Has Borderline Personality Disorder

People involved with partners who have borderline personality disorder (BPD) or who suffer from strong borderline traits often don't realize they are being emotionally abused. They may know they are unhappy in their relationships, but they blame themselves or are confused about what is causing the continual disruption. They are often blamed for the relationship problems or made to feel that if they would only be more loving, more understanding, more sexual, or more exciting, their relationships would improve. To the contrary, it's often the case that the partner of a borderline is actually codependent or dependent, causing him or her to be extremely patient and willing to put up with intolerable behavior.

Partly because they are constantly being blamed for things they didn't do, people involved with borderline individuals often come to doubt their own perceptions or their sanity. Frequently accused of behaving, thinking, or feeling in ways that upset their partners, they tend to adapt a careful style of living that the authors Paul Mason and Randi Kreger call "walking on eggshells." The constant worrying about whether they will upset their partners with BPD can cause people to develop physical ailments such as stomach problems, ulcers, headaches, insomnia, and other conditions associated with stress. Many come to believe that they are not only the cause of their relationship problems but the cause of their partners' emotional problems as well.

QUESTIONNAIRE

*Does Your Partner Suffer from Borderline
Personality Disorder?*

The following questions, adapted from *Stop Walking on Eggshells* by Paul Mason and Randi Kreger, will help you to determine whether your partner suffers from BPD or has strong borderline traits.

1. Has your partner caused you a great deal of emotional pain and distress?

2. Have you come to feel that anything you say or do could potentially be twisted and used against you?

3. Does your partner often put you in a no-win situation?

4. Does your partner often blame you for things that aren't your fault?

5. Are you criticized and blamed for everything wrong in the relationship or everything that is wrong in your partner's life, even when it makes no logical sense?

6. Do you find yourself concealing what you think or feel because you are afraid of your partner's reaction or because it doesn't seem worth the hurt feelings or the terrible fight that will undoubtedly follow?

7. Are you the focus of intense, violent, and irrational rages, alternating with periods when your partner acts normal and loving? Do others have a difficult time believing you when you explain that this is going on?

8. Do you often feel manipulated, controlled, or lied to by your partner? Do you feel as if you are the victim of emotional blackmail?

9. Do you feel as if your partner sees you as either all good or all bad, with nothing in between? Does there seem to be no rational reason for the switch in his or her perception of you?

10. Does your partner often push you away when you are feeling close?

11. Are you afraid to ask for things in the relationship because you will be accused of being too demanding or be told there is something wrong with you?

12. Does your partner tell you that your needs are not important or act in ways that indicate that this is how she or he feels?

13. Does your partner frequently denigrate or deny your point of view?

14. Do you feel you can never do anything right or that his or her expectations are constantly changing?

15. Are you frequently accused of doing things you didn't do or saying things you didn't say? Do you feel misunderstood a great deal of the time, and when you attempt to explain, does your partner not believe you?

16. Does your partner frequently criticize you or put you down?

17. When you try to leave the relationship, does your partner try to prevent you from leaving by any means possible (for example, declarations of love, promises to change or get help, implicit or explicit threats of suicide or homicide)?

18. Do you have a hard time planning activities (social engagements or vacations) because of your partner's moodiness, impulsiveness, or unpredictability? Do you make excuses for his or her behavior or try to convince yourself that everything is okay?

If you answered yes to many of these questions, your partner likely has traits associated with BPD. As you can see from this list, many of the previous behaviors have already been described in this book as Jekyll and Hyde behavior and as emotionally abusive (for example, constant criticism, unreasonable expectations, constant chaos, emotional blackmail, gaslighting). What you were probably unaware of was that many of these behaviors are also symptoms of a personality disorder. While it is impossible to diagnose people without seeing them, I can say with a great deal of certainty that if your partner thinks, feels, and behaves in many of these ways, she or he probably suffers from BPD. For more information on the characteristics of BPD, refer to the books listed under "Recommended Reading."

Twin Fears: Abandonment and Engulfment

At the core of all these feelings and behaviors are the twin fears of abandonment and engulfment. Those who suffer from BPD or have strong borderline tendencies almost always experienced some form of abandonment when they were infants or children. This abandonment may have been physical (for example, the hospitalization of a parent, the death of a parent, being put up for adoption, being left in a crib for hours at a time) or emotional (for example, having a mother who was unable to bond with her child, being an unwanted child whose mother neglected her, having a detached and unloving father). This physical or emotional abandonment causes the borderline individual either to be extremely afraid of being rejected or abandoned in an intimate relationship and having to feel the original wounding all over again or to be distant and detached as a way of defending himself or herself from the potential pain of intimacy. In many cases, borderline individuals actually vacillate from one extreme to the other. At one point in time, they may be emotionally smothering—desperately clinging to their partners, demanding a great deal of attention, begging their partners never to leave them. At another point in time, perhaps only hours or days later, the same person can be overwhelmed with the fear of being engulfed. She may become distant and withdrawn for no apparent reason or she may push her partner away by accusing him of not loving her, of being unfaithful, of no longer finding her attractive. She may even accuse him of being too needy.

This vacillation between clinging behavior and rejecting behavior is actually quite common in people with BPD. Over the course of a relationship, the most typical pattern that emerges is that a borderline individual will "fall in love" very quickly and will push for instant intimacy. For example, a woman with BPD may seem to have few, if any, boundaries—insisting on seeing her lover every day, sharing her deepest darkest secrets, even pushing to marry or live together right away. But once she has captured her partner's heart and received some kind of commitment from him, a typical borderline individual may suddenly become distant or critical or have second thoughts about the relationship. She may stop wanting to have sex, saying that she feels they had sex too early and didn't get to know each other in other ways. She may suddenly become suspicious of her partner, accusing him of using her or of being unfaithful. She may begin to find fault in everything he does and question whether she really loves him. This distancing behavior may even verge on paranoia. She may begin to listen in on her partner's phone calls, check on his background, or question past lovers.

This behavior on the part of the person suffering from BPD may cause her partner to question the relationship, or it may make him so angry that he distances himself from her. When this occurs, she will suddenly feel the other fear—the fear of abandonment—and she will become needy, clingy, and instantly intimate once again. For some partners, this vacillation may be merely perplexing, but for many it is extremely upsetting. In some cases, it will cause the partner to want to end the relationship. When this occurs, there will no doubt be a very dramatic scene in which the borderline individual may beg her partner to stay, threaten to kill herself if he doesn't, or even threaten to kill him if he tries to leave her.

Even though many of the typical behaviors of a person suffering from BPD are clearly emotionally abusive (for example, constant chaos, constant criticism, unreasonable expectations), often the relationship becomes mutually abusive because the borderline person pushes her partner to his limit, and he ends up acting out in frustration and anger. This kind of vacillating behavior is very difficult for most people to cope with, and few come away from the situation without losing their tempers or resorting to abusive tactics themselves. When someone is sobbing and clinging to your legs as you try to walk out the door, it's difficult to squelch the desire to either gather her up in your arms or kick her away. If you gather her up in your arms and promise to never leave, it will be difficult for you to ever respect your partner again. You may stay, but you will never see her as an equal again, and this will be an open invitation for you to become emotionally abusive toward her. If you kick or push her away, you may be accused of being physically abusive. Or she may become so enraged with you for rejecting her that she physically attacks you and you are forced to defend yourself. If you are a man, you'll have a difficult time explaining why you kicked or hit an innocent woman. If you really lose your temper and hurt her, you may end up staying with her out of guilt, but you're very likely to repeat your abusive behavior the next time she frustrates you.

Strategies to Help You Cope with a Borderline Partner or Parent

1. Acknowledge what you are getting out of being in the relationship. Women and men who become involved with partners who suffer from BPD soon discover that their partners are deeply unhappy people. Many of them learn that their partners had desperately unhappy childhoods, often suffering from either physical or sexual abuse or severe neglect and abandonment. If this is true of your situation, it's natural for you to want to be a positive influence in your partner's life and to somehow make up for the severe pain and loneliness he or she has experienced. Unfortunately, this may have led you to put up with unacceptable behavior and to swallow your anger and ignore your own needs. This is what is commonly referred to as codependent behavior on your part (codependents typically avoid their own problems by focusing on those of someone else).

   You are not helping a partner with BPD by subordinating your own needs and by putting up with unacceptable behavior. In fact, this enables, or reinforces, inappropriate behavior on the part of your partner. With no negative consequences for his or her actions, your partner has no motivation to change.

   You also need to recognize why you were attracted to someone with BPD in the first place and what you sought to gain from the unhealthy relationship. It may very well be that one of the reasons you were attracted to someone with BPD was that you liked to see yourself as the Knight in Shining Armor who was going to rescue this person. Perhaps you got a boost in your self-esteem when you realized that this person needed you so much, and you liked the idea of being able to save someone so helpless or troubled. Underneath this Knight in Shining

Armor persona of yours is probably a need to be in control. Instead of focusing on yourself and your own problems, it may have been a lot easier to focus on someone else.

2. Stop trying to fix the person with BPD. Instead, start focusing on yourself and on making the changes in yourself that will contribute to the betterment of your relationship. Take responsibility for your part in the relationship. Again, it's very important that you don't confuse this with believing that you *caused* your partner's problems. You did not. But there are inevitably behaviors on your part that *enable* your partner to continue acting out in negative ways. You must address these behaviors in order to take back control of your life. For example, your instincts may tell you that you need to rescue the person you care about, while the exact opposite is probably true. You need to back away and allow your partner to take responsibility for his or her behaviors and emotional health. The person with BPD will be more than happy to allow you to continue your old behavior of rescuing him or her—it's probably one of the reasons she sought you out. This, however, won't help either of you.

3. Voluntarily climb off your pedestal. One reason you were probably attracted to someone with BPD was that this person put you on a pedestal in the beginning of the relationship. He or she thought you were wonderful—so accomplished, so funny, so loved by others. This felt great—who doesn't want to be adored like this? But as you undoubtedly discovered, the higher up on a pedestal you are put, the farther you have to fall, and fall you did. The only way to avoid these extremes is to voluntarily refuse to be put on a pedestal. When your partner or parent is overcomplimenting you or is building you up too much while talking to others about you, say that you are uncomfortable being placed on a pedestal. Remind the person that what you did was not all that great and that although you appreciate his or her compliments, you believe you acted as many others would have done in the situation. By voluntarily climbing off the pedestal, you will avoid the situation of having to fall off the pedestal quite so far. Yes, you will still experience

being pushed off your pedestal when the borderline person splits and sees you as "all bad," but you won't fall off quite so far.

4. Let go of your victim mentality. If you are with someone who is a borderline Jekyll and Hyde who frequently flies off the handle and becomes emotionally, verbally, or physically abusive, you have, in fact, been victimized. But being a victim of abuse and developing a victim mentality are not the same things. Developing and maintaining a victim mentality will only keep you feeling trapped, powerless, and out of control. In some cases, this is actually the intention of those who have BPD—they want to keep you off balance.

   In order to change your situation and take back your power and control, you must refuse to tolerate unacceptable behavior, and you must set and enforce your boundaries. You can't do this if you are being a victim. This doesn't mean that you won't sometimes feel weak and helpless. That's normal when you are involved with someone who has this disorder. But you must not give in to these feelings for too long a period of time. You must remain firm in your resolve not to fall back into behaving like a victim, no matter how hard the person with BPD tries to force you back into that role.

5. Identify your partner's triggers. Borderline individuals tend to react spontaneously and sometimes intensely to certain situations, words, or actions. These are called triggers. Knowing what your partner's triggers are can help you avoid some conflicts. Since perceived abandonment is a huge trigger for people with BPD, know ahead of time that, by setting limits, you will likely be perceived as shutting your partner out. Your need for time away from the relationship will likely be perceived as your pulling away or even as your ending the relationship. Knowing this may help you to anticipate the borderline person's reaction, be more sensitive to the person's feelings when he or she reacts, and help you to stay detached and not get sucked into his or her drama. Of course, you cannot avoid all of the triggers all the time, and you must keep in mind that your partner's behavior

is his or her responsibility, not yours. See chapter 11 for a list of common BPD triggers.

6. Try to find patterns in your partner's behavior. Some people suffering from BPD are actually quite predictable if you know what to look for. For example, notice the circumstances surrounding their outbursts, depressions, or bouts with anxiety. Were there factors such as the time of day, the presence or the absence of alcohol (in you and in your partner), or the presence of a specific person? Behavior that is predictable can be much easier to handle than behavior that seemingly comes out of nowhere. Taking the time to know your partner and your partner's moods will help you to understand that person better, avoid conflicts, and stop taking his or her outbursts personally.

7. Get a reality check. If you become confused as to whether you are guilty of the behavior or the attitude that your partner is accusing you of, check it out with close friends or family members. While it isn't usually advisable for partners in a relationship to involve others in their domestic problems, in your situation it may be the only way you can stay clear as to what is the truth about you and what is a projection or a fantasy of your partner's. Since borderline individuals can also be very perceptive about others and may be the only people who are willing to tell you the truth about yourself, it can be even more confusing.

For example, your partner may complain to you that you are insensitive to her needs and too focused on yourself. You may not feel that this is true since you spend a great deal of time trying to make her happy, but after hearing this complaint over and over, you might come to doubt your perceptions. It's time for a reality check. It's quite possible that you are rather self-focused, since it's common for people who suffer from BPD and those with narcissistic personality disorder to become involved with one another. Yet it's also possible that your partner is projecting (attributing her own denied qualities onto you) or confusing you with her parents. Of course, you can't depend on your friends or family to always tell you the truth, but if you let them know it's important and that you would appreciate their honesty, they will likely tell you how they really perceive you. While you might be different with your friends and family than you are with your partner, more than likely they have observed you in many different situations and with previous lovers, and you can probably trust their perceptions of you.

8. Determine your personal limits and set appropriate boundaries. There are entire books written about boundaries and limits, and I have listed some of them at the back of this book. For our purposes, it is important to understand that the goal is to create flexible boundaries that are not too thin or too thick. When boundaries are too thin, you tend to take on the feelings and responsibilities of others and lose sight of your own. When your boundaries are too thick, you become too rigid. You are disconnected from the feelings of others and from your own feelings as well.

Personal limits are not about controlling or changing other people's behavior but about what you need to do to take care of yourself. People with weak or nonexistent limits can have difficulty distinguishing between their own beliefs and feelings and those belonging to others.

People with BPD tend to change the rules, act impulsively, and demand attention on their schedule. Limits can help you deal with these behaviors so that you don't feel like a puppet on a string. Without limits, BPD behavior can get drastically out of control, so setting limits is not just for your own mental health, but it can actually benefit the borderline in your life. In fact, when you allow the borderline to violate your boundaries, you may actually make the situation worse.

Show by your actions that you have a bottom line, that there are limits to the type of behavior that you will accept. Communicate these limits clearly and act on them consistently. For example, refuse to continue an argument if the other person starts yelling, and remove your child from the situation if your partner or parent becomes verbally or physically abusive. It is best to be specific when communicating about your personal limits. For example, instead of asking the borderline to "treat you with more respect," ask him or her to stop calling you names. And it is also best to communicate one limit at a time instead of bombarding the other person with a list of demands. If you find that you are unable to establish a bottom line or follow through with the limits you've set, you may want to seek the help of a therapist.

9. Disengage if your limits aren't observed or if you or your partner is losing control. If your partner is unable to or refuses to honor the limits you have set or if a situation arises that threatens to get out of hand, the best thing you can do is to emotionally or physically disengage from him or her. Don't stubbornly continue to assert your point of view when you can see that it is triggering your partner or causing him or her to become enraged. In this emotional state, your partner won't be able to really hear you or take in your perspective anyway, and if you persist, he or she is likely to resort to name-calling, character assassination, or suicidal threats. Also, don't feel obligated to continue a discussion that has eroded into an argument just because your partner wants to continue it. Here are some suggestions for ways to disengage:

- Change the subject or refuse to continue the discussion.
- Say no firmly and stick to it.
- Leave the room or the house if necessary.
- If the discussion or argument occurs on the phone, hang up and refuse to answer if your partner calls back.
- Stop the car or refuse to drive until your partner has calmed down.
- Stop seeing your partner for a while.
- Suggest that you continue the discussion in your therapist's office.

There will be times when none of these suggestions work, when your partner has completely lost control. Your suggestion to table the discussion or your attempt to walk away may be interpreted as rejection or abandonment, and your partner may become enraged, may attempt to prevent you from leaving, or may threaten suicide. In these situations, you should stop trying to handle the situation yourself. If your partner is in therapy, call the therapist. If your partner is not in therapy, call a crisis hot line. If your partner threatens suicide or violence toward you, call the police.

BPD is a serious personality disorder. Many people suffering from the disorder don't just threaten suicide; they actually go through with it, and some can become extremely violent if they feel provoked. It's very important that you seek outside help from a competent mental health professional if your attempts at coping with the situation and stopping the emotional abuse seem to upset your partner to the point that he or she threatens suicide or your life.

10. Make a distinction between the things you can control and the things you cannot. No matter how hard you try, a partner with BPD may not respond as you would like during any particular emotional exchange, discussion, or disagreement. This is beyond your control. What is within your control is how you chose to react to the situation, whether you did all you could to take care of yourself in the relationship, and whether you did your part in helping to eliminate the emotional abuse in your relationship.

11. Work on your own issues such as codependency, a need to be in control, alcohol abuse, or low self-esteem. If you are codependent, join Codependents Anonymous, or CODA; read books on codependency; or enter therapy to work on your issues. If you have control issues, particularly if you have the need to make everyone happy, work to discover the origin of this need so that you don't continue taking responsibility for your partner's happiness. You may focus on the needs of others in order to avoid your own unresolved issues, you may feel it is up to you to make others happy because this was the message you received from your parents, or you may have an investment in avoiding your own unhappiness. If you have low self-esteem, enter therapy to discover the causes and to develop ways to build up

your self-confidence and improve your self-image so that you will be in a better position to depersonalize and deflect your partner's criticism.

12. Don't blame all of your problems in the relationship on your partner's BPD. Before you conclude that your partner's strong reaction is merely a symptom of his or her disorder, ask yourself whether your behavior would have caused others to be upset. If you and your partner are going through a particularly difficult time, such as when your partner is feeling especially insecure, ask yourself if your own behavior or attitude could be contributing to the situation. If your partner accuses you of something, before you write it off as typical blaming and criticizing, ask yourself whether there is any truth to what he or she is saying. Those with BPD can be very intuitive, and many are extremely sensitive to cues such as body language and tone of voice. Certain borderlines are even capable of picking up on something someone is feeling before that person is aware of it. Being honest with yourself and owning up to how you truly feel will help your partner to trust you and may defuse a potentially explosive situation.

Remember that you both play a part in the problems in your relationship. By acknowledging how your behavior may have contributed to the problem, you can act as a healthy role model for your partner. Don't, however, take on more than your share of responsibility. As much as you don't want to blame your partner for everything based on his or her BPD, you also don't want to fall into the trap of allowing your partner to blame you for all the problems in the relationship.

Seek Outside Help When Needed

You cannot be your partner's or your parent's therapist. Neither can you force this person to go to therapy. What you can do is to make sure you seek out therapy to help you to cope when things get too painful. You need someone to talk to, someone who will understand what you are going through.

You don't need to tell your partner or your parent that you are seeking help unless you want to. Therapy is a private act, and it is no one else's business. Often, your act of starting therapy can cause a borderline partner's or parent's behavior to worsen. Many borderlines are threatened by therapy and therapists.

If you have a parent who is borderline, it's essential that you seek professional help. As Christine Ann Lawson, the author of *Understanding the Borderline Mother*, explains:

> Children of borderlines cannot become healthy, autonomous adults unless they find a way of understanding their experience. Like children who are born deaf and blind, children of borderlines have no way of organizing their emotional life. They do not realize that they are different, that other children are born into a world of sound and light. The lack of consistency in their emotional world creates a sense of meaninglessness, as if life itself is nonsense. Therapy helps children of borderlines organize and express their feelings, and helps them find meaning in their own existence.

Deciding Whether You Will Continue the Relationship

The next chapter is devoted to this question, but the following advice applies specifically to those involved with borderline partners: don't stay in the relationship because you feel sorry for a borderline partner or because you feel you are the only one who can help or save him or her. You have a right to experience a happy, healthy relationship and not sacrifice your own life for someone else's. And you may not be helping your partner as much as you think. In fact, you are a trigger of the illness. Rather than making the situation worse, it actually might help both of you if you were to leave. Your presence can inadvertently make your partner worse, since people with BPD tend to relive previous traumas through their significant others, alternating between paradoxical feelings of fear of engulfment and fear of abandonment. While you don't cause these feelings, your presence can exacerbate your partner's response.

You should also not stay in the relationship because your partner threatens to commit suicide if you leave. Some BPD partners use the threat of suicide to prevent their biggest fear: abandonment. Yet while threatening suicide, they may also be looking for someone to replace you or putting money away for the impending divorce. Some BPDs can actually become suicidal when they are faced with abandonment, however, so you should not hesitate to call in medical help and the police if you feel there is a real possibility that your partner may follow through with his or her threats. The same is true if your partner cuts or otherwise mutilates his or her body. Self-mutilation is a well-known BPD trait whereby the person hurts himself or herself in an effort to escape inner pain. Alert medical authorities, your partner's therapist, or both, if you see this happening or even if it is merely threatened.

Coping if Your Partner Is a Narcissist

Despite his aura of grandiosity and his bubble of self-sufficiency, the narcissist is extremely thin-skinned. Narcissistic people constantly take offense at the way others treat them (for example, people don't treat them with enough respect or don't appreciate them enough), and they frequently feel mistreated. This may be the only chink in their otherwise thick armor, the only clue that there is something wrong with them. Don't be fooled, though; people with NPD are suffering from a serious psychological disorder. While narcissists may not feel the emptiness in their lives, their behavior and attitude cause suffering in everyone with whom they have intimate contact. Typically, people who suffer from NPD or who have strong narcissistic traits seek treatment only when they fail to live up to their own expectations of greatness or when their environment fails to support their grand illusions. At this time, they will likely become depressed and seek psychotherapy to ease the pain.

QUESTIONNAIRE

Is Your Partner Suffering from Narcissism?

1. Does your partner seem to be constantly wrapped up in himself—his interests and projects—and have little concern about what is going on with you? Even when he does take an interest, is it short-lived?

2. Does your partner like to be the center of attention? Does she become bored or rude when someone else has the floor? Does she tend to bring the conversation back to herself?

3. Does he seem to feel that he is entitled to special treatment from you and others?

4. Does she seem to lack empathy and compassion for other people? Does she seem to have particular difficulty feeling other people's pain, even though she expects others to feel hers?

5. Does your partner feel that his opinions and beliefs are always the right ones and that others (including you) really don't know what they are talking about?

6. Does she think she is smarter, hipper, more attractive, or more talented than almost anyone else?

7. Does he seem to have an inordinate need to be right, no matter what issue is being discussed? Will he go to any lengths to prove he is right, including browbeating the other person into submission?

8. Is she very charismatic, charming, manipulative, or any combination of those qualities when she wants something, only to be dismissive or cold after a person has served his or her purpose?

9. Have you come to distrust your partner because you have frequently caught him in exaggerations and lies? Do you sometimes even think he is a good con man?

10. Does she often appear to be aloof, arrogant, grandiose, or conceited?

11. Can he be blisteringly insulting or condescending to people, including you?

12. Is she frequently critical, belittling, or sarcastic?

13. Does your partner become enraged if he is proven wrong or when someone has the audacity to confront him on his inappropriate behavior?

14. Does she insist on being treated a certain way by others, including by waiters and waitresses in restaurants, by store clerks, and even by you and your children?

15. Does he frequently complain that others do not give him enough respect, recognition, or appreciation?

16. Does she constantly challenge authority or have difficulty with authority figures or with anyone who is in a position of control or power? Is she constantly critical of those in power, often insinuating that she could do better?

17. Does your partner seldom, if ever, acknowledge what you do for him or show appreciation to you?

18. Does she instead seem to find fault with almost everything you do?

19. Even when he is forced to acknowledge something you've done for him or a gift you've given him, does he somehow always downplay it or imply that it really didn't meet his standards?

20. Does your partner focus a great deal of attention on attaining wealth, recognition, popularity, or celebrity?

21. Is your partner charming and manipulative when he wants something, only to be aloof and dismissive when his needs have been satisfied?

If you answered yes to more than half of the questions, your partner may be suffering from NPD or may have strong narcissistic personality traits. For more information on this disorder, refer to chapter 11 and to the books listed under "Recommended Reading."

Strategies to Help You Cope with a Narcissist

It's important when dealing with narcissists or people with strong narcissistic traits to keep remembering that they are not very conscious human beings, especially when it comes to their own behavior. Although much of their behavior can be experienced as emotionally abusive (for example, their arrogance, their dismissive attitude, their need to be right), they aren't necessarily trying to make you feel bad about yourself. In fact, the primary goal of narcissists is to make themselves feel good, even at the expense of others. Their inattentiveness, their brashness, their insensitive comments may give the impression that they are deliberately trying to hurt you when, in reality, most of the time they frankly couldn't care less about how you feel. Most narcissists are oblivious to others and to the feelings of others. The only time you become important is if you upset the status quo in any of the following ways:

- They need you in some way or want something from you.

- You confront them.

- You threaten to change things.

- You threaten to end the relationship.

For this reason, it's important not to take what a narcissist says or does personally. This, of course, is a very difficult task. But if you can try to remember that in a narcissist's world, he or she is the center of the universe and everyone else is but a mere satellite revolving around him or her, it might help. This doesn't mean that narcissistic people don't have feelings or that they aren't capable of caring about others, but it does mean that their needs will always come first.

The only time most narcissists deliberately try to hurt others is when they feel criticized or threatened in some way (for example, if you dare to question their ability or knowledge, if you tell them they are wrong about something, or if you challenge their authority). This is when you will feel their full wrath. Narcissists can cut you to your core in seconds by using just the right words that can wound you the most.

Coping with the Emotional Abuse

Here are some suggestions and strategies to help alleviate a great deal of the emotional abuse that can occur in a relationship with a narcissistic person:

- Recognize that narcissists have a tremendous need for personal space. If you insist on too much closeness, they will feel smothered and will lash out at you in order to push you away.

- If they become critical of you, call them on it immediately. The more you allow them to criticize you, the more they will disrespect you and the more they will continue to criticize you. Narcissistic individuals only respect those they feel are their equals. While they may seek out relationships in which they can feel superior and in which they can control other people, these people are mere puppets to them. In order for a narcissist to truly care about another person, he or she must respect that person.

- Begin to recognize their tendency to criticize as a sign that they (1) need some space from you, (2) are feeling critical of themselves, or (3) are testing you to see whether you are their equal. Confront them about their criticalness, ask them whether they need more space, and certainly don't buy into their criticalness by asking questions or arguing with them.

- If you have a complaint, state it clearly and strongly. Don't beat around the bush; don't try to be sensitive and say it subtly. This will only enrage them. And don't whine. Narcissists hate it when people whine or act like victims, and they lose all respect for people who do.

- When you have a complaint, follow it with a clear statement of how you would like the narcissist to change. For example, say something like, "I don't like the way you dismissed my comment as if it had absolutely no merit. My opinions are as valid as yours."

- Refuse to allow yourself to be charmed or used by your partner. Do only what you really feel like doing, and don't allow yourself to be talked into anything you don't really want to do.

- Take more responsibility for making sure you get a chance to talk. Instead of sitting patiently while the narcissist goes on and on about personal interests and projects, tell him or her you'd like to share something that happened to you. If the person refuses to stop talking, say something like, "I've been listening to you now for quite some time. I'd appreciate it if you'd give me a turn to talk." If this still doesn't work, say something like, "I'm tired of listening to you and not being heard. I'm going to go now" (or "Let's go").

- Realize that while narcissists can dish out criticism, they can't take it, especially if it involves "pulling their covers"—exposing the vulnerabilities and weaknesses under their facades. In fact, even constructive criticism is experienced as deep wounding in narcissists. This feeling of being wounded is so profound and so specific to narcissists that there is a psychological term for it—*narcissistic wounding*. When you suggest or point something out to them, don't be surprised if they take it as a criticism and react very strongly. They may lash out at you, they may huff out of the room, or they may give you the silent treatment. You may be able to help the situation by saying to them at a later time, "I didn't mean to hurt your feelings. I was only trying to make a suggestion," or "I'm sorry if I hurt your feelings. I was only trying to point something out that might help you."

- In spite of this sensitivity, you must stop narcissists from abusing you in any way. Even though they may not have intended to hurt your feelings, even though they may react very negatively at the time, confronting them is the only way to stop their abusiveness and the only way to gain or retain their respect.

- If they do make positive changes in their behavior, be sure to acknowledge it. Don't belabor the point since doing so may cause them to feel too vulnerable, and their pride may rise up, causing them to be angry with you. Just acknowledge the change briefly, and thank them for making it.

Unfortunately, once a narcissist loses respect for you, it may be nearly impossible for you to regain it. It depends on how much you've allowed him or her to control you or abuse you in the past, how much whining and groveling you've done, and how much you've allowed him or her to see your neediness and vulnerability. If the person shows no signs of respect for you whatsoever—he sighs and rolls his eyes when you talk, he laughs at you when you try to stand up to him, or he challenges you to try to live without him—then there is little chance of ever gaining his respect, and any relationship with him will continue to be abusive. Your best bet is to work on gaining enough strength to end the relationship.

If you choose to stay, all you can do is cut off the aggressiveness and abusiveness by confronting it at the moment and work on building a strong enough sense of self that your partner cannot erode your identity.

Above all, seek professional help to assist you in overcoming your anger and shame—shame at not being loved, shame at having accepted this person's humiliation for so long, and shame at what you have submitted to and undergone.

Should You Tell Your Partner That You Suspect He or She Has a Personality Disorder?

After reading this chapter and discovering that your partner may suffer from a personality disorder, you may feel eager to share this information with him or her. This is understandable since you probably feel relieved to learn that there is a reason for your partner's behavior, and you may assume that your partner may feel relieved to learn it as well. Unfortunately, however, this is usually not the case. Most partners become angry and defensive, and some respond with such shame and despair that they try to hurt themselves.

It's usually best if people learn about their disorders from a therapist, not from their partners. The only exception to this rule is if people are actively seeking answers as to why they act and feel the way they do. If you do share this information with your partner, make sure you do so in a loving and caring way.

One of my goals for this chapter is to humanize these two personality disorders since they have both been demonized by the media and even by some in the professional community. Many people view those suffering from personality disorders as freaks who are beyond help, but this is absolutely not true. Those who suffer from borderline personality disorder or narcissistic personality disorder suffer from an illness as surely as do people with depression or schizophrenia, and many were victims of severe emotional, physical, or sexual abuse as children. Since the descriptions and the behavior of people who suffer from both BPD and NPD seem so negative, anyone diagnosed with either of these disorders tends to feel very stigmatized. For this reason, it's important to realize that these disorders are something that people have, not something they are.

Understanding that your partner has a personality disorder will explain a great deal. It doesn't excuse his or her behavior, but it makes sense out of it. By understanding the disorder and its probable cause, some partners can gain the necessary empathy that will be required for them to try to work out the problems in the relationship. For others, of course, it will mean that they now have a legitimate reason to leave the relationship and in certain severe cases, this is probably the best option.

Learning that your partner has a personality disorder doesn't give you an excuse to stop working on your own issues and stop taking responsibility for your part in your relationship problems. This is especially true because the partners of people with personality disorders often have personality disorders themselves.

If You Are Dealing with a Sociopath

It is important to realize, whether the sociopath in your life is your intimate partner, a parent, a sibling, or your own child, that a person without a conscience experiences emotions very differently from the way normal people do. This includes the fact that they don't experience love at all. As painful as this is to accept, it's crucial that you do so. Otherwise, you are setting yourself up for more heartache and perhaps endangering yourself and your other loved ones. It's particularly important that intimate partners grasp this information because otherwise you may continue to modify your own behavior in the hopes of finally winning his or her love. The truth is, no matter what you do, no matter how hard you try to please a sociopath, you cannot make this person love you. The sociopath simply is not capable. You may, however, serve a purpose in this person's life (for example, the appearance of a normal, happy marriage can help the person in his or her career; the sociopath may not want to be alone).

Because sociopaths cannot really love, life is reduced to an endless game of attempts to dominate other people. Sometimes their attempts to dominate are primarily confined to the business world, to a profession, or to a position in government. Other times, sociopaths focus on exploiting those in their personal relationships. Perhaps most important, you should realize that sociopaths can become physically violent, that they cannot be cured, and that even if there was a cure, most of them don't wish to change.

Facing these cold, hard facts can be difficult, but to protect yourself and the ones you love, you must face them if you are dealing with a sociopath. Facing these truths will also be your first step in deciding whether you need to completely sever your ties with this person or find safer ways to deal with him or her.

If you decide to continue the relationship, it's vitally important that you don't join in on his or her game of domination. Don't become tempted to compete with a sociopath in any way—don't try to argue or debate with this person or outsmart or psychoanalyze him or her. You will only reduce yourself to the sociopath's level and, most important, distract yourself from protecting yourself from him or her.

As Martha Stout, the author of *The Sociopath Next Door: The Ruthless versus the Rest of Us*, so aptly put it, "The best way to protect yourself from a sociopath is to avoid him, to refuse any kind of contact or communication." Rarely do I, or do other psychotherapists, recommend something so harsh, but in this case it is absolutely necessary. Remember, there is no changing a sociopath—you can't change this person, and he or she doesn't want to be changed even if it were possible. The longer you continue a relationship with a sociopath, the more you put yourself in danger of being hurt, manipulated, conned, used, or betrayed.

You don't have to worry about hurting a sociopath's feelings by excluding this person from social events, by ending the relationship, or even by refusing to speak to him or her. The sociopath simply doesn't have any feelings to hurt—although he or she may try to convince you otherwise. In the case of a family member, others in the family may not understand why you are being so harsh and may try to make you feel bad about your actions. Remind yourself about the inherent danger in maintaining a relationship with a sociopath, and stay strong in your conviction.

If the sociopath in your life does try to manipulate you into feeling sorry for him or her, remind yourself that pity should be reserved for innocent people who are in genuine pain or who have fallen on misfortune. Pitying someone who consistently hurts you or other people and then actively campaigns for your sympathy is a waste of time.

If, in the process of ending your relationship with a sociopath, he or she begs you for a second chance (or a third, a fourth, or a fifth chance, for that matter), remind yourself that second chances are for someone who is able to change and who has a conscience. Don't fall into the trap of wanting to rescue a sociopath. This person can't be rescued. If you want to save something or someone, rescue a dog from a shelter. If you really want to help someone, help people who truly want to be helped.

As Stout admonished in her book, never agree, out of pity or for other reasons, to help a sociopath conceal his or her true character. Once you have discovered who this person really is, the sociopath in your life may beg you not to tell anyone else. But don't join sociopaths in their deceits by agreeing to conceal their real character. Other people deserve to be warned, especially when it comes to child abuse, partner abuse, stealing, and other, more dangerous, pursuits of sociopaths.

7

Deciding Whether to Continue the Relationship

You never know what is enough unless you know what is more than enough.

—William Blake

Deciding whether you should continue a relationship with a Jekyll and Hyde is difficult, especially if there are times when the person can be considerate, loving, and supportive. People with children have an especially difficult time when one parent has this syndrome. The other partner must then decide whether to stay or go. A similar quandary exists for anyone with a parent who is a Jekyll and Hyde. The information, the exercises, and the questionnaires in this chapter will help those of you who are undecided determine whether you should continue the relationship or end it.

For the most part, your decision to stay or leave will come down to the following issues:

- How much damage you have sustained due to the emotional (or physical) abuse you have experienced from your involvement with a Jekyll and Hyde.

- Whether there is any real hope for change (that is, whether your Jekyll and Hyde is willing to admit he or she has a problem and is willing to seek professional help).

- Whether the person is sincere in his or her attempts to change or is manipulating you.

Let's address these items one by one.

The Damage

Depending on the type of Jekyll and Hyde in your life, you may have sustained so much emotional damage that you really can't afford to remain involved with this person. If the Jekyll and Hyde in your life is so cruel and so critical that he or she has worn away much of your self-esteem and sense of self, if his or her constant personality changes have confused you to the point where you can't trust your own perceptions, it's best that you disconnect from this person as soon as you possibly can. It's not a question of "giving him another chance" or "believing she can change." It's not even a question of whether you love this person or whether he or she truly loves you. It's a question of survival for you. As one client told me, "I honestly don't feel I can go another round with my husband. He promises me that he is going to change this time. He's even started therapy. But I just don't feel strong enough to withstand any more criticism from him. I'm just too fragile at this point. If I hear one more criticism about the way I act, I think I will break."

This woman knew her limits. She had already put up with far too much, but she knew that she couldn't tolerate any more, and, thankfully, she cared enough about herself to honor her instincts. You have the right to put yourself first, to put your emotional well-being ahead of the Jekyll and Hyde's. You can't save this person, but you can save yourself.

EXERCISE

List the Damage

It can be difficult to assess the damage because we tend to forget or deny painful events. It will help if you take some time to make a list of all the times when the Jekyll and Hyde in your life has hurt you due to erratic, eruptive, abusive, dishonest, or conflicting behaviors.

1. Start with the most recent events and work your way backward, listing every major event you can remember. (For example, your partner blew up and berated you in front of the kids).

2. After you have made your list, slowly read over it again. Allow yourself to really take in the reality that this person has done these things to you or treated you in these ways.

3. Starting with the latest incidents, write down the negative consequences for each event: how it made you feel, the ways in which you or your children suffered, any losses you experienced (friends, money, respectability). For example, "When she berated me in front of the kids, I felt so much shame. I'm sure my kids lose respect for me each time she does that. And I think it teaches my kids that it is okay to berate your partner."

Is There Hope for Change?

In order for people with the Jekyll and Hyde syndrome to really change, they must first recognize that their behavior is not normal. They must be able to admit that they have a problem and must be willing to seek help for it. This means that if they are emotionally or physically abusive, they must be willing to acknowledge this fact and seek out an abuser's program or professional therapy. If they abuse alcohol, they must be willing to go to Alcoholics Anonymous or an alcohol treatment program. If they are bipolar, they must be willing to go to a psychiatrist and take the medicine that is prescribed. If they have borderline personality disorder, they must be willing to seek out a psychotherapist who works with this disorder. The same is true for anyone who suffers from narcissistic personality disorder.

Next, these people must be able and willing to recognize how their behavior has caused you and others pain and damage. Many abusive Jekyll and Hydes, for example, will tell you that they understand that they have been abusive and that they are determined to change, but often this is merely manipulation. Many Jekyll and Hydes are excellent at convincing you that they have good intentions when in fact they are merely trying to get you back.

Is the Person Sincere in His or Her Attempts to Change?

Some Jekyll and Hydes are very charismatic and very clever. They know exactly what to say to get you to soften, they know what your weaknesses are, what will "push your buttons" in terms of feeling sorry for them, and so on. When you tell a Jekyll and Hyde that you are thinking of ending the relationship, this person may pull out all the stops, so to speak, and create a campaign to get you back. During this time, the Jekyll and Hyde can appear to be very sincere, saying the things you always wanted to hear, showing you a completely different side that you wish you could have seen all along.

You must realize, however, that many Jekyll and Hydes, by the sheer nature of their personalities and their disturbance, are extremely manipulative. As was the case in the story of Dr. Jekyll and Mr. Hyde, the darker side of their personality is very powerful and does not want to be annihilated, so to speak. It will fight to stay in existence. If this means manipulating you into believing that they have changed, so be it. If it means lying and telling you that they are going to therapy when they are not, or that they have stopped their extramarital affairs when they have just become better at hiding them, they will do so.

Fortunately, if you are alert and you look closely, you can often see the cracks in their veneer even in the midst of their attempts at convincing you they will change. During a couples session with an abusive man, whom I will call Carl, and his wife, Nadine, I witnessed this very phenomenon. Carl had been telling us how motivated he was to change and how much he loved Nadine, and he had seemed very sincere. Then Nadine shared with me another of Carl's behaviors that troubled her. Carl shot Nadine an angry, almost evil glance. The look expressed so much rage and hostility that it belied his sincerity. Fortunately, his wife also saw the glance and called him on it in the moment.

As much as Jekyll and Hydes try to hide their darker nature, it will seep out—especially as you begin to set limits or confront them on their behavior. This is what occurred with my clients Irene and Mark. Irene and Mark had been married for three years when Irene came to see me. She started off telling me how wonderful her husband was, how kind and considerate and generous he was, but then she broke down and cried and told me that he was also unbelievably cruel: "Every few weeks he turns into another person. He starts nitpicking at every little thing I do wrong. I don't clean the house well enough. I don't iron his shirts right. It goes on and on. If I try to reason with him, he won't listen to me. I'm always wrong, and he's always right. His biggest complaint is that I'm not affectionate enough with him and that I don't want to have sex with him often enough. But the truth is, when he's in his other personality, I just don't feel attracted to him. And his temper is so bad, I've become afraid of him. Who wants to have sex with someone you are afraid of?"

Irene wanted to know if I would see her and her husband in therapy. "Maybe it's me. Maybe I'm too cold. I don't like doing domestic stuff [Irene had a full-time job] so I know I don't put enough effort into it. Maybe I bring out the worst in him. After all, he can be so wonderful."

I agreed to see Mark to get his perspective and to consider seeing them for couple's therapy. During my initial session with him, he seemed very sincere about wanting to change. He owned up to his nitpicking behavior and seemed to be as troubled by his periodic personality changes as his wife was. "I really want to find out what causes me to change like that. I love Irene, and I don't want to be picking at her like that. I don't know what comes over me."

I agreed to see Mark and Irene in couples therapy since Mark seemed to be so willing to change. I noticed, however, that Mark often came into our sessions very agitated. He usually started right in complaining about something Irene had done (or not done). When I confronted Mark about this, he tried to justify his complaints—he really didn't hear me. When I stopped him and gave him feedback that I didn't feel he had heard, Mark stared at me blankly and then began to complain again. It was as if I had said nothing, as if absolutely nothing was getting through to him. I asked Mark to stop, to take some deep breaths, and to just be quiet for a few minutes. He couldn't do it.

I pointed out to Mark that he always started our sessions very agitated and critical of Irene and that if he loved her so much and wanted to save the marriage so badly, this seemed to be having the opposite effect. Mark once again simply stared at me and made no comment.

After three sessions of couples therapy, it became clear to Irene that Mark had serious issues that didn't involve her. Because she felt some support coming from me, she began to get stronger. It became more and more obvious to Irene and to me that Mark wasn't in therapy because he wanted to change. He was there because he wanted Irene to change.

From my experience working with Jekyll and Hydes, I have found that those who really can change need to be able to do the following:

1. Believe their partners when the partners tell them about their two sides and how severe their personality changes actually are.

2. Admit they have a problem and seek help. It is safe to say that all Jekyll and Hydes need professional therapy to help them resolve the inner conflicts that created their split. In addition, some of them need support groups such as Alcoholics Anonymous, Debtors Anonymous, and so on.

3. Take complete and utter responsibility for their erratic, explosive, or abusive behavior. This means that they do not blame their partners (or children) for causing them to react the way they have.

4. Apologize to their partners (or children) for their behavior.

A word of caution: Even Jekyll and Hydes who do start therapy and exhibit some real signs of improvement often fall back into their old patterns as soon as they get their partners back. For this reason, it's important to insist that your partner stay in therapy for at least a year (if your partner has a personality disorder, he or she needs to continue for several years).

Good Reasons to Leave a Jekyll and Hyde

The following are good reasons you should seriously consider either ending the relationship or separating from your loved one until things change.

- The Jekyll and Hyde refuses to admit he or she has a problem.
- The person refuses to get help.
- The Jekyll and Hyde continues to blame you for his or her abusive behavior.
- You made it clear that you will no longer tolerate abuse of any kind, but this person has continued to be abusive.

    You definitely need to leave when:

1. Your partner is physically abusing you or is threatening to do so. Many people start out by emotionally abusing their partners and work their way up to physical abuse. The more emotional abuse you take, the more permission your partner feels he or she has to become even more abusive, including physically abusive. As your partner's anger intensifies and as the relationship deteriorates, he or she may resort to physical violence as a way of gaining control. If he or she has already hit you, even if it was "just a slap," you are in danger. The same holds true of behaviors such as pushing, shoving, pinning you down, or holding you captive against your will. All of these behaviors indicate that your partner has lost control of himself or herself, and they are danger signs for you. In some cases, they may indicate that your partner has become mentally unstable.

2. You have reached a point where you are becoming physically abusive. You may have become so frustrated and angry because of your partner's or parent's erratic Jekyll and Hyde behavior

that you have reached a breaking point and have begun to act out your anger in a physical way. If this is the case, you could hurt your partner or parent seriously next time or push him into hurting you. Either way, it's time to leave.

If you honestly feel that you are not an abusive person by nature but that your partner has pushed you into becoming violent, then the best thing for both of you is for you to end the relationship. Even if your partner suffers from a mental or emotional disorder of some kind, you are not helping either of you by staying.

3. You have begun to fantasize about harming or killing your partner or parent. If you have reached this point, you feel trapped and believe there is no way out of your abusive relationship. But it is important to realize that this is a symptom of the emotional abuse you have been suffering—it is not reality. The reality is that there is a way out. You will need to get professional help in order to gain the courage and the strength to leave, or if you are afraid for your physical safety, you need to contact the police or a battered women's shelter. In either case, you need to realize that there is certainly a better way out than risking being in prison for the rest of your life or being overwhelmed with guilt for the rest of your life because of the physical harm you caused your partner.

4. You are seriously questioning your sanity. If your partner is using gaslighting techniques on you (for example, denying that things have occurred, telling you that you are imagining things, or accusing you of being crazy), and you are beginning to distrust your own perceptions, it is time to leave the relationship. The longer you stay, the more you will doubt yourself and your sanity, and the more your mental health will be jeopardized.

If You Can't Leave for Yourself, Leave for Your Children

If the Jekyll and Hyde in your life becomes overly controlling, domineering, critical, or rejecting of you, it isn't too much of a stretch to realize that this person will treat your children the same way. Unfortunately, most partners and other loved ones (adult children, siblings) of a Jekyll and Hyde try to fool themselves into believing otherwise. They tell themselves that they are the only ones who are being affected by the Jekyll and Hyde's erratic or abusive behavior. But the truth is that when Jekyll and Hydes have sudden shifts in behavior, they affect everyone who is close to them. If you become disoriented, confused, or afraid when your partner or your parent suddenly goes on a tirade or shifts into another personality, how do you think your children feel? Your children are far less equipped to handle erratic behavior, especially when it comes from a parent or a grandparent.

Don't continue to be blind to the way the Jekyll and Hyde in your life treats your children or to make excuses for his or her behavior. If you can't walk away from the abuse, get professional help. Therapy will help you build up your self-esteem and gain the courage to do what you know is right for you and your children. Remember that you are who you are today primarily because of the way your parents (or other caretakers) treated you. Don't continue the cycle of abuse by exposing your children to the same unacceptable behavior you grew up with.

When You Resist Leaving

Even though deep inside you may know that you need to end this relationship, you might find yourself vacillating about whether you should stay or leave. Here are some common thoughts and behaviors that may interfere with your ability to make a clear decision.

- *False hope.* You may continue to hope that things will get better. Your partner may try to convince you that he now understands what you have been trying to tell him and that he's going to change. But you need to remind yourself of how many times you thought things were getting better, only to be disappointed when he reverted back to his abusive, or "Mr. Hyde," behavior.

- *The way we were.* You may hope that things will go back to the "way it used to be." You may find yourself remembering how your partner behaved when you first fell in love and wishing that she would treat you that way again. You may have even seen glimpses of her old behavior during one of her "good" cycles. Remind yourself, though, that each good cycle is usually followed by a bad cycle. In many cases, there may not be a return to the good cycle, and the behavior or abuse may actually worsen.

- *Unclear thinking.* Those who are in a Jekyll and Hyde relationship are often under such stress, confusion, and trauma that they are not thinking clearly. It can be extremely confusing when your partner alternates between terrible rages and normal, loving behavior, and if you are being abused emotionally or physically, it's very common to be confused and traumatized. For this reason, you may need to get feedback from your friends and family members about your partner and his or her behavior. They may actually have a clearer picture of your partner and the situation than you do. You also need to seek therapy to help you clarify your thinking.

- *Fear that your partner might commit suicide if you leave.* This may sound cold, but you must remember that you are not responsible for anyone else's actions. Some Jekyll and Hydes may use the threat of suicide to try to control you, to make you feel sorry for them, or to show you how much they love or need you, but most of them don't carry through with it. There are some exceptions, however (most notably, people who have borderline personality disorder). If a threat is actually attempted, don't hesitate to bring in both medical personnel and the police. If your partner is in therapy, also contact his or her therapist.

- *Emotional and physical exhaustion.* Having to deal daily with the fear of a blow-up or a personality change can be extremely stressful and draining. You may feel as if it takes all your energy just to get through the day. Having to make such a life-changing decision or having to cope with the pain of ending the relationship may seem like too much for you to do right now. Unfortunately, the longer you stay in the relationship, the more exhausted you will be. Therefore, it's very important that you find a way to take some time alone to think about your situation from a distance. Perhaps you could take a short vacation to visit family or go away for a weekend with friends so that you can create some physical and emotional distance from your partner. This will help you to get a break from the turmoil and gain perspective on the situation.

- *Substance abuse.* If you are indulging in substance abuse (alcohol or drugs) in order to help you cope with a Jekyll and Hyde, do your best to taper off or quit. You won't be able to think clearly as long as you are under the influence. Recognize that resorting to this way of coping is further evidence of how the relationship is harming you.

- *Loneliness.* Many people resist leaving because they are afraid of being alone and being overwhelmed with loneliness. Others have been led to believe that all they have are their Jekyll and Hyde partners or that no one else will ever want them. Many Jekyll and Hydes have pushed away friends and family members or encouraged their partners to do so. You may have contributed to your own isolation by focusing too much attention on your relationship and on your efforts to avoid conflict. And you may have your own dependency needs as well. Make an effort to reconnect with friends and family to help avoid feelings of isolation, and seek therapy to gain an opportunity to connect with someone on a deep emotional level.

- *Feeling as if you can or should help.* You may feel as if you need to stay in order to help your partner to recover. Just as it is with alcoholism, however, Jekyll and Hydes cannot get better until they decide they want to do so. Your primary responsibility is to yourself, not to your partner. The fact is, you need help in order to heal from the damage caused by being with a Jekyll and Hyde. Instead of focusing on helping your partner, seek therapy for yourself. This will also set an example for your partner.

Sometimes you know you should leave but are unable to do so. You may know the relationship isn't going to get any better, know that the abuse will only get worse, and even know that you are in physical danger or are in danger of losing it and hurting your partner—yet you're still unable to leave. If this is the case, I strongly urge you to seek professional psychotherapy in order to gain the courage to leave. There are plenty of reasons to leave, even if your partner is not physically abusing you or the children, the most important of which is that your children are being negatively affected by observing your partner's mood swings and erratic behavior. If you have such low self-esteem that you can't understand that you deserve to be treated better, then you need to work with a professional therapist who can help you build up your self-esteem.

If You Decide to Stay

If your partner has done all the right things—admitted he or she has a problem, taken complete responsibility for his or her mood shifts, erratic behavior, or betrayal; and sought professional help for the problem—you may decide to stay.

Unfortunately, even though you decide to stay, it can still be difficult to move forward without fear, resentment, or anger continuing to pollute the waters of your relationship. Once someone has been victimized or betrayed by a partner, it's hard not to live in fear that it will occur again. As one client told me, "I always have one foot out the door." In actuality, this fear can be a good thing. Your partner needs to prove to you that he or she can be trusted and that it's safe for you to let your guard down, and you need to keep your options open in case your partner doesn't change.

Eventually, though, you will need to move forward in your relationship, and to do this, you both must be willing to trust and to forgive. This is a tall order for anyone. It takes time to rebuild trust, and it can try the patience of both you and your partner when you realize that the trust is just not there. You may become impatient with yourself, thinking that you should be over it by now, and your partner may begin to feel that he or she is constantly being punished for past actions and is not being given another chance.

If you cannot forgive your partner for betraying you or emotionally abusing you in the past, your anger and resentment will make it impossible to move forward. While you have every reason to be angry, you need to take responsibility for finding constructive ways of releasing your anger—otherwise, your anger will continue to seep out, creating a wedge between you and your partner and triggering defensiveness and anger from him. Your partner can't be expected to tolerate your anger indefinitely, nor is it fair to expect him or her to. Forgiving is different from forgetting. Certainly, you can never forget how your partner treated you. Nor should you. Remembering the abuse will keep you on your toes and will strengthen your resolve never to allow it to happen again. But when you forgive, you say to your partner that you are willing to give him or her another chance—that you recognize we all have our issues and that we can't expect perfection from one another. Unfortunately, some survivors will discover that they are unable to rebuild trust in their partners and are unable to forgive their partners for the abuse, even though they have given themselves time to do both. If this is the case, it will be important to admit this to yourself and to your partner. Once this reality is faced, one or both of you may come to realize that it is time for the relationship to end.

You will also need to forgive yourself for allowing the abuse to continue. There is no need for you to continue to chastise yourself for being so passive or weak or foolish—whatever labels you've put on yourself. You likely put up with the abuse for the same reason your partner abused you—because you were abused or neglected as a child.

Although it's important for you to work at rebuilding trust in your partner, it's far more important that you trust yourself. If you trust yourself to take care of yourself—meaning that you trust yourself to speak up if your partner ever crosses the line and becomes abusive again—then you both can relax in the relationship and let time show you whether your partner has, in fact, stopped his or her Jekyll and Hyde ways.

Continue to Identify and Confront Jekyll and Hyde Behavior

Even though you have decided to continue the relationship, you still need to make an effort to identify and confront Jekyll and Hyde behavior in your partner. The following suggestions will help to keep you on track:

1. Pay attention. You don't need to be hypervigilant, but you do need to be cognizant of how your partner treats you on a daily basis.

2. Trust your perceptions and honor your feelings. At this point, hopefully, you are able to determine when your partner acts inappropriately. The more you trust your perceptions, the less confused you will be and the better able you will be to take care of yourself.

3. Continue to speak up. You simply can't afford to let things slide. You need to speak up each and every time your partner becomes abusive or acts in inappropriate ways; otherwise, you're sending the message that it is okay.

8

How to Avoid Getting Involved with a Jekyll and Hyde in the Future

Men will never disappoint us if we observe two rules:
(1) To find out what they are; (2) To expect them to be just
that.

 —George Iles

Be not swept off your feet by the vividness of the impression, but say, "Impression, wait for me a little. Let me see
what you are and what you represent. Let me try you."

 —Epictetus

Those who have been in a relationship a Jekyll and Hyde tend to continue the pattern of getting involved with this type of person. In this chapter, I provide specific, multidimensional steps that people can take to break this pattern. These include:

- Learning to spot a Jekyll and Hyde.
- Avoiding the repetition compulsion.
- Completing your unfinished business from the past.
- Taking it slow next time.

- Continuing to work on yourself.

- Choosing to have equal relationships.

- Learning to own your dark side. Sometimes people tend to get involved with abusive people as a way of avoiding their own dark side. Instead of addressing their own darker impulses, they get involved with people who will control them or act out their Shadow for them. They can then focus all their attention on the other person's dark side and ignore their own.

- Not placing people on pedestals.

Learning to Spot a Jekyll and Hyde

Learning to spot Jekyll and Hydes in the future can be a very difficult undertaking since most of them don't show you their true selves early on in a relationship. Nevertheless, here are some red flags to look out for:

1. Are they moody? Have you noticed that they can suddenly get in a bad mood and not be able to explain why?

2. Have you noticed that they change considerably when they have had a few drinks?

3. Do they seem secretive or illusive?

4. Do they keep important things from you? For example, do they ask you to call them at work instead of giving you their home phone numbers? Are they illusive about what they do for a living? Do they seem to dodge the question "Have you ever been married?" or "How many times have you been married?"

5. Do they change their minds often?

6. Do they seem hypocritical at times, saying they believe one thing but behaving in a completely different way?

7. Are they hypersensitive? Do they constantly feel slighted, injured, or insulted?

8. Do they often complain about how others have slighted, disappointed, or angered them?

9. Do they experience extreme highs and lows in a short period of time?

10. Do they rant incessantly?

11. Do they tell you that they sometimes feel like two different people or that others have told them they act like two different people at times?

12. Do they tend to be distant, for no apparent reason? Does this seem to happen most often after you've had a particularly good time together or after you have become intimate?

In addition to these questions, refer back to the questionnaire in chapter 1.

How to Avoid an Abusive Jekyll and Hyde

Abusive Jekyll and Hydes are often masters of deception. They are great at presenting themselves as caring, considerate, and cooperative when they are actually self-absorbed, opportunistic, and confrontational. Most abusive Jekyll and Hydes mistreat only people they are closest to (their partners, their children). To the rest of the world, they can appear to be rational, composed, and even kind. Because of this, many people find themselves involved with abusive Jekyll and Hydes before they have a chance to discover the true nature of these individuals, and by that time, it is often too late. Yet abusive Jekyll and Hydes are not as difficult to spot as you might think. All you need to do is look for some subtle and not-so-subtle telltale signs. The following are characteristics of abusive Jekyll and Hydes:

- They tend to build themselves up by bragging about their accomplishments and achievements.

- They tend to blame their mistakes and failures on others or on the world at large.

- They tend to be too eager and to get involved too quickly.

- They can be overly flattering and tend to idealize their partners (at least in the beginning).

- They tell you constantly that you make them feel good.

- They don't respect your boundaries or privacy.

- They need to be in control of the situation.

- They can have a physical posture that exudes an air of superiority, mysteriousness, hidden powers, or amused indifference.

- They have a sense of entitlement—they ask for and expect special treatment (don't want to wait their turn, insist on talking directly to authority figures as opposed to assistants or secretaries).

- They tend to talk a lot about themselves. They aren't really interested in others, although they may feign interest in the beginning of a relationship or in order to win over new acquaintances.

- They tend to be easily bored and impatient unless they are the topic of conversation.

- They tend to lack a sense of humor when it comes to themselves.

- They are easily hurt and insulted. Even the most innocuous remarks or acts can be interpreted as belittling, intruding, or insulting, and they feel constantly misunderstood.

By spotting these behaviors, attitudes, and traits, you can avoid becoming involved with an abusive partner. The following list of questions will also help.

QUESTIONNAIRE

How to Identify a Potential Abuser

1. Does he tend to blame everyone else for his mistakes or shortcomings?

2. Does she treat service people or those who are weaker than herself (such as the poor or animals and children) impatiently or cruelly?

3. Does he experience "instant intimacy" with you? Does he declare you are the love of his life on the first date? Does he push for marriage after knowing you for only a short time?

4. Is she jealous when you merely cast a glance at another woman?

5. Does he neglect to ask you what you would like to do or eat (by ordering for you at a restaurant, or choosing a movie without consulting you).

6. Does she disrespect your privacy and boundaries (show up unexpectedly without calling, go through your belongings).

7. Does he have to be in control at all times?

8. Was she abused as a child or raised in a violent household?

9. Does he drink excessively? Abuse drugs?

10. Is she jealous of your other relationships—not just with other women but with your male friends and family members as well?

11. Does he keep tabs on you? Does he want to know where you are at all times?

12. Does she expect you to spend all your free time with her? Does she act unusually possessive of you and your time?

13. Does he lose his temper frequently and more easily than seems necessary? Does he overreact to small problems?

14. Does she become enraged when you don't listen to her advice?

15. Does he become angry if you don't fulfill his wishes or if you cannot anticipate what he wants?

16. Is there a sense of overkill in her cruelty or her kindness?

17. Does he believe in a gender-specific supremacy or hold a strong stereotype of gender roles in the family?

18. When she becomes angry, do you become afraid of what she will do?

19. Has not making him angry become an important part of your behavior?

20. Does she punch walls or throw things when upset?

21. Does he use violence to solve problems? Does he get into fights with others?

22. Does she have a history of violent offenses?

23. Does he keep guns or other weapons? Does he threaten to use them when he's upset with someone?

If you answered yes to any of questions 1 through 12, you may have a reason to be concerned, especially if you answered yes to more than one question. If you answered yes to even one of questions 13 through 23, you definitely have a reason to be concerned. This person has an abusive personality and is very likely to become physically abusive toward you.

How to Avoid Becoming Involved with a Borderline Jekyll and Hyde

Although there are several different types of borderlines, in general, the following are common characteristics and behaviors of people with borderline personality disorder (BPD).

1. They want "instant romance" or "overnight commitment." There is a joke among lesbian women: Where do two lesbians go on their second date? To the U-Haul store. The reason this is a joke is that many lesbians move in together after being involved for a very short time. This joke could also apply to some types of borderlines who open up far too easily. They may tell you their histories right away, sharing intimate details of their lives that are embarrassing or painful to hear. They may push for more intimacy than you are comfortable with, perhaps wanting to have sex on the first date. They may tell you that they are in love with you after only one or two dates and may even tell you it was love at first sight. They may shame you into wanting to see them, perhaps calling you if you haven't called for a few days, sending you cards, or leaving little gifts at your doorstep.

2. Extreme withholding behavior. This type of borderline is just the opposite of the type described above. These borderlines are reluctant to tell you about themselves and

can be elusive about their history. They may be uncomfortable with signs of public affection (even though you are having sex) and often have little eye contact with you. You may feel that you need to persuade them to trust you or to have a relationship with you.

3. They exhibit a great deal of ambivalence or uncertainty, especially concerning whether they want to have a relationship with you or what type of relationship they want to have (for example, friendship versus romantic). One type of borderline is extremely reluctant to commit to a relationship. This type is fearful of being hurt, of losing himself or herself in a relationship, or of being smothered or engulfed in a relationship.

4. They have difficulty making decisions. They agonize over the simplest decisions, such as where you should go for dinner, and change their minds often.

5. They fluctuate between wanting instant intimacy and needing space. This type of borderline exhibits the twin fears that most borderlines experience—fear of abandonment or rejection and fear of engulfment or smothering. One day these borderlines may tell you they are crazy about you, that they can see the two of you being together for a long time, and the very next day they may tell you that they think you are going too fast.

6. Closely related to the above is a sense of their either constantly pushing at you for more involvement or commitment or their pushing you away. If you call them every day, they may tell you they need a break. If you don't call as often, they may insist that you are losing interest.

7. They have a heightened sense of sensitivity, and their feelings are easily hurt. People with BPD often tend to feel they are being ignored or short-changed, and they tend to misinterpret what you have said or what you meant by what you said. You may often feel as if you have to explain yourself more than usual or that your motives are constantly being questioned. This can lead to the feeling of

having to "walk on eggshells" around the person—the phrase so often used by partners of borderlines.

8. They have a tendency to rage and punish.

9. They withdraw love or attention or both when they don't get what they want.

10. They lack empathy or compassion for others.

DANIEL: THE IMPORTANCE OF NOTICING RED FLAGS

If a person you are involved with has any of the previous characteristics, view these as giant red flags. If you don't, you are likely to end up in a relationship with someone who not only suffers from BPD but who will make your life miserable. This was the case with my client Daniel, who began a roller-coaster ride of a relationship with a woman after they connected on an Internet dating site.

Daniel and Marie corresponded for several months, often by telephone. "Marie told me that she wanted to go slow—that she had broken off a long-term relationship a year ago and had been very hurt by the break-up. I certainly didn't want to rush into anything either, so I was okay with getting to know each other gradually over time."

After a few months they seemed so compatible that Daniel told Marie that he would like to come visit her (he lived two hundred miles away). Marie initially said that she'd love to meet him in person, but whenever he tried to pin her down as to when it would be convenient, she always seemed to have some reason that the time wasn't right.

Eventually they set a date, and Daniel drove up to Marie's hometown to meet her. They both were aware that there was the potential for disappointment on one or both of their parts once they actually met face-to-face, but their first meeting seemed to go exceptionally well—at least from Daniel's perspective. He found himself very attracted to Marie, and she seemed to feel the same about him. They talked nonstop and were both very affectionate. Although they didn't have sex during their first visit, they did kiss quite often and seemed to have a difficult time saying goodnight. When Daniel left, he couldn't wait until he saw Marie again.

When Daniel got home, though, he found an e-mail from Marie stating that she felt very pressured by his physical advances and needed to slow the relationship down. Although she had planned on visiting him in two weeks, she told him she was canceling her trip. This surprised Daniel because he had made no overt sexual moves toward her. "She seemed like she was responding to my kisses. She never tried to pull away. I thought we were both on the same page."

Daniel tried to talk to Marie about the situation, but she seemed very closed down. Hurt, he decided to back off for a while and let Marie make the next move. After he didn't e-mail or call her for a week, he received an e-mail from Marie, asking him if he was seeing anyone else. "I was kind of hurt that she would assume this. I told her no, that I was just confused about whether she really wanted to pursue a relationship with me or not and was taking a break to think things over. She told me that that sounded to her like I was 'giving up on her.' I told her I was doing no such thing—that if she was interested in me, I still wanted to see her. She told me she would be down to see me the following weekend."

When Marie came to visit Daniel, she seemed like a different person. "I was very reticent about touching her, but she was all over me. In fact, she wanted to have sex that first night. I couldn't believe how passionate she was. We had a really wild night! When she was getting ready to leave at the end of the weekend, she broke down and cried. She told me she was falling in love with me and didn't want to leave me."

Guess what happened once Marie got home? That's right—she had cooled down considerably. Daniel called her that night to see if she had gotten home okay, but Marie was very distant. When he told her what a good time he had with her and how he was looking forward to their next visit, she snapped at him, "All you want me for is the sex. Maybe you should get a hooker." Once again, Daniel was shocked at this turn of events. But instead of taking her radical mood shifts as a giant warning, Daniel felt it was important to be understanding and patient with Marie. "I knew she'd had a rough life and that other men had really hurt her. I thought that maybe I was paying for their cruelty, and while this wasn't fair, I thought I could take it."

This began what turned out to be three years of misery for Daniel, due to Marie's ups and downs. By the time he came into therapy, Daniel was nearly a basket case. Marie had been so cruel to him at times that his self-esteem was flattened. He was madly in love with her but knew he had to find a way to get away from her. "She is no closer to making a commitment to me than she was three years ago, but she won't let me go. I feel like a yo-yo. Every time I break up with her, she comes crying back to me, telling me she can't live without me. I even started dating another woman, but Marie ruined it for me by practically stalking the woman at her home and job. It was a nightmare. I've got to get away from her. Please help me!"

I was able to help Daniel break away from Marie. And Daniel learned two important lessons—to honor his intuition and not to fool himself into thinking he could rescue or change someone. As Daniel lamented to me, "I should have trusted my instincts about Marie. I sensed right away that there was something wrong with her. I thought it was because she had been hurt by other men. I thought I would be the one who could treat her with kindness and patience, and I could make up for what those other guys did, and this would help her to trust a man again."

How to Avoid a Narcissist

A person suffering from narcissism will tend to choose either a fellow narcissist as a partner or someone who feels inadequate and invisible and needs to hide in a relationship. This suits the narcissist just fine, since he or she doesn't want to recognize the existence of another person. In her book *Trapped in the Mirror: Adult Children of Narcissists in Their Struggle for Self*, Elan Golomb, Ph.D., explains:

> Often, her mate is the child of a narcissist, already indoctrinated to regard exploitation and disregard as love. Others lured by the narcissistic aura are those in whom healthy childhood exhibitionism has been repressed. . . . If the

parent puts the child to shame for showing off, the need for attention gets repressed into the unconscious. Repression means that the need is not satisfied and continues to press for expression in the adult without her being aware of it. The repressed adult may select an exhibitionistic mate to achieve vicarious satisfaction.

In other words, you are at risk of attracting a narcissistic partner if you have repressed your own need for expression and attention. If this seems to apply to you, I encourage you to continue working on your own childhood issues (reading *Trapped in the Mirror*, if you had a narcissistic parent, is a good first step). It will also help if you look for ways to express yourself (through creativity or public speaking) and if you own up to your need for attention instead of pretending that it doesn't matter to you. Refer back to the questionnaire "How to Identify a Potential Abuser" earlier in this chapter for more information on avoiding a narcissist.

How to Avoid a Sociopath

Sociopaths are masters at manipulation through flattery and charm. They love to sweep you off your feet with their counterfeit charm and false flattery. Even though it massages your ego to receive such flattery, don't be so hungry for an ego boost that you allow someone to manipulate you with it. You'll only end up acting foolish, and it will set you up to be taken advantage of.

Martha Stout, the author of *The Sociopath Next Door*, recommends that when considering a new relationship of any kind, you practice what she calls the "Rule of Threes" regarding the claims and the promises a person makes, and the responsibilities he or she has: "One lie, one broken promise, or a single neglected responsibility may be a misunderstanding instead. Two may involve a serious mistake. But *three* lies says you're dealing with a liar, and deceit is the linchpin of conscienceless behavior. Cut your losses and get out as soon as you can. Leaving, though it may be hard, will be easier now than later, and less costly."

Avoid the Repetition Compulsion

The truth is, even with these tips, you may still find yourself attracted to a Jekyll and Hyde. Many people develop a pattern of becoming attracted to and getting involved with abusive partners even though they try not to. The reason for this is that they were abused in childhood and have not worked in therapy to heal the damage. This is due to what is called the repetition compulsion.

So how do you avoid reenacting your childhood abuse experience in a romantic, intimate relationship? How do you avoid getting involved with someone who is a replica of a parent or another abuser?

Because we tend to surround ourselves with people who are similar to those in our families of origin or to our abusers, to take on the same roles we had in our families, it's often necessary to reevaluate our relationships in order to break the cycle.

The first thing you need to do is to identify your pattern. When you look back on your previous relationships, do you notice that many of your partners were similar in temperament, personality, and possibly even physical characteristics? Have you found that you pick the same kind of partner over and over—for example, someone who is excessively critical, like your father, or someone who is extremely moody, like your mother? If you have difficulty seeing the parallels between your choice of partners and your parents or another original abuser, the following exercise will help.

EXERCISE

Discover Your Pattern

1. Draw a vertical line down the middle of a piece of paper. On one half of the page, list the positive personality traits of your most recent lover; on the other half, list his or her most predominant negative personality traits.

2. On another piece of paper, do the same for your mother.

3. Repeat this same procedure to list your father's personality traits.

4. Notice whether there are similarities among the traits of your most current partner and those of your parents. Pay special attention to whether he or she shares negative, abusive traits with one or both of your parents.

5. Now, once again, on separate sheets of paper, list the positive and the negative personality traits of your previous three lovers (if you have had that many).

6. Notice whether your previous lovers share any personality traits, particularly negative ones.

7. Compare these traits with those of your parents.

8. Circle the negative traits that your partners (both present and past) have in common with your parents (or other primary caretakers).

Most people with a history of abuse or neglect notice a close correlation between the traits of their partners and those of their parents. With only a few exceptions, the traits that match up most closely tend to be the negative or abusive traits. This means that if you have developed a pattern of becoming involved with an abusive, a borderline, or a narcissistic Jekyll and Hyde, the chances are very high that one of your parents or primary caretakers was this type of Jekyll and Hyde as well.

While it may seem logical to look for partners who compensate for, rather than duplicate, our parents' inadequacies, the fact is that we tend to do the opposite—we attempt to recreate the conditions of our upbringing in order to correct them. We attempt to return to the scene of our original wounding in an effort to resolve our unfinished business.

Now that you know your pattern, be on guard when you meet "your type." If you become enormously attracted to someone right away, beware! This person is probably a replica of your original abuser. If you feel as though you've known someone all your life, it may be because you have.

The repetition compulsion is so powerful that even after you become aware of having developed a pattern of choosing a particular type of person, you can still fall into the trap. For this reason, it's important to make a list of your new partner's characteristics and compare them with the list of your parent's characteristics each time you enter a new relationship.

Complete Your Unfinished Business from the Past

Once you recognize these patterns, they can be broken by completing your unfinished business from the past. This includes releasing your anger toward your parents or others for their neglectful or abusive behavior in constructive ways (such as an "anger" letter you don't send), confronting those who have harmed you (if it is safe), and then working toward forgiveness. For more information on completing your unfinished business, read my book *Breaking the Cycle of Abuse*.

Take It Slow Next Time

In order to establish a healthy relationship you need time—time to get to know the other person, time for him or her to get to know you, and time to determine whether you are compatible with each other. We all try hard to impress potential partners at the beginning of relationships, and it takes time before we are willing to let down our false personas and risk exposing our real selves. This is especially true for Jekyll and Hydes, who can initially be quite charming. Don't let yourself be fooled again. Take time to get to know the real person—not the superficial, beginning-of-the-relationship personas that we all project. This will only be revealed over time, as layer after layer of defensiveness is stripped away, and the other person's false self melts away.

The problem with instant romance is that by the time you finally get to know your partner, you are already emotionally and sexually involved and can no longer be objective. This makes it nearly impossible for you to perceive the person for who he or she really is. This is particularly true for women. When women have sex, a chemical called oxytocin, which is a bonding agent, is released into the body. This same chemical is released when a woman nurses her baby, and, again, the purpose is to help her bond with her baby.

Continue to Work on Yourself

To prevent future abuse or betrayal, you will also need to continue working on becoming the most assertive, independent person you can be. Don't fool yourself into thinking that it was all your partner's fault and that if you choose a different type of partner next time, you have nothing to fear. If you are a dependent type of personality who is drawn to "take-control" types of partners, you are bound to slip right back into unhealthy ways of relating that will encourage abuse.

If you're going to avoid abusive relationships, you have to learn to make your own decisions. You must learn to speak your mind and get over your fear of offering your opinions and stating your preferences. You'll need to realize that your thoughts, ideas, perceptions, and needs are as important as anyone else's.

If you are a woman, refer to my book *Loving Him without Losing You* for more information on how to learn to make decisions, speak up, and state your preferences, as well as how to go slow in the beginning of a relationship and how to avoid losing yourself in relationships.

Choose to Have Equal Relationships

Make sure you choose a partner who is your emotional equal. Unfortunately, many people choose partners whom they perceive as their superiors as a way to compensate for their inner sense of defectiveness. Others are driven by hunger for the protection and care they did not receive as children. In a quest for rescue, they may seek out powerful authority figures who seem to offer the promise of a special caretaking relationship. Also haunted by the fear of abandonment and exploitation, they may choose people who appear to offer security and undying love.

When you get involved with someone you perceive as being more powerful or "better" than you are in some way, either because he seems more intelligent, more successful, or more attractive, you will tend to give in to him far more than if you felt you were his equal. You will tend to keep quiet when you should speak up, to tolerate unacceptable behavior, and to generally allow him to control the relationship. You may bend over backward to please your partner, which includes putting up with abusive behavior. This is particularly true for women. Since most women have a strong motivation to maintain harmony in their relationships, they tend to make the changes their partners request, even when the requests are unreasonable.

When you become involved with a partner who has more power or perceives himself or herself as being more powerful or better than you are, this person will tend to expect and demand more from you and will tend to take advantage by pushing limits, taking you for granted, or trying to dominate you. If you are the one who holds the most power, you will undoubtedly behave the same way. It is human nature.

Therefore, it is vital that you aim for equal relationships—ones in which both you and your partner view one another as equals. This doesn't mean that you are equal in all respects, but that overall, your qualities balance each other out. More important, it means that you each have equal power in the relationship.

Own Your Dark Side or Shadow Personality

There is no such thing as a totally innocent person. We all have the capacity to deceive, manipulate, use, and abuse others. There is a part of ourselves that we hide away not only from others but from ourselves. One of the reasons you have been attracted to a Jekyll and Hyde in the past is that you may have disowned your own Shadow—those traits, characteristics, attitudes, experiences, fantasies, and feelings that have been repressed into the unconscious. We often become involved with people who can act out our Shadow for us.

For example, let's say that you were raised by an authoritarian father who frightened you so much that you could never express your anger toward him. The very thought of showing him your anger may have been so threatening that you felt you must deny and repress any signs of anger in order to protect yourself from your father's wrath. Instead, you presented a face of submission, obedience, and pleasantness. This face was a false face, masking your true feelings. As time went by and you continued to mask your anger with pleasantness, the mask became thicker and your Shadow became larger. In time, the process of falsifying your feelings became second nature and was totally unconscious.

Thus, anger became part of your Shadow, and pleasantness became part of your persona. Since anger was not an acceptable emotion for you to express, you may have become attracted to a person who expresses his or her anger openly, if not abusively. Or, you may have become involved with someone who has the same inner conflict you have about anger—a Jekyll and Hyde who also puts on a false front to others but is secretly seething with anger.

Our Shadow usually begins to form early in childhood when we learn from our parents and other authority figures that certain emotions and certain behaviors are unacceptable. In order to avoid punishment and gain approval, we learn to repress these emotions and avoid these behaviors. For example, girls often learn that the expression of anger is unacceptable; boys often learn that crying is unacceptable. Thus, anger and assertiveness often become part of a girl's Shadow, and vulnerability and weakness become part of a boy's Shadow.

Women, in particular, often hide their dark side behind a mask of sweetness, innocence, and fragility. While looking honestly at your dark side may threaten you, it will also enlighten and empower you, as well as help you to recognize your own tendency to lie, dominate, control, and even abuse. You may, in fact, have the very same qualities that you find so unacceptable and repulsive in the Jekyll and Hyde in your life.

For example, your intolerance for the shallowness, the self-centeredness, and the manipulative qualities of the narcissist may be a signal that you have buried or rejected these very qualities within yourself. Dr. Carl Jung, the famous psychoanalyst who first brought the importance of the Shadow, or dark side, to our attention, explained that when we feel repulsed by a quality or a characteristic of another person, it is because we are confronting something in ourselves that we find objectionable, something with which we ourselves struggle.

EXERCISE

Identifying Your Shadow

1. List all the qualities you don't like in other people (for example, conceit, selfishness, short temper, greed, bad manners).

2. Take a look at your list and note which of these characteristics you find most offensive in others—the qualities that you not only dislike but despise, hate, or loathe. Circle these items.

The items you have circled are a fairly accurate picture of your own personal Shadow. For example, if you circled selfishness as one of those traits that you simply cannot stand, and you tend to adamantly criticize others for this quality, you would do well to examine your own behavior to see if perhaps you too tend to be selfish.

Not all criticisms of others are projections of our own undesirable Shadow traits, but any time our response to another person involves excessive emotions or overreaction, we can be sure that something unconscious has been activated. If your partner is sometimes selfish, for example, there is a certain degree of reasonableness about your being offended by his behavior. In true Shadow projection, however, your condemnation of him will far exceed his demonstration of the fault.

Let's talk more specifically about how owning your Shadow can help to explain why you chose a Jekyll and Hyde in the past and how it can help prevent you from choosing one again in the future. I will once more share a case example to illustrate my points.

Jessica was raised in a very conservative Catholic home where she was taught that sex outside of marriage was a tremendous sin. Masturbation was also considered a sin. Yet Jessica was born with a strong sex drive, and she sexually matured very early. This meant that she had to put her sexual desires into her Shadow in order to prevent herself from acting on her sexual urges. Although it was extremely difficult, Jessica managed to remain celibate until she was married, and she didn't even masturbate in the meantime. She married a very upstanding man who shared her religious beliefs and who was also celibate when they got married.

Ten years into their marriage, Jessica discovered that her husband was having an affair. She was devastated and shocked to learn that the man she married, the man she admired so much and who shared her values, could stray so far from his beliefs. She was also deeply hurt that this man could have lied to her and deceived her in the way that he did. Even members of her church believed that she had every right to divorce him, and this is what she did.

Jessica came to see me because she felt she needed help in getting past the pain of her ex-husband's betrayal. She was also concerned about marrying another man who could deceive her again. "I am so afraid I will marry another two-faced hypocrite like my ex-husband. I don't know if I can ever trust a man again."

In addition to encouraging Jessica to vent her anger in safe, constructive ways, I also encouraged her to look at her Shadow. I asked her about her sexuality. Had she and her husband had a satisfying sexual relationship? Was she still happy that she had waited until marriage to have sex? Did she masturbate, and, if so, did she have sexual fantasies? Jessica was shocked by my questions, but since we had established a trusting relationship, she sheepishly answered them.

It turned out that she and her husband had sex only periodically, and it had never been satisfying for Jessica. From the beginning of their marriage, her husband had suffered from premature ejaculation. Early in the relationship Jessica didn't realize he had a problem. She assumed that every man climaxed as quickly as her husband did, and she was so naive that she didn't know about foreplay. Years later, however, she learned more about sex and began to resent her husband for what she considered to be his selfishness at not taking his time so that she could reach an orgasm. She had also tried to introduce the idea of foreplay, to no avail. As she talked, it became more evident that Jessica had a lot of anger toward her ex-husband for not seeking help for his problem and for not being more open to pleasing her. She also had a lot of regrets about her only sexual relationship being so unsatisfying. "You know, the only good thing that has come out of my husband's infidelity is that

I may have another chance at a good sex life," she confided to me.

Then we talked about her sexual fantasies. Jessica admitted to me that starting when she was a teenager, she often had elaborate fantasies about being with different men sexually. "It was the only way I could cope with my decision to remain celibate and not to masturbate. I never touched myself, but my fantasies were so real that sometimes I had orgasms," she told me sheepishly. "And yes, I continued having my fantasies after I got married and our sex life was so bad."

It was a tremendous relief to Jessica to be able to talk about all this and to confess her so-called sins. By talking about her sexual fantasies, she was bringing them out into the light—one of the most significant ways of healing the Shadow. And interestingly, she told me that she felt less angry toward her husband. "I didn't have an affair, but the truth is I might have if I'd had the chance. I've been so sexually frustrated. I think some of my anger toward him is that he did what I wished I could do." This is another way we tend to deal with our Shadow. We often judge and are critical of people who are doing what we secretly wish we could do.

By acknowledging her sexual fantasies and appetites, Jessica was taking back a disowned part of herself. Only by finding and redeeming those wishes and traits that we chronically deny in ourselves can we move toward wholeness and healing. Jessica needed to own her sexuality and her sexual desires and not continue to see them as sinful or evil. Instead of being overwhelmed by our darker urges, we can learn to coexist with them. This is what happened with Jessica. Although she remained a Catholic, she admitted to herself that she no longer believed that sex outside of marriage was a sin. She decided that she had denied herself a good sex life long enough and that if she met a man whom she was attracted to and whom she respected, she would engage in premarital sex. "Frankly, I don't want to end up with another man with a sexual dysfunction. I believe I deserve a good sex life, and if I can't have it with one man, I'll find someone else that I can have it with."

Owning your Shadow doesn't mean pretending that the dark doesn't exist. Neither does it mean embracing the dark, as some practitioners of black magic or Satanism teach. What it does mean is that you work toward taking back all those forbidden thoughts, feelings, undesirable and rejected personality traits, and all the violent and sexual tendencies we consider evil, dangerous, or forbidden.

Shadow-work forces us to take another point of view, to respond to life with our undeveloped traits and our instinctual sides, and to live what Jung called the tension of the opposites—holding both good and evil, right and wrong, light and dark, in our own hearts.

As Connie Zweig and Jeremy Abrams so eloquently wrote in their book *Meeting the Shadow: The Hidden Power of the Dark Side of Human Nature*:

> Doing shadow-work means peering into the dark corners of our minds in which secret shames lie hidden and violent voices are silenced. Doing shadow-work means asking ourselves to examine closely and honestly what it is about a particular individual that irritates us or repels us; what it is about a racial or religious group that horrifies or captivates us; and what it is about a lover that charms us and leads us to idealize him or her.

Stop Placing People on Pedestals

Our Shadow includes not only our forbidden thoughts, feelings, fantasies, and undesirable and rejected personality traits, but *any* aspect of ourselves that we have denied. This includes our talents, ambitions, and dreams. Just as we project our anger, greed, lust, and rage onto others as a way of denying these qualities within ourselves, we also project our talents, ambitions, and dreams. This is at the core of our need to idealize others and put them on pedestals.

When we put someone on a pedestal, we don't see the person for who he or she really is. If you have had a history of idealizing romantic partners and being blind to their faults, you will need to stop doing this. Open your eyes and see the real person instead of holding on to a fantasy about him or her. Be careful not to be blinded to this person's charm, false promises, or bigger-than-life persona.

When you put someone on a pedestal, you are bound to become disappointed. In addition, by doing so you negate your own worth. By idealizing others, you devalue yourself.

Envy is at the core of our exaggerated respect for other people and the celebration of their achievements. At the same time, it's a rejection of the good things within ourselves, for when we envy, we unconsciously project our own positive attributes onto others. The tragedy is that our envy blinds us to the good that is within ourselves.

Envy is our longing for what another person has. It's what we feel when we ache for the possessions, the position, or the perceived happiness of others. Envy and jealousy are often confused. When we are jealous, we want to possess a lover or a friend and to get rid of our rival. By contrast, when we feel envy, we want to defeat our rival, not out of love for a third party but because we begrudge our rival anything we cannot possess. Jealousy is clearly a three-person relationship, whereas envy involves only two: the envied and the envier.

When we envy someone, we not only want what the other person has but we feel that, by rights, what that person has belongs to us. In our minds, it is almost as if the other person stole from us the very things we envy.

When we envy others for what they have been able to achieve, our own unique gifts and talents are lost to us. Instead, we see our own neglected talents in others and feel that somehow people who possess them have taken these talents from us.

The Shadow can be positive, particularly when you are not living up to your potential. The personal Shadow contains psychic features that are unlived or scarcely lived. Jung said that the Shadow is a gold mine of depth, mystery, richness, substance, knowledge, creativity, insight, and power—the very qualities we all seem to be striving for, the very qualities we admire and envy in others. Therefore, only if our Shadows are recognized and integrated into our personalities can we actualize our full potential. The following exercises will help you come closer to connecting with your Shadow and your full potential.

EXERCISE

Mining for the Gold of Your Shadow

1. On a piece of paper or in your journal, list the qualities you most admire in other people (for example, strength, confidence, ambition).

   Although you may be convinced that you could never possess such attributes, they are undoubtedly part of what is referred to as your Golden Shadow. Begin looking for these qualities in yourself. No matter how deeply they are buried or how undeveloped they are, they are hidden somewhere inside you. You can find them if you keep digging.

2. List the qualities you most admire in your current partner. If you are not in a relationship, list the characteristics you most admired in your last relationship or in the men or the women you are currently attracted to.

   These qualities are likely to be the very attributes that you have denied within yourself. Caught up in desire for their lovers, many people project their own unconscious positive attributes onto the men or the women they become romantically involved with. While these wonderful traits may in fact be in your partner to some degree, usually they are present nowhere to the degree that you perceive them to be. In fact, the admired traits may lie more within you than in the person you admire.

3. Give yourself credit for your positive attributes. List five of your most positive characteristics—the attributes that you feel best about and are most proud of. If you cannot think of five things, continue thinking about it and observing yourself until you can. If you still cannot think of five positive attributes, ask a close friend to tell you what she values and admires most in you. Write these attributes down on an index card, and place it in a conspicuous place where you can look at it often (some people have placed the cards on their dashboards or on their mirrors at home). Stop to read your list at least twice a day. Take a deep breath after reading each item. As you breathe, take in the knowledge that you possess each quality.

PART III

If You Suffer from the Jekyll and Hyde Syndrome

9

Confronting and Healing Your Jekyll and Hyde Behavior

I would rather be whole than good.
> —Carl Jung

Be aware that a halo has to fall only a few inches to be a noose.
> —Dan McKinnon

A spiritual life cannot save you from shadow suffering.
> —Suzanne Wagner

If you are reading this chapter, it's because either your partner or another loved one has confronted you about your Jekyll and Hyde behavior or you have begun to suspect, on your own, that you have this syndrome. You may even have bought this book suspecting that someone you are close to has the syndrome, but discovered that you also suffer from it. In either case, I commend you for your courage. It takes a strong person to face the fact that he or she suffers from the Jekyll and Hyde syndrome and all that it implies (for example, that you have been abusive toward your loved ones, that you have a personality disorder, that your drinking has crossed the line into alcoholism). You will need to call on that courage and strength as you continue reading the book and completing the exercises.

In this chapter I offer general advice and guidelines no matter which type of Jekyll and Hyde you are. In chapter 10 I provide specific advice to those of you who are abusive Jekyll and Hydes and in chapter 11 advice for people who have a personality disorder.

Trust the Perceptions and the Feedback of Others More Than Your Own

Very few Jekyll and Hydes recognize just how severe their mood shifts or erratic behavior can be. Even fewer are able to grasp just how abusive their behavior can be once they have shifted into their Mr. Hyde personality. For this reason, most of them need to rely on the feedback they receive from their loved ones. This can be difficult for anyone to do, but it will be especially hard for someone with the Jekyll and Hyde syndrome. No one wants to admit that they cannot trust their own perceptions or that their perceptions are actually distorted, but this is exactly what you will need to do in order to recover from this syndrome.

Some Jekyll and Hydes suffer from a form of dissociation when they switch from one personality to another. This dissociation can be triggered by something in the environment—a sound or a smell, being treated a certain way, viewing a scene that reminds them of a previous, most likely, traumatic event. When you are in a dissociative state, you may not be aware of how you are behaving because you are so disconnected from your body and, in some cases, your self. When people dissociate, they can actually feel as if they are leaving their bodies and going somewhere else. Many people who suffer from dissociation talk about leaving their bodies and being able to look down upon them from above.

Alcohol and drugs can also cause you to be unaware of your Jekyll and Hyde behavior. Whether you are in a blackout or not, alcohol and drugs can fog your memory and prevent you from knowing when you have become abusive or otherwise Mr. Hyde–like.

When borderline Jekyll and Hydes are faced with stressful situations (for example, the loss of a job, relationship problems, feelings of rejection or abandonment), they may become paranoid and lose touch with reality. They may become disconnected from their body and their memory may be impaired. They can lose track of time, lose awareness of their surroundings, and become disoriented. If they abuse alcohol or drugs, their behavior can become abusive to themselves or others.

Many Jekyll and Hydes are not aware of the changes in their moods or even in their personalities because they have in essence begun to "channel" the behavior of one of their parents. This is actually a rather common cause of abusive episodes. When you channel a parent, you begin to act like that parent, even though you may not have any conscious awareness that your behavior has changed.

CAROL THE CHANNELER

A few years ago I was asked by the director of a victim's advocate group to speak at a fund-raising event. The director, whom I will call Carol, picked me up at the airport and proceeded to complain to me for more than an hour about how the group of volunteers working with her had suddenly turned on her. She was convinced that the revolt had been spearheaded by one individual in particular, and that this person was then able to turn everyone against her. She felt that her part in the problem stemmed from her pattern of not being assertive enough and of allowing others to walk all over her.

Later on, when I met the group of volunteers, I heard a completely different story. From their point of view, the director had become emotionally abusive in her treatment and demands of them. She repeatedly berated and shamed them for not working hard enough to raise money. She continually criticized their fundraising attempts, and it seemed to them that no matter how hard they tried, they couldn't please her. She even went so far as to attend events and to sit in the back of the room shaking her head disapprovingly while they gave their speeches.

In the course of our drive from the airport, Carol had also told me that she had been mercilessly criticized by her mother and that this was why she tended to be nonassertive and to be repeatedly victimized in her life. Remembering this, I came to the conclusion that Carol was "channeling" her mother without any conscious awareness and that this is what led her to become abusive to her volunteers in much the same way her mother had been to her.

Because she had opened up to me so much on the drive from the airport, I wondered whether she would be receptive to any feedback on our drive back to the airport several days later. I began by telling her that the woman she assumed had turned the group against her had actually been her strongest advocate until recently. Carol was surprised by this but didn't seem willing to change her mind about the woman. I then gingerly asked her whether she was open to hearing some feedback. She told me that she was tired of talking about the problems. In essence, she was telling me that she was unwilling to change. This was sad because she was blind to her own behavior and would surely repeat this kind of scenario again and again in her life.

Don't make the mistake that Carol did. Listen to the feedback of your partner, your children, or others who are close to you. Believe them when they tell you about your behavior and how it has affected them. Even if you have no memory of an incident, believe the people who tell you about it. After all, why would those who are close to you make up such stories? People who have personality disorders tend to have huge trust issues and understandably will be reluctant to believe their partners. For this reason, you may need to check with others close to you—your children, your close friends—to see if what your partner is saying has some validity. Don't simply dismiss your partner's feedback, though. Jekyll and Hydes are seldom aware of how their behavior affects others.

Discover Your Primary Conflict

If you are a Jekyll and Hyde, it means you are in conflict. As mentioned earlier, that conflict may be any of the following:

- A conflict between your public and your private self

- A conflict between your self and your idealized self

- A conflict between good and bad—when your behavior doesn't match your beliefs

- A conflict between your ego and your Shadow.

Although you may identify with each of these conflicts, you no doubt resonate with one more than the others. When I asked my client Lyle which conflict he felt was strongest within himself, he immediately said, "Oh, the conflict between being good and bad. I sometimes feel like there are actually two people inside me. There is the one who urges me to do good things, who is loving and understanding, who would never want to hurt anyone, and then there is the one who encourages me to do bad things, who secretly hates people and wants to hurt them." Just as it was with Lyle, the conflict that you resonate with the most will determine in some ways what you will need to focus on to heal the split inside you.

A Conflict between Your Public and Your Private Self

As mentioned earlier in the book, we all create a public persona in order to gain acceptance from others socially and to fit into society. Yet when our public self and our private self become too different, when our public self is mostly a false self—a mask we put on in order to avoid exposing our true self—we are in trouble. Why? Because the more we hide our true self from others, the greater the risk that we will lose track of who we really are. This is what my client Ian shared with me about this very situation: "I'm getting so I don't know who the real me is. I've pretended so often to be confident and competent, to be in control. Everyone seems to rely on that from me—my wife, my kids, my employees. Now I'm realizing that I need to let down my defenses and reconnect with my emotions and my true self, but I can't do it. I've lost touch with how I really feel at any given time."

I advised Ian to begin by taking small steps: being more vulnerable with his wife and kids, sharing his fears with his wife, and relinquishing control once in a while. If this is your primary conflict, I suggest you do the same.

A Conflict between Your Self and Your Idealized Self

The best way to begin to resolve this conflict is for you to become far less critical of yourself and far more compassionate. While it's good to keep striving to be the best you can be, it's unrealistic to think that you can ever reach the goal of perfection. Start by being more realistic about what you are really capable of at this time in your life. Make an honest evaluation of your strengths and weaknesses, and set reasonable goals. When you reach a goal, give yourself lots of credit, but when you fall short, don't chastise yourself mercilessly. Instead, ask yourself whether you did the best you could under the circumstances. If the answer is yes, then let yourself off the hook.

A Conflict between Good and Bad

If you feel that your major conflict is between good and bad, it's vitally important that you understand that the very nature of being human is to be both good and bad. We are all a combination of good and bad qualities; we all share the capacity to do both good and bad. Ironically, it is often people who stand out as the *most* moral, the *most* kind, and the *most* magnanimous who are the *most* likely to develop the Jekyll and Hyde syndrome. It is a rule of nature that the higher up on pedestals we allow others to put us, the farther we have to fall. The more devout, respectable, and altruistic we seem to be in the eyes of others, the more likely it is that we have dark sides just waiting to get out.

People in the helping professions are particularly vulnerable to this phenomenon. This is true for several reasons. First of all, those who choose these professions often have a strong and abiding need to be seen as "good." Helping others becomes their primary way of gaining approval and love from others and of boosting their self-esteem. In addition, they may sacrifice themselves for others to the point of losing all sense of right or wrong, and they frequently begin to identify with the personas projected upon them by others. Society also sets certain people up to be "good." Ministers, priests, nuns, and other religious leaders are expected to have exemplary characters, to always put the needs of others before their own, and to dedicate themselves to goodness.

Celebrities are also put on pedestals, and many of them find that life up there is just too precarious. Michael Jackson is a good example. We all fell in love with the little boy/man who talked to us in the breathy, innocent voice. Many saw him as a near saint because of his good works. But for many people, that love has turned to hate and disgust because of his most recent behavior and the allegations that he molested children. Michael is such a master of disguises that it seems we will never know the truth about who he really is. One thing is certain, however: he is neither all bad nor all good. As Margo Jefferson, the Pulitzer prize–winning critic for the *New York Times*, wrote in her book *On Michael Jackson*: "But who is Michael Jackson's double? Is it the brown-skinned self we can no longer see except in the old photos and videos? Is he a good man or a predator? Child protector or pedophile? A damaged genius or a scheming celebrity trying to hold on to his fame at any cost? A child star afraid of aging, or a psychotic freak/pervert/sociopath? What if the 'or' is an 'and'? What if he is all these things?"

If the primary cause of your Jekyll and Hyde behavior has been an overly zealous need to be good, you will need to give yourself permission to be bad at times—not by betraying your spouse, not by cheating your business partner or by breaking the law. Being bad may mean speaking up when you don't agree with someone. Being bad can be telling your child no once in a while. You can't expect yourself to be agreeable and accommodating all the time. You need to learn to say no to unreasonable demands and say yes to taking care of yourself.

The Conflict between Your Ego and Your Shadow

If you identify this as your primary conflict, you will need to work toward taking back those disowned aspects of your self that you rejected or repressed in order to be acceptable to your parents and society in general. Earlier I wrote about the age-old battle, well known in mythology and literature, of the opposing twins—one good and the other bad—who symbolize the ego and the alter ego. The way toward wholeness is for the ego to assimilate the disowned self. The following exercise will help you to do this.

EXERCISE

Meeting Your Twin

1. Lie down or sit comfortably in a room where there are no distractions. Take some deep breaths and relax as much as possible.

2. Imagine that you are sitting on a bench in a beautiful garden or a park. Notice the bright colors of the flowers and plants, the clear blue sky, the feeling of the gentle wind.

3. Imagine that you have a twin brother or sister that you were separated from at a very early age. Even though this person is your twin, you look and act very differently since you were raised in different environments and by different parents. In fact, in many ways your twin has ended up being the opposite of you. Today you are going to meet each other again after all these years.

4. You are positioned in such a way that you can see your twin approaching before he or she sees you. What does he or she look like? Notice his or her posture, the way he or she walks, the clothes he or she is wearing.

5. Now your twin sees you and walks toward you. How do you feel? Are you uncomfortable or happy to see him or her?

6. Your twin sits down beside you on the bench and tells you something very important. What is it?

7. You begin to talk to each another. What is the sound of his or her voice? Is he or she critical or kind? Selfish or caring? Timid or outgoing? Take a moment to fully experience your twin and how it feels to be together again.

8. For the next few hours, try acting as if you were this twin. Notice how it feels. Are there aspects of your twin that you would like to bring into your life?

Discover the Cause of Your Jekyll and Hyde Behavior

In addition to having an internal conflict, other related factors also propel you into Jekyll and Hyde behavior. It's safe to say that the cause of your Jekyll and Hyde behavior, as well as the origin of your primary conflict, lies in your childhood. If you experienced either emotional, physical, or sexual abuse as a child and have not dealt with your past, you will undoubtedly discover that it *will* catch up to you. Unfinished business has a way of sneaking up on us, invading our lives in insidious ways, which include causing us to act in a Jekyll and Hyde manner.

Unfortunately, many people believe that they can leave their childhoods behind and with them all feelings of anger, fear, shame, and pain. Yet the feelings that we repress don't get left behind; instead, they become part of our Shadows or dark sides.

RICHARD BERENDZEN

In his book *Come Here: A Man Overcomes the Tragic Aftermath of Childhood Sexual Abuse*, Richard Berendzen, a past president of American University, wrote,

> I believed in the power of my own will. Self-determination I learned about later on reading about leaders I admired. Man is the master of his fate. Whenever the abuse came into my mind, I would say, "I'm not going to think about this." It was my way to fight back. I couldn't stop the abuse, but I could, through force of will, stop myself from thinking about it. Denial became synonymous with survival. How could it hurt me if I didn't think about it?

Yet Richard's past was hurting him, and signs of it began to seep through the cracks. After his father's death, he started making phone calls to strangers who had placed ads in newspapers to provide child care. He usually chatted briefly with these people and then insinuated something about children and sexuality. For example, he mentioned that in his home his children bathed with his wife and him, or that they slept in the same bed. Usually, the other people expressed no interest or said they didn't do such things in their homes. Most calls were no longer than ten minutes, and then he quickly ended the conversation.

This continued for several years, but in 1990 Richard began to suffer from feelings of depression and started to make the calls more frequently. One day, he called the wrong woman. This woman didn't end the conversation when he hinted at parents and children being sexually involved. Instead, she spoke to him at length and encouraged him to call again. When he did call her back, he made up stories about bizarre sexual activities that he and his wife did with their children.

Unbeknownst to him, the police had attached a device to her phone to record and trace his calls. "As much as I found the calls repulsive, the compulsion to call again grew even stronger," Richard confessed. "Part of my life had spun out of control. I was too ashamed and baffled to tell anyone about it. How would I begin? Ninety-nine percent of me was the man the world saw: university president, husband, father. But the other one percent was a bomb about to explode and destroy everything I stood for and had worked to achieve."

Many people try to repress and deny their feelings concerning the abuse or the neglect they experienced in childhood. As Richard explained, "I had no idea—and could not have been persuaded— that something from so long ago suddenly could take over my life. I want others to know what I learned—if you have been traumatized by abuse, you must find a way to understand and resolve it. Even if your life seems fine at the moment, unresolved trauma neither goes away nor diminishes over time. It can erupt at any time."

The Family Legacy and How It Can Create the Jekyll and Hyde Syndrome

Jekyll and Hydes beget Jekyll and Hydes. If you had a parent who was constantly having tirades, you may have grown up to be an adult who does the same. If you had a borderline parent, the chances are very high that you will become borderline yourself or at least have very strong borderline tendencies. The same is true if one of your parents suffered from narcissistic personality disorder.

The first step in preventing yourself from reenacting the abuse or the neglect that you experienced as a child or stopping behavior you have already begun is to make a clear connection between your current behavior and the behavior of your abusers. The following exercise will help you connect the dots in order to clearly see how much your current behavior is a repetition of either your parent's or an abuser's behavior.

EXERCISE

What Do You Have in Common with Your Parents?

1. On a piece of paper or on a page of your journal, write down the ways in which your mother was neglectful or abusive toward you or others. Be sure to include attitudes and verbal comments, as well as behaviors.

2. On a second piece of paper, write down any behavior on your father's part that was neglectful or abusive.

3. If you were raised by anyone other than your parents (foster parents, grandparents, aunts or uncles, etc.), make a separate list of this person's behavior.

4. On another piece of paper, write down the ways you have been abusive toward your children, your partner, or anyone else in your life. No one else needs to read this list but you. Making this list will no doubt be difficult and painful, and you may want to put it aside or attempt to lie to yourself, but

imagine how much more difficult it will be to face the damage you continue to inflict on your loved ones if you aren't honest with yourself now.

5. Compare your lists. Notice the similarities between the ways you have been abusive and the ways your parents were neglectful or abusive toward you or others.

If you find that you are repeating the abuse or the neglect that you suffered as a child, you must make a commitment to yourself to work on expressing the pent-up emotions associated with such neglect or abuse. Please think seriously about entering psychotherapy, where you will be able to tell your story to an objective listener, receive encouragement and help in releasing your repressed and suppressed emotions surrounding the trauma, and learn to come to a place of acceptance and even forgiveness. Only by doing this can you stop reenacting the abuse you sustained.

Discover How Your Shadow Was Created

All children undergo a socialization process that involves learning what is acceptable and unacceptable in their families and in their cultures. While this is an important process, it is responsible for creating our Shadow personality. The so-called unacceptable qualities don't cease to exist in the child; they are merely repressed. The qualities that are denied expression fester inside each of us and form the Shadow or dark side, becoming more powerful as time goes by.

When I was growing up, my mother often told me this story. One day, as she dropped me off at the babysitter's and gave me her usual admonishment—"Now you be good for Mrs. Jones today"— I turned to her and said, "I have to be good for Mrs. Jones, I have to be good for you, I have to be good for my teachers, I have to be good at church. When can I be bad?"

My mother always laughed when she told this story, since in many ways she loved my precociousness. But I doubt that she truly appreciated what I was trying to tell her—that I felt too much pressure to be good.

My personal Shadow was created by my mother's insistence that I "be good" at all times. Because it wasn't acceptable to ever be "bad" (which meant not bothering my mother, not being loud, not insisting on getting my way, not being selfish, not wanting attention, and so forth, and so on), I learned to repress my anger, take on a "good girl" stance, and continually try to please my mother.

I've already discussed how the Shadow is created when a child is taught that certain behaviors are not acceptable. In addition, though, many parents teach their children to repress their feelings, thus making these feelings part of the Shadow as well. A little boy falls and hurts himself and is told, "Big boys don't cry." A little girl becomes angry with her brother and screams at him, and she is told, "Nice little girls don't get angry." An exuberant child bursts into the house after school, talking a mile a minute, and is told by an irritated parent, "Don't get so excited. Calm down." Thus a child can be led to the idea that his or her feelings are unacceptable and must be controlled. Unfortunately, all too often this requires the child to disown these feelings and to put them into his or her Shadow.

Other times children can be taught that their feelings are actually dangerous. If a little boy gets beaten because he dared to disagree with his father, he will learn that expressing his feelings directly is unsafe. If a little girl is locked in her room because she felt too full to eat all her dinner, she will learn that even her body can betray her.

EXERCISE

*The Role Your Parents Played in Your
Jekyll and Hyde Behavior*

1. Make a list of all the messages you remember hearing from your parents or other primary caretakers that may have led to the repression of your emotions.

2. Make a list of all the messages from parents or other caretakers that encouraged you to hide or disown other aspects of your self.

Own Your Dark Side

The next and most important step is for you to own your dark side. Only by owning it can you gain control over it. We've all heard the saying "It's what we don't know that can hurt us," and this couldn't be more true for people with the Jekyll and Hyde syndrome. Once you are aware of your dark side, you can exercise real control over it—not by suppressing it, but by respecting it, finding constructive outlets for it, and setting limits.

How do we meet the Shadow? By conceding that there are parts of ourselves that we abhor, despise, or deny; by acknowledging those parts of ourselves, no matter how horrific they are; and by seeing that we are still ourselves.

The medical model of immunization offers a parallel to this process. When we are immunized against disease, our bodies know instinctively how to make good use of the poison or the disease-producing substance that in larger amounts would harm us. The ability to admit the Shadow, to allow it into consciousness in manageable doses, similarly allows us to immunize the psyche.

It is a paradox of consciousness that allowing and admitting the Shadow reduces its power, producing the opposite of what we feared. By making ourselves vulnerable to it, we achieve an immunity to its deadliness. Instead of being overwhelmed by our darker urges, we learn to coexist with them, nodding knowingly when they appear, gratefully taking the lessons they give us, and turning them into healthy emotional or creative expressions. In my practice I've seen time and time again that recognizing the dark side produces a powerful and beneficial change in consciousness.

We find our Shadows:

- In our exaggerated feelings about others ("I just can't believe he would do that!")

- In negative feedback from others who serve as mirrors

- In the interactions in which we continually have the same troubling effect on several different people

- In our impulsive and inadvertent acts ("Oops, I didn't mean to say that.")

- In situations in which we are humiliated
- In our exaggerated anger about other people's faults

Step One: Solicit Feedback from Others

Begin by looking beyond the mirror to discover who you really are. As William A. Miller so eloquently stated in his book *Your Golden Shadow: Discovering and Fulfilling Your Undeveloped Self*: "Looking in a mirror we see only the reflection of ourselves as we choose to see it. Looking beyond the mirror we see ourselves as *we are seen*."

We all know that it is easier to see the faults of others than it is to see our own. The same goes with our Shadows. We are often amazed at how oblivious others are to their less-than perfect behavior. One of the most effective methods for gaining insight into our personal Shadow is to get feedback from others as to how they perceive us. This is related to, but also different from, what was discussed earlier in the chapter.

The very thought of getting this kind of feedback from others can be threatening. We would much rather continue to assume that others see us as we see ourselves. If you really want to see yourself clearly, however, and not continue to be at the mercy of your Shadow, you will need to take this risk. People who are in the best position to help us see our Shadow are those who know us well (our close friends, our partners, our colleagues, or fellow workers).

Although our Shadow is as much a part of us as our persona is, it is often a stranger to us. While others may hear and see manifestations of our "hidden side" ("Why can't she see how judgmental she is?"), we are often blind and deaf to it ("I'm a very open-minded person"). This is why the Shadow so often surprises us and causes us so much confusion when our words and actions don't match our perceptions of ourselves or what we think we know about ourselves.

When you know your hidden self—your Shadow—you are more in charge of it. You can prevent your Shadow from acting out in ways that will embarrass you or cause you problems in your life. Also, you won't be as likely to become attracted to someone with a very big Shadow who will act out your Shadow for you.

Step Two: Own Your Projections

Projection is the act of attributing to others the feelings and reactions that we ourselves are having but don't want to acknowledge or, in some cases, feelings that we fear we may have or have had in the past. Just as a movie camera projects an image onto a screen, we project onto others all those aspects of ourselves we are fearful of or ashamed of.

Why do we project? Projection is an unconscious defense mechanism. Therefore, we are not necessarily aware of our behavior. In fact, more often than not, we are unaware of it. Projection happens whenever a trait or characteristic of our personality that has no relationship to consciousness becomes activated. As a result of the unconscious projection, we observe and react to this unrecognized trait in other people. We see in them something that is a part of ourselves but that we fail to see in ourselves.

In order to take back your Shadow projections, you must first identify them. The following exercise will help you to do so.

1. List all the qualities you don't like in other people—for instance, conceit, short temper, selfishness, bad manners, and greed.

2. When your list is complete, extract the characteristics that you not only dislike in others but hate, loathe, or despise.

This shorter list is a fairly accurate picture of your personal Shadow. This means that the qualities in others that you despise the most, the ones that repulse you, are actually the qualities in yourself that you have repressed and hidden away into your own dark side.

Of course, not all of our criticisms of others are projections of our own undesirable qualities, but any time our responses to other people involve excessive emotion or overreaction, we can be certain that something unconscious within us is being prodded. For example, you may feel that your partner is selfish and self-absorbed, and if this is the case, it is reasonable for you to find this behavior offensive. In true Shadow projection, however, your condemnation of your partner will far exceed his or her demonstration of the fault, in which case it would be wise for you to examine your own behavior for selfishness.

Conflict situations are especially fruitful in helping you to discover your Shadow projections because they bring up strong emotions and highlight important issues. The next time you are in an argument with your partner and find yourself expressing intense feelings about one of his or her characteristics, look within yourself to see if you can find that very same attribute tucked away in some corner inside yourself.

Step Three: Come Off Your Pedestal

For many people who suffer from the Jekyll and Hyde syndrome, healing lies in being willing to come down off their pedestals and joining the ranks of the common man and woman. It is the person who needs to see himself or herself as better than others who is most vulnerable to the Jekyll and Hyde syndrome.

This is particularly true for those who have made a career out of being good: priests, ministers, doctors, nurses, psychologists, and others in the helping professions, as well as philanthropists and social activists. As a society, we have a need to put these people up on pedestals, attributing qualities to them that no human being could possibly embody, and requiring of them exemplary behavior that is impossible to sustain. Priests and ministers must be saints, doctors are expected to be all-knowing and incapable of mistakes, and psychotherapists are supposed to have it all together. Those in the helping professions who believe these expectations can become conceited, pompous, and unreachable. And those who accept the personas handed to them by others and who adopt them as their own, molding their conscious personalities around them, lose part of themselves in the process.

How to Integrate Your Jekyll and Hyde

As I mentioned early on in the book, generally speaking, those who suffer from the Jekyll and Hyde syndrome are in conflict. This conflict is often centered around their attempts to be good people in spite of the fact that they may have critical, judgmental, harsh, demeaning, or other types of abusive feelings, thoughts, and behaviors. In their attempts to be good people, they may have tried to bury, deny, repress, or suppress these abusive tendencies. Unfortunately, these repressed and suppressed feelings, thoughts, and behaviors cannot be buried permanently. Instead, they continually pop up unexpectedly, often without a person's conscious awareness or control. This, in essence, is what causes your Jekyll and Hyde behavior. Your dark side or Shadow—those repressed tendencies—will continue to surface until you address them directly, discover their source, and then find constructive, creative, and positive avenues for them to be expressed.

Returning to the Story of Dr. Jekyll and Mr. Hyde

In Stevenson's story, Mr. Edward Hyde is described as young, small, and somehow deformed, full of hellish energy—a person who evoked hatred in others at the very sight of him. Hyde's small size and deformed appearance is symbolic of the fact that, as the Shadow personality, Hyde has not lived very much in Jekyll's outer life. Having dwelt for the most part in the darkness of the unconscious, he is deformed in appearance, much like a tree forced to grow among the rocks and in the shadow of other trees.

Hyde has a black, sneering coldness and is incapable of human feeling. He is without any twinge of conscience and so is incapable of guilt. This lack of conscience is also characteristic of the Shadow personality. The Shadow leaves moral feelings and obligations up to the ego personality, while he or she strives to live out inner and forbidden impulses. At first, Jekyll has seen in himself only a certain "gaiety of disposition," a pleasure-seeking side that might have led to mischief but nothing more, but once he has become Hyde, he realizes he is far more evil than he ever supposed. From this description, we can see that the Shadow personality begins with one's personal dark side, but at some point it contacts a deeper, more archetypal level of evil. In the hands of this archetypal evil, the pleasure-seeking mischief in which Jekyll wanted to engage soon led to truly evil activity, as exemplified in the hellish murder of Dr. Carew. This was done for the pure love of evil and destruction.

(We can see this same evil or "satanic" quality emerging in situations in which a person cold-bloodedly kills others without any evidence of remorse. It is an archetypal evil that both shocks and fascinates us.)

And so we see why living out the darkest impulses of the Shadow cannot be the solution to the Shadow problem. Once he decides to be Hyde, even if only for a while, Jekyll tends to become Hyde. In other words, the deliberate decision to do evil leads to our becoming evil (if you have a problem with the concept of "evil," substitute "lying" or "living a duplicitous life"). As Jekyll finds himself involuntarily turning into Hyde, he becomes more and more aware of this danger. He had expected to move from Jekyll to Hyde and back again at will, but now he finds that Hyde is taking over. His former confidence, which led him to say, "the moment I choose, I can be rid of Mr. Hyde," is now gone.

How many times have you heard yourself say to yourself or to others, "I can quit drinking any time I want," or "I can stop gambling whenever I want"? Many people who decide to live in two worlds fool themselves into thinking they are in control and can stop their aberrant behavior whenever they want, but the proof of how false this kind of thinking really is, is that they do *not* stop the behavior, and eventually the behavior takes over their lives.

It is Jekyll's careless disregard for the powers of evil, together with his desire to escape the tension of his dual nature, that paves the way for his ultimate demise. Just as many of us have done, Jekyll resolves to have nothing more to do with the Hyde part of his personality. He will banish Hyde from his life. He returns to his old life and becomes more dedicated than ever to doing good works.

Jekyll, like many other "sinners," looked to the church and religion to save him. This, too, is a common strategy for those who are trying to battle their darker urges. But because Jekyll isn't sincere and doesn't really connect with God, his attempts, of course, fail. Many who suffer with the Jekyll and Hyde syndrome often use religion in the same way, especially the religions that decry men's sins, threaten the sinner with punishment, and encourage good deeds as the pathway to salvation. This kind of religion tends to attract people who are consciously or unconsciously struggling to hold in check their Shadow personalities. Jekyll's attempt doesn't work, and Hyde has grown still stronger within him and is now, more than ever, struggling to be free—to possess Jekyll's personality so he can live as he wants.

What Is the Answer to the Shadow Problem?

So, how do we deal with our Shadow? The answer is not in allowing ourselves to completely be taken over by our Shadow and neither is it in attempting to banish it completely from our lives. Both tactics leave the personality split in two. The answer is to embrace the tension of the opposites within ourselves.

As we see in the story of Dr. Jekyll and Mr. Hyde, Henry Jekyll was aware of his dual nature. Had he been willing to hold the tension of the opposites—that is, allow himself to grapple *consciously* with the fact that he was both good and bad—he would have been able to develop a healthy, integrated personality (individuation). Instead, he chose to escape this tension by creating the drug that allowed him to be both Jekyll and Hyde and have the pleasures and the benefits of living out both sides of his personality without guilt or tension. Dr. Jekyll felt no responsibility for Mr. Hyde; he had in essence, been able to completely disown a part of himself, thus allowing that part of himself to run amok.

Jekyll's failure can provide us with tips on how to resolve our own Shadow conflicts successfully. If attempting to escape the pain leads to psychological disaster, carrying the pain may give the possibility of wholeness.

John A. Sanford, in an article in *Meeting the Shadow*, explains it this way: "If we consciously carry the burden of the opposites in our nature, the secret, irrational, healing processes that go on in us unconsciously can operate to our benefit, and work toward the synthesis of the personality. This irrational healing process, which finds a way around seemingly insurmountable obstacles, has a particularly feminine quality to it. It is the rational, logical masculine mind that declares that opposites like ego and Shadow, light and dark, can never be united. However, the feminine spirit is capable of finding a synthesis where logic says none can be found."

What does this mean exactly? It means that the answer to our Shadow problem is not going to come from our rational, logical sides. Although all of us were taught that there is good and bad, light and dark, right and wrong, the truth is that life is not that simplistic or regimented. Something or someone can be both good and bad. An action can be both right and wrong, depending upon the circumstances and our perspectives. We can find truth in two opposing ideas. For example, there is truth in both of these beliefs: (1) child molesters are horrible monsters who should be locked up for life, (2) child molesters were usually sexually abused themselves. They are human beings who are out of control of themselves, and they deserve to be treated with some compassion. Most people feel that they have to choose between these two ideas—they have to make one idea wrong and the other right. Accepting that there is truth in both statements makes us feel uncomfortable. Ambivalence makes us uncomfortable. Not knowing something for certain makes us uncomfortable. We are far more comfortable when we feel certain, absolute. It can be maddening to see the truth of both sides of an issue. (Remember how frustrated Tevye from *Fiddler on the Roof* became as he flip-flopped back and forth between one truth and the other: "On the one hand," "On the other hand"?)

What happens when we are able to hold two opposing truths at the same time? Yes, we experience discomfort, but the tension of the opposites creates a space for a deeper understanding of humankind. It encourages us to develop more personal depth and more human compassion.

The same can be true when we begin to face the truth about ourselves—that we are neither good nor bad. We have some good qualities and some bad ones. We have done some wonderful, caring things in our lives, and we have done some hurtful, selfish things. Facing and carrying the truth of this will transform us. When we stop trying to fight the truth about ourselves—that we can be selfish, cruel, deceitful—we are able to take on a wonderful feeling of self-acceptance and self-compassion. When we admit that we have dark impulses—to cheat on our spouses, to steal from our friends, to lie to our business partners—we actually become better able to manage and control these dark impulses. Carrying the knowledge and the pain of our darker natures is difficult, but it makes us less judgmental, of ourselves and of others.

EXERCISE

The Good and the Bad in You

1. Make a list of your worst qualities and character traits.

2. Make another list, this time of your best qualities and traits.

3. Now list the worse things you have done in your life. Include the times when you have hurt or disappointed people, the times when you have lied or betrayed the ones you love.

4. Finally, make a list of the best things you have done in your life. Include the times when you have unselfishly helped someone, the times when you have sacrificed your own happiness for that of someone else.

5. Compare your "good" lists with your "bad" lists. If you are like most people, you will discover that the lists somewhat balance each other out. You aren't all bad any more than you are all good.

The Next Steps

At the beginning of this chapter, I commended you on your courage for facing this issue. I told you that it takes courage and strength to be willing to look at yourself so honestly. Now you will need your courage and strength to do something else as well. You will need it to reach out for help beyond this book. If your mood shifts have become problematic to your life or damaging to your loved ones, you need to enter psychotherapy to get the help you need. This is especially true if you suspect that your Jekyll and Hyde behavior may be the result of childhood abuse or a personality disorder.

If your Jekyll and Hyde behavior comes up when you are drinking, you will need to reach out to Alcoholics Anonymous or another alcohol treatment program. You may have been fooling yourself for quite some time, telling yourself that you don't have a drinking problem, but if you have developed the Jekyll and Hyde syndrome because of your drinking, it's time to come out of denial. Those who exhibit severe personality changes when they are under the influence of alcohol clearly have an alcohol problem. Even if you don't have other warning signs of alcoholism, this behavior alone can tell you that you have the disease.

10

If You Are an Abusive Jekyll and Hyde

It's hard to fight an enemy who has outposts in your head.
— Sally Kempton

The only person you can control is yourself.
— Marian Wright Edelman

If you are an abusive Jekyll and Hyde, meaning that you not only have a duality to your personality but that you also become abusive in some way (such as having emotional outbursts, suddenly becoming critical of those around you, or withdrawing from your loved ones for no apparent reason), you not only need to resolve the conflict within you and own your dark side, but you also need to work on ending your abusive behavior. The first step is for you to understand why you become abusive.

When you are being verbally, emotionally, or physically abusive to your partner or children, you are essentially projecting anger and shame onto them. There are several reasons why you might do this.

1. As a child you were taught that anger was unacceptable, and so it became part of your dark side or Shadow.

2. You learned negative ways of expressing anger from your parents (for example, you witnessed one of your parents physically abusing the other, you often heard your parents yelling at each other).

3. You had an angry, abusive parent, and now you are "channeling" that parent (acting and sounding just like that parent in your interactions with your partner or children).

4. One or both of your parents were abusive toward you, and you often become triggered by situations in your present life that remind you of this abuse.

5. You are taking the anger you have at your parents or another significant caretaker out on your partner or children.

6. You were abused as a child and identified with the aggressor—you chose to become just like your abusive parent as a way to avoid feeling like or becoming a victim.

7. You were abused as a child and are projecting your shame onto your partner or children.

You will notice that many of the reasons for projecting your anger and shame onto others suggest that you were abused yourself. Not everyone who becomes abusive was abused as a child. Some were neglected or abandoned, and some witnessed the abuse of others. Nevertheless, abuse does beget abuse. The following information will help you discern why you took on this particular way of coping with your own abuse or neglect in childhood.

- *Repetition compulsion.* This is the most common way that people who are abused or neglected in childhood attempt to resolve their feelings of hurt, anger, and fear. To a large extent, the repetition compulsion explains why, if one of your parents was verbally abusive to you, you will tend to be verbally abusive to your partner or your children (or both). If one or both of your parents were controlling and domineering, you will tend to treat your partner or children (or both) in a controlling and domineering way. And if one or both of your parents were physically abusive, you may end up becoming a batterer yourself. This is how abuse gets passed down from one generation to the next. In far too many cases, in spite of our best intentions, we unfortunately do become our parents.

Trauma therapists have offered several explanations as to why survivors reenact their traumatization: (1) to give a happy ending to a story whose horror still plagues them; (2) to prove to themselves that they now know how to handle such situations; (3) to relive the moment of escape or reprieve, which is the moment when the survivor felt most aware of how precious life is; or (4) to assuage their trauma-induced biological addiction to the brain's defensive response to overwhelming fear and helplessness.

- *Identifying with the aggressor.* The experience of being abused challenges one's most basic assumptions about the self as invulnerable and intrinsically worthy and about the world being just and orderly. Assuming responsibility for the abuse allows feelings of helplessness to be replaced by an illusion of control. Identifying with the aggressor (including taking on his or her characteristics) replaces fear and helplessness with a sense of omnipotence.

- *An attempt to rid yourself of shame.* It is the belief of Alice Miller and others that victims of childhood abuse and neglect reenact their abuse in an attempt to rid themselves of their fear. It is my belief, and that of others, that they also do so in order to rid themselves of their shame. This is especially true with those who were sexually abused as children or adolescents, but it's also true of anyone who was neglected or abused in any way. The cycle of abuse continues when abusers, overwhelmed with their own shame, pass it on in desperate attempts to rid themselves of it.

You are no doubt carrying shame from your own experiences of being abused as a child, as well as shame concerning your own abusive behavior toward others. Shame plays a significant role in the cycle of abuse in the following ways:

- People who abuse others are often trying to rid themselves of their own shame.

- Shame can cause emotional outbursts. It is often shame that triggers the kind of rage that causes abusiveness.

- It is shame that causes a person to humiliate and degrade his or her partner or children.

- It is often shame that prevents people from believing that they deserve to be treated with love, kindness, and respect.

Action Steps for Changing Your Abusive Behavior

The following steps are vitally important if you are going to be able to make any real changes in your behavior.

Step One: Discover the Root of Your Anger

Anger is, of course, one of the biggest culprits in causing abusive behavior. If you have an abusive side to your personality, you must, I repeat, *must* discover the seeds of your anger. The most likely place to begin your search is your childhood. Most people with the abusive Jekyll and Hyde syndrome either had negative role models when it comes to anger or were mistreated as children by angry, hostile, or abusive parents or caretakers. Some of you may already be aware of these influences in your life; others may still be in denial about them. The following questionnaire will help you to determine whether having poor role models is at the root of your anger problems.

QUESTIONNAIRE

How Did Your Parents Interact When They Were Angry?

1. Did your parents discuss problems rationally, or did they tend to blow up at each other?

2. Did they express emotions easily, or did they hold in their feelings?

3. Did your parents tend to blame each other for their problems?

4. Did your parents fight often?

5. Did your parents give each other the silent treatment?

6. Did your parents yell at each other?

7. Did your parents punish each other?

8. Did your parents emotionally abuse each other?

If your parents were not poor role models in how they handled anger, it is very likely that your anger problem comes from experiencing neglect or abuse in your childhood. Neglect and abuse are violations against the human spirit and therefore make children very angry. Many of them carry this anger into adulthood for several reasons. First of all, most children are unable to express their anger at the time, for fear of further abuse or rejection. Second, this repressed or suppressed anger is often reignited when they themselves become intimately involved with partners or when they have children and reexperience some of the same feelings and experiences they did as children. Third, anger is a major avenue for repeating the cycle of abuse. We tend to repeat the way our parents disciplined us, the way they expressed their anger, and the way they misused or abused their anger against other people.

Victims of child abuse often reenact their own experiences of abuse by becoming abusive to others. This may occur because of unconscious motivations, but it also happens because abuse victims are enraged. Parental abuse, in particular, creates intensely angry reactions in children. That rage bursts out of them whenever they are shamed, when they are under stress or under the influence of alcohol or drugs, or when they are triggered (reminded of their own abuse). Those who were abused also tend to repress their anger at their abusers for fear of abandonment, rejection, or punishment. This anger is stored in the unconscious and is expressed only when something in their current lives triggers the memories. At these times they are likely to strike out without warning at those nearest to them, most especially their children and their partners.

Step Two: Learn Constructive Ways of Releasing Anger

For you to stop being abusive to others, you need to learn constructive ways of releasing your old rage toward your original abusers.

Writing "anger" letters is one of the best ways to release old anger. Say everything that you feel; don't censor yourself. No one needs to read what you have written. You can tear up the letter or burn it for another experience of catharsis. Or walk around your house when no one is at home and have an imaginary conversation with your parent. Tell him or her everything that you feel. Don't hold anything back. It may help if you look at a picture of your parent while you are releasing your anger. Physical release is also effective, especially if you don't tend to be a physically abusive person. Go to the batting cage and hit some balls, shoot hoops, play a one-person game of racquetball, or hit some tennis balls. Express your emotions through art, sculpting, or other creative outlets. For more information on how to release your anger in healthy ways, consult my book *Honor Your Anger: How Transforming Your Anger Style Can Change Your Life*.

You also need to take responsibility for changing your unhealthy ways of dealing with anger and stress. The following information will help you begin to understand and manage your anger in more positive ways.

- Think about what you are really feeling under all that anger and criticism of others. Recognize that your partner or child is separate from you and therefore has a right to have different reactions and opinions about things, to be in a different mood than you are in at any given time, to have different tastes than you, and to make choices that you might not make.

- Realize that you cannot control anyone else. Even if your partner allows you to control him or her, the price you pay for this compliance is the loss of that person's love. No slave ever loved his master. No prisoner ever loved his jailer. There is no room for true love or devotion in the hearts of people who are scrambling for their lives every day. There is only room for hatred and dreaming of the day when they will finally be free.

- Recognize that your feelings of anger probably have more to do with you than they do with your partner. Instead of ruminating about what your partner has done or how she or he has upset you, take a look within yourself—at your current life and your personal history—for answers as to why you are so upset.

The following is my nine-stage process to avoid becoming abusive with your anger, taken from my book *Honor Your Anger: How Transforming Your Anger Style Can Change Your Life.*

1. Identify what you are feeling under your anger or what feeling is causing your anger. Ask yourself, "What am I really feeling in this situation? Do I feel threatened, afraid, humiliated, rejected, hurt, or jealous?

2. Once you have identified the feeling beneath your anger, communicate your feelings to the person you are upset with. Communicate what you are feeling using "I" messages and avoiding sarcasm, name calling, or vindictiveness. For example, if you feel humiliated, say something like, "I feel so humiliated when you tell your friends about our problems. I don't think it is any of their business, and it makes me really angry. I don't want you to do it again."

3. Avoid making statements that can devastate the other person or destroy your relationship. Making derogatory statements like "You're a whore," or "You're a loser," can devastate a person's self-esteem. Threatening to end a relationship, quit a job, or get a divorce can cause irreparable harm. Make sure you don't say anything in the heat of an argument that you can't take back.

4. Avoid making sarcastic remarks, insults, or put-downs in order to get back at someone. If someone has done or said something to anger you, instead of coming back at the person with sarcasm or insults, tell this person what you are feeling and that you don't like what he or she said. You may discover that the other person didn't mean to upset you or wasn't aware that what he or she said or did would upset you. This also makes it clear to the other person that you don't want to be spoken to or treated like that again.

5. Think through your responses. Aggressive people tend to jump to conclusions and act on impulse. The next time you find yourself in a heated discussion, slow down and think through your responses. Think carefully about what you want to say instead of saying the first thing that comes to your mind. At the same time, listen carefully to what the other person is saying.

6. Avoid hitting, pushing, shoving, shaking, grabbing, or physi-
    cally abusing another person in any way. If you feel that you
    can't control yourself, leave the scene. You don't have to explain
    yourself; just get away as fast as you can, for your protection as
    well as for the protection of the other person.

7. If necessary, take a cooling off period. If you find that you are
    losing control, take a time-out. Take a short walk, or go some-
    place where you can sit and think things out. When you have
    calmed down, discuss the situation that upset you.

8. Find constructive ways to vent your anger. Sometimes a con-
    versation with the person who upset you is not possible, or you
    continue to be so upset that a discussion is not a good idea. In
    these situations, physical exertion and sports are good outlets
    for your anger.

9. Examine what part you had in creating the incident. Taking
    responsibility for your part in any situation will prevent you
    from blaming others so often and will actually help you to feel
    more in control of your life.

Step Three: Heal Your Shame

In addition to healing your anger, you will also need to heal your
shame if you wish to stop your abusive behavior. This is because
shame can trigger abusive reactions. It can cause us to compensate
by needing to have power over others.

Identifying the emotion of shame isn't as easy as it is with some
of our other emotions. When we feel strongly shamed, it's common
for us to want to hide. In fact, the word *shame* is thought to derive
from an Indo-European word meaning "hide." Checking in with
our bodies can help us discover our shame. We tend to feel shame
in our bodies as a sense of dread, an overwhelming desire to hide or
cover our faces, a pain in the pit of our stomachs. Some people
blush (a hot or red face), and others experience feelings of jitteri-
ness, nervousness, or a choking or suffocating sensation. Certain
people experience what is commonly referred to as a "shame-
attack," in which they feel completely overwhelmed with shame.

Reactions commonly reported by those having a shame attack are feeling dizzy or spacey, disoriented, and nauseated.

EXERCISE

Your Experience of Shame

1. How do you know when you are feeling shame?
2. Identify where you feel shame in your body and how you experience it.

Defending against Shame

Some abusive Jekyll and Hydes defend against shame by projecting it out on others and by raging at others. If you tend to lash out at people or have sudden, unexpected fits of rage, ask yourself the following questions. Do you put other people down because you feel rejected by them? Do you go on a verbal rampage in an attempt to shame anyone who dares to criticize you? Do you yell at anyone who makes you feel inadequate? Do you become difficult or insulting when you feel like a failure?

People tend to react to shaming experiences (such as child abuse) in very predictable, yet unhealthy ways. As you read the following ways of defending against shame, see if you can recognize the methods you have used in your life:

- *Rage.* Rage occurs spontaneously and naturally following shame. It insulates us against further exposure and keeps others away so we can avoid further occurrences of shame. Whether held inside or expressed more openly, rage serves the purpose of defending against shame. It may also, secondarily, transfer the shame to another. This can create an abusive style of relating to others.

- *Identifying with the aggressor.* A related way that victims suppress their feelings of helplessness is by identifying with the aggressor. I discussed this phenomenon earlier in the chapter. This phenomenon is particularly common with boy victims. In most societies it isn't acceptable for men to be perceived as victims. A boy who is sexually molested, for example, will likely blame himself rather than face the shame of having been a victim. He will also be less likely to tell anyone about it, for fear of being further shamed. Because he has told no one and because he comes to blame himself and even to convince himself that he may have wanted it, he may also begin to identify with the aggressor—that is, become like his abuser. The only way left for him to discharge his shame and aggression is to do to others what was done to him.

- *Turning shame into blame.* When a child is often blamed for things that go wrong or frequently observes a parent blaming others for his or her own problems, this child is likely to take on blaming as a defending strategy against shame. In a blame-oriented family environment, attention is focused not upon how to repair the mistake but on whose fault it was and on who is to blame. The child learns to blame in order to counter blame received from others.

  These children may grow up to perceive the source of all that goes wrong to lie outside of themselves and, paradoxically, beyond internal control. Although they resent the resulting feeling of powerlessness, they never recognize that they have colluded in the very process of creating that powerlessness. This is a typical pattern for male batterers.

  While full control is not available to us as human beings, we do have control over how we face life, how we handle what comes our way, and how we internally experience ourselves. Although blaming others may help us to escape culpability for wrongdoing or mistakes and thus avoid shame, we render ourselves powerless by doing so.

- *Contempt.* Contempt, unlike rage, is not a naturally occurring affective response to shame. The most essential requirement in developing contempt as a defense against shame is experiencing a parent who is skillful in the modeling of contempt. When children experience contempt directly at the hands of a parent, they experience themselves as offensive to the parent and feel utterly rejected and disgusting to the parent. When children observe a parent treat someone else contemptuously (that is, the other parent, a sibling), they become vulnerable to taking on this way of treating others themselves. By looking down upon others and perceiving them as lacking, lesser than, or inferior beings, a once-wounded self can become securely insulated against further shame. We then see the beginnings of a judgmental, fault-finding, or condescending attitude.

- *Striving for power.* As Gershen Kaufman stated in his book *Shame: The Power of Caring*: "While rage keeps others away and contempt both distances the self from others and elevates the self above others, the striving for power is a direct attempt to compensate for the sense of defectiveness which underlies internalized shame. To the degree that one is successful in gaining power, particularly over others, one becomes increasingly less vulnerable to further shame."

  By reaching a position of real power over others, we not only become less vulnerable to having our own shame activated, but we are in a good position to transfer blame to others. In the same way, parents can both wield power over their children and blame the children for any mistakes they make with them. Power-seeking individuals also prefer to remain in control in any interpersonal situation and to gain control in their intimate relationships. They will even seek out people who are weaker or less secure to gain influence or power over.

  For these individuals, power not only becomes a way to insulate themselves from further shame but a way to compensate for shame internalized earlier in life. By gaining power over others, they in essence reverse roles from the way it was early in life. This power strategy may or may not include longings for revenge. For these individuals, security is to be won through control and self-esteem gained through power.

- *Striving for perfection.* Instead of striving for power, some people fight against shame by striving for perfection. Like power-seeking, this is a way to compensate for an underlying sense of defectiveness. The reasoning goes like this: if I can become perfect, I am no longer vulnerable to being shamed. Unfortunately, the quest for perfection is doomed to fail, and the realization of this failure reawakens the already-present sense of shame the person was trying to run from in the first place. Since the person already feels that he or she is inherently not good enough as a person, nothing this person does is ever seen as good enough.

- *Trading shame for guilt.* Since shame is so debilitating, it makes sense that we would do almost anything possible to try to avoid it. Human beings strive to stay in control. We are raised to believe that we are responsible for what happens to us and that we can control our own lives. When something goes wrong, we tend to feel ashamed that we have lost control of our lives. This is especially true of trauma victims who, instead of simply believing that something bad "just happened," tend to believe that they somehow caused or contributed to the events and are therefore responsible. Being victimized causes us to feel helpless, and it is this helplessness that leads us to feel humiliated and ashamed. As a protection against feeling helplessness and shame, we take personal responsibility for our own victimization; in other words, we trade guilt for shame.

  Shame is often confused with guilt, but it's not the same emotion. When we feel guilt, we feel badly about something we did or neglected to do. When we feel shame, we feel badly about who we are. When we feel guilty, we need to learn that it's okay to make mistakes. When we feel shame, we need to learn that it's okay to be who we are.

- *Turning shame to anger.* Turning shame to anger can actually be a positive way of reacting to shame. Instead of taking the negative energy in, against oneself, the energy is directed outward, against the person who is doing the shaming or causing the shame. Most children are unable to do this due to their tendency toward self-blame.

- *Becoming shame bound.* Sometimes a child has been so severely shamed or has experienced so many shame-inducing experiences that he or she becomes what is referred to as "shame-bound" or "shame-based," meaning that shame has become a dominant factor in the formation of the person's personality. Shame-based people are commonly survivors of severe physical discipline, sexual abuse, emotional abuse, neglect, and abandonment, which all send the message that the child is worthless, unacceptable, and bad. Shame-based people suffer from extremely low self-esteem and feelings of worthlessness and self-hatred. They feel inferior, unacceptable, and different from others. They were often taught that they were worthless or bad by hearing adults say such things to them as "You are in my way," "I wish you were never born," or "You'll never amount to anything."

Shame-based people tend to defend against any feeling of shame with anger. While most people react with anger whenever they are made to feel humiliated, devalued, or demeaned, shame-based or shame-bound people tend to be extremely sensitive and defensive, and they go into rages when they feel criticized or attacked—which is often. Because they are so critical of themselves, they believe everyone else is critical of them. And because they despise themselves, they assume everyone else dislikes them. If you are shame-bound, one teasing comment or one well-intentioned criticism can send you into a rage that lasts for hours. Because you feel shamed by the other person's comment, you may spend hours making the person feel horrible about himself or herself—in essence, dumping shame back on the other person.

Shame-based people feel very vulnerable underneath all their defensiveness. Another way a shame-based person uses anger as a defense is by attacking others before they have a chance to attack him. It's as if he or she is saying, "I'll show you. I'll make you feel like shit because that's what you think of me."

If you are shame-bound, you may also use anger to keep people away from your vulnerability by raging at them. In essence, you are saying, "Don't get any closer to me. I don't want you to know who I really am." This raging works—it drives people away or keeps them at a safe distance. Of course, this also makes you feel even worse when you realize that others are avoiding you.

How Shame Has Affected You

The following questions will help you gain a deeper understanding about the role shame has played in your Jekyll and Hyde behavior.

- Think about how you reacted to the shaming experiences of your childhood. How did you defend against the shame? Did you blame yourself? Did you become angry?

- How has shame contributed to your style of relating to others?

- If you have externalized shame, think about the ways you have projected your shame onto others.

- Some people defend against shame by projecting it out on others and by raging at others. If you tend to do this, particularly if you lash out at people or have sudden, unexpected fits of rage, pay attention to the ways in which you convert shame into anger. Do you put other people down because you feel rejected by them? Do you go on a verbal rampage in an attempt to shame anyone who dares to criticize you? Do you yell at anyone who makes you feel inadequate? Do you become difficult or insulting when you feel like a failure?

Your Shame Inventory

By focusing on the following questions, you will not only gain a deeper understanding of how shame dictates your behavior, but you will be able to learn to better manage shame when it is triggered.

- Notice what triggers shame in you today. Is it criticism from others, is it being called on your "stuff" (or, as one client described it, "Having my covers pulled"), or is it being rejected?

- When are you most likely to feel shamed? Is it when you feel the most insecure? Is it when you are trying to impress someone?

- Who is most likely to trigger shame in you? Is it the people you care about the most? Or is it those you are trying to impress? How about the people you feel inadequate around or those who have rejected you in the past?

Strategies for Coping with Shame in a Healthy Way

Next, you will need to learn healthy ways of coping with shame. The following suggestions will help you with this process:

1. Break the shame/rage cycle. The first thing you need to do is to break the shame/rage cycle. To do this, you must ask yourself, "What am I ashamed of?" each and every time you get angry. Think of your anger as a red flag signaling the fact that you are feeling shame. This is especially true whenever you experience sudden bursts of anger or when you become enraged. It may be difficult to find your shame at first, and you may not feel shame each and every time you feel angry, but with some practice you will be able to recognize the times when you feel ashamed and discover what has triggered it in you. Once you've identified the shame/rage connection, you will need to break it. This means you will have to stop yourself from becoming angry as a way of defending against your shame.

2. Learn to deal with shame attacks. If you are having a full-blown shame-attack, you may need to talk to a trusted friend or someone else close to you (your therapist, your sponsor, a member of your support group, someone at a hotline). Explain that you are having a shame-attack and that you feel horrible about yourself. Don't blame the person who triggered your shame for making you feel bad; take responsibility for your own shame. Try to make a connection between this current incident and what it reminds you of (from your childhood, from a more recent traumatic shaming). Ask your friend to remind you that you are not a horrible person by telling you of at least one good attribute you have. If you can't find someone you trust to talk to, write your feelings down on paper or in a journal. Describe what you are feeling in detail, including your physical reactions. Trace these reactions back to other times and incidents when you felt similar feelings. If you find a connecting incident, write about it in detail. Then spend some time reminding yourself of your good qualities and accomplishments.

3. Discover your triggers. Each of us has buttons that get pushed, triggers that set us off emotionally. They may be situations that remind us of the past or things that people say that remind us of what someone from the past said to hurt us. Getting your buttons pushed, or "being triggered," can send you into a tizzy

without warning, causing you to become enraged, deeply hurt, fearful, or depressed. Make a list of your triggers. The next time your partner does something to trigger you, such as using a particular phrase, tell your partner that you don't want him or her to use it again, that it hurts you deeply and reminds you of the past. If your partner seems to be sympathetic, you may wish to share your entire list, explaining why each item upsets you so much. While you're at it, ask your partner to make his or her own trigger list and share it with you. The following exercise will help you to discover what your shame triggers are.

EXERCISE

Discover Your Triggers

1. Take some time to create a list of the most embarrassing experiences in your childhood or adolescence. Include the times when you felt humiliated or shamed by someone else.

2. Once you have completed your list, read through it slowly. Pay attention to how you feel emotionally and how your body feels as you read each item.

3. Put a checkmark beside each item on your list that you still feel an emotional charge about.

Think about the possibility that these items might be your triggers. For example, if you remembered an experience where you were chastised or punished in front of a group of people when you were a child and thinking about the event (or the events) still makes you feel humiliated, angry, or both, it's possible that when you experience any kind of public embarrassment, it may trigger the memory of this event. This may then cause you to have a shame attack and to overreact to the situation in the present.

4. Stop putting yourself down. While it's important to take responsibility for your actions, constantly putting yourself down for your past actions will only increase your shame. Research shows that painful and debilitating feelings of shame do not motivate constructive changes in behavior. In

fact, shame serves to escalate the very destructive behavior we aim to curb. This is true whether someone else is shaming you or you are shaming yourself.

Step Four: Work on Your Tendency toward Perfectionism

Perfectionism is closely related to shame and is the cause of a great deal of abusive behavior. In particular, perfectionism can cause people to become overly critical of their partners or children and is often the cause of nit-picking behaviors so common among Jekyll and Hydes. If one or both of your parents were perfectionistic, you will tend to be perfectionistic as well. You'll expect yourself to do things right the first time, and when you make a mistake, you won't be forgiving of yourself. Instead, you'll berate yourself with comments like, "What's wrong with you?" and "Stupid, you can't do anything right." If you expect perfection from yourself, you will continually be disappointed in yourself and continually damage your self-esteem. If you expect perfection from others, you will end up being demanding and critical. If you do this with your children, you will be emotionally abusing them.

Step Five: Take Responsibility for Your Own Reactions and Moods

Because they were so shamed, many Jekyll and Hydes tend to project their negative feelings about themselves onto others. Each time their shame is activated, they immediately try to rid themselves of these horrible feelings by focusing on the shortcomings (or, more accurately, the *imagined* shortcomings) of others.

Many Jekyll and Hydes live with a great deal of internal anxiety. As one client explained, "It's as if I have a cyclone going on inside me most of the time. I constantly feel all churned up." This internal anxiety comes and goes with virtually no warning, and most Jekyll and Hydes have little or no idea why they suddenly become anxious. Unfortunately, instead of going inside and asking themselves, "What is going on with me? Why am I feeling so anxious?" they tend to focus outside themselves. Instead of taking responsibility for their own reactions and trying to discover what they are feeling, they blame their environment, and most often their partners or children for their distress. Their thinking is like this: "If I'm not feeling comfortable, if I am feeling anxious, it must be someone else's fault."

This kind of thinking is at the core of a very common form of abusive Jekyll and Hyde behavior—criticism and nitpicking. Partners and children describe it like this: "All of a sudden, my husband will start picking at me. If we're out somewhere, he'll focus on what I'm wearing—'Do you have to wear such sexy clothes? You look like a tramp.' If we are at home, he'll start criticizing the way I clean house or the way I cook. 'I'll bet you haven't cleaned inside this refrigerator for months. You're probably poisoning us with all this rotting garbage in here.'"

In reality, it isn't the way this man's wife dressed or the way she cleaned the house that really bothered him, but since he didn't spend any time focusing on himself, he couldn't discover what had really created his anxiety. Not only did he upset his wife, causing her to grow more distant and angry with him, but he didn't get any real relief from his troublesome anxiety. Criticizing his wife was merely a momentary distraction; it didn't solve his anxiety problem. Not only that, but on top of his anxiety he now had his guilt to contend with and a distant, angry wife.

How do you learn to switch your focus from outside to inside? It is difficult. You've been focusing outside yourself for a long time, probably most of your life. This is how I helped my client Seth begin to change his pattern.

I started by asking Seth to recount his most recent upset with his wife. It turned out to be the previous weekend when he and his wife had his parents over for dinner. "My wife was taking forever to get the table set, and I didn't like the centerpiece she had made. I told her I thought it looked cheap. She got upset with me and told me to please not start with her. That made me more upset. I told her that I at least wanted the table to look good because I knew the food would be terrible. With that, she fired back, 'I don't know why I even try to do nice things for you,' and she stormed out of the house. I had to make excuses to my parents why she wasn't there. It was so embarrassing."

I then asked Seth to try to remember how he felt just before he became critical of his wife. "I was feeling anxious—I'm not sure why, though."

I asked whether he felt nervous about having his parents to the house.

"No, they've been over for dinner several times since we got married. There was nothing out of the ordinary happening this time."

I wasn't certain, however, that Seth wasn't more nervous about pleasing his parents than he thought. "Are you sure you weren't worried about impressing your parents? You made such a big thing about the centerpiece."

"Well, now that I think about it, maybe I was. My mother's house is immaculate—a showroom. And she is a gourmet cook. I didn't expect Virginia to cook as well, but I didn't want my parents to think she was a bad wife. They are pretty particular. I guess that's why I started getting anxious."

I asked Seth how he thought it would have worked if he had gone to his wife and told her about his nervousness, telling her something like, "Honey, I'm getting so anxious about what my parents are going to think about the dinner. I know it shouldn't matter, but somehow it does."

"She might have tried to console me. She's pretty good about that kind of thing. She probably would have tried to reassure me that the dinner was going to be good and that my parents just wanted to visit with us—that they weren't expecting a gourmet meal."

"And how would that have felt to you?"

"It actually would have felt a lot better than what happened. It would have been like we were in it together—as a team."

"That's right. And you would have been taking responsibility for your own anxiety instead of projecting it onto her."

Think about the last time you started criticizing someone close to you. Try to imagine how it might have worked if you'd gone inside yourself to look for the cause of your anxiety or discomfort instead of assuming that someone else was doing something to you to make you feel bad.

The truth is, just because something upset you doesn't mean that the other person did something wrong. This is a very difficult concept for most people to understand, especially those with abusive or neglectful backgrounds. It only stands to reason that if we are upset with someone, that person must have done something wrong, right? Otherwise, why would we be upset with them? The answer is that we can become upset with someone else for reasons that have nothing at all to do with that person.

11

If You Have a Personality Disorder

Although the world is full of suffering, it is also full of overcoming it.

    —Helen Keller

If you bring forth what is within you, what you bring forth will save you. If you do not bring forth what is within you, what you do not bring forth will destroy you.

    —Jesus

In this chapter I offer step-by-step guidance as to how people with borderline personality disorder (BPD) or narcissistic personality disorder (NPD) can work toward curbing characteristics and tendencies that create havoc in their relationships and may cause them to be emotionally abusive to their partners or children, as well as how they can take care of their own needs better in a relationship. Although the chapter was written specifically for people with these disorders, I also encourage partners and adult children to read it in order to better understand the unique problems that someone with a personality disorder must face.

For those of you who suspect that you suffer from BPD or NPD but still aren't certain, the information and the questionnaires offered in this chapter may help. Of course, to be absolutely certain, you will need to be diagnosed by a qualified health-care provider.

Do You Suffer from Borderline Personality Disorder?

Although it will be extremely painful and embarrassing to admit that you suffer from BPD, once you have done so, you are on your way toward healing it. As mentioned earlier in the book, according to the *DSM-IV*, BPD is characterized by a pervasive pattern of instability of interpersonal relationships, self-image, and affects (moods), and marked impulsivity beginning by early adulthood and present in a variety of contexts. Refer back to chapter 3 for a list of symptoms as outlined by the *DSM-IV*. Also, refer to chapter 6 for a questionnaire that will help you further determine whether you may suffer from this disorder or from borderline tendencies.

How Borderline Personality Disorder Leads to Jekyll and Hyde Syndrome and Emotionally Abusive Behavior

People who suffer from BPD or strong borderline tendencies most often become emotionally abusive due to their tendency to project or transfer their own feelings, behaviors, or perceived traits onto others. Projection is a defense mechanism that we all use from time to time, but those suffering from BPD use it in excessive ways. Because they tend to be overwhelmed with self-criticism, self-loathing, and self-blame, and because they cannot contain these feelings without sometimes dire consequences (deep depression, self-mutilation, or suicide attempts), borderline individuals tend to project their feelings of self-hatred outside themselves, onto others. This can cause them to be extremely critical or judgmental of others, particularly of people closest to them. Because they feel as if something is wrong with them, they accuse others of being inadequate and incapable. Often, their self-hatred comes out as verbal abuse, constant criticism, or unreasonable expectations.

Those suffering from BPD also accuse others of having feelings and thoughts that really belong to them. They often project their self-hatred by experiencing others, particularly their partners, as disapproving of their actions or being judgmental or critical of aspects of their personalities. This can cause them to become almost paranoid, constantly assuming that their partners are criticizing them when the partners are merely stating preferences or opinions.

Because people with BPD feel so innately bad about themselves, they cannot imagine how someone could love them. This can cause them to demand constant reassurance and proof of their partners' love and to become extremely jealous and possessive. They often demand all of their partners' attention and accuse their partners of being unfaithful when there is absolutely no proof that any such infidelity has occurred.

Projection also works in another way. If you suffer from BPD, you may accuse your partner of doing something that you are actually doing. Many people with this disorder accuse their partners or children of talking behind their backs when, in actuality, they often do this themselves.

EXERCISE

Making the Connection

In addition to projection, if you suffer from BPD or have strong borderline traits, there are many other aspects of your personality that can lead to Jekyll and Hyde behavior or abusive behavior. Put a checkmark next to each of the following personality traits that describe your behavior:

- *Inappropriate, intense anger or an inability to control your anger.* This includes frequent displays of temper or sudden outbursts, constantly being angry, getting into physical fights.

- *Feelings that vary dramatically from moment to moment* (for example, being flooded with emotions or being numb to your feelings, which can manifest into total silence or explosive screaming). This fluctuation of feelings is magnified greatly by the next personality trait.

- *A tendency to forget what you felt prior to the present.* This "amnesia surrounding emotions" prevents you from remembering past experiences and from appreciating that pain is temporary and can be survived. Whatever feeling-state you are experiencing at the moment seems to last forever, and you can't recall ever feeling differently. As a result, your last encounter with your partner may be recalled as the whole of your relationship. You forget all the good times you've had with your partner and may threaten to end the relationship based on one bad incident. With this black-and-white quality of feelings, disappointment often turns to rage, which may be directed at others in fits of temper or physical attacks. (Rage may also be turned against the self in the form of self-abuse, self-injury, or suicidal threats or behavior).

- *A tendency to alternately idealize and devalue a person or to view a person as either "all good" or "all bad."* As long as you feel that your partner is paying enough attention to you, appreciating your efforts and behaving in ways that cause you to respect him or her, you will likely perceive your partner as "all good." Yet as soon as your partner rejects you, disapproves of something you've done, or does something that you disapprove of, you may suddenly see this person as "all bad." This may cause you to belittle or berate your partner, sometimes in front of others (character assassination), or threaten to leave him or her (emotional blackmail).

- *Unpredictable responses.* Because of an inconsistent sense of self, you may also seem to set up no-win situations for your partner. You may react one way to your partner's behavior one time and an entirely different way the next. Or you may ask your partner to treat you a certain way, and then when he or she does, you may get angry with your partner for it. In this way, you keep your partner completely off-balance since he or she cannot predict how you will react. Your partner may grow to feel that no matter what he or she does, it will be wrong.

- *You may resort to using alcohol or drugs, binge eating, impulsive sexual encounters, compulsive shopping, gambling, shoplifting, or other behaviors* as a quick fix for painful, seemingly endless, emotions, such as loneliness and anger. Under the influence of alcohol or drugs, you may display erratic Jekyll and Hyde behavior or become emotionally or even physically abusive to your partner or children.

- *A need to control your partner and your environment.* Those who suffer from BPD need to feel in control of other people because they feel so out of control of themselves. In an attempt to make your world more predictable and manageable, you may order your partner around, require him or her to do things a certain way, insist on being the one in charge, or try to make your partner over.

- *Intense fear of rejection or abandonment*, which may cause you to be extremely possessive, jealous, and controlling or to react in extreme, sometimes outrageous, ways, such as bursting into a rage when your partner tells you he or she is going on a business trip or desperately clinging to a girlfriend or a boyfriend who is threatening to end the relationship. This same fear of abandonment may cause you to be hypervigilant, looking for any cues that might show you that your partner doesn't really care about you. If and when your fears seem to be confirmed, you may erupt in a rage, make outrageous accusations, seek revenge, or engage in some kind of self-destructive act.

- *Your feelings may become so intense that they distort your perception of reality.* You may imagine that others, including your partner, are deliberately persecuting you. You may accuse your partner of plotting against you with others or of deliberately trying to upset or undermine you when in reality he or she has merely let you down.

- *Emotional blackmail.* You may threaten to end the relationship, move out of the house, or kick your partner out of the house whenever there is a fight or a disagreement. While you may change your mind as soon as you cool down, your threats take a toll on your partner and on your relationship. People suffering from BPD also threaten to hurt or kill themselves in order to get their way or to get their partners to take them back.

- *Constant chaos.* Your insecurity, accusations, jealousy, possessiveness, emotional outbursts, and depression create constant chaos and drama in the relationship. You start fights, become depressed, and cry for hours, then you want to make up as if nothing had happened and you beg your partner to take you back. You hate your partner one day and love him or her the next. You may alternately cling to your partner out of a fear of abandonment and push your partner away out of a fear of being smothered. Those with BPD or borderline tendencies often experience a great deal of anxiety—a constant nervous feeling or the feeling that there is a whirling cyclone going on inside them. This feeling of anxiety is so uncomfortable that they create drama as a way to distract themselves from it. Other BPDs prefer to create upheaval in their lives rather than be forced to face the horrible feelings of emptiness they might otherwise experience.

- *Constant criticism and continual blame.* You may criticize your partner as a way of creating distance so that you can ward off feelings of engulfment, or you may criticize as a way to cope with abandonment fears. You may feel defective at a core level and fear that your partner will one day discover this and reject you completely. Therefore, you find fault in your partner as a way of deflecting his or her judgments and criticism. If your partner is the one who is always wrong, you can't be. You may also criticize your partner for things you yourself are guilty of (projection).

- *Gaslighting.* Although it is not necessarily your intention, your behavior can cause your partner to question his or her own sanity. You forget you said or did something and thus deny it when your partner brings it up. You have an emotional outburst and then deny it ever happened (it is quite common for people suffering from BPD to dissociate while in a rage). Even when you realize you've done something, such as when you catch yourself being inconsistent, you may be too ashamed to admit it. You may try to portray your partner as the one who is mixed up or even imply that he or she is crazy.

Begin to Change Your Erratic or Emotionally Abusive Behavior

Changing your behavior when you suffer from BPD or strong borderline traits won't be easy. It isn't as if you can simply *will* yourself to change. Much of your abusive behavior is unconscious, based on strong defense mechanisms. Even when you are consciously aware of your erratic or abusive behavior, it may feel at the time that it is the only thing you can do to protect yourself (for example, verbal abuse) or to hold onto your partner and your relationship (for example, lie, manipulate). For some of you, especially those who suffer from a more extreme version of BPD, professional psychotherapy is the only way you can make the kind of substantial changes to your personality that will interrupt your abusive patterns. For others, particularly those who suffer from a milder form of BPD or who have only borderline tendencies, the following suggestions can help you begin to change your behavior immediately.

Step One: Become More Conscious about Your Jekyll and Hyde Behavior

You need to become more aware of your erratic or abusive behavior and of the effect it has on your partner, your children, and others. This can be an extremely difficult task in itself, and it will take a leap of faith on your part, as well as tremendous courage. You will need to ask those closest to you to give you feedback about your behavior. This step, of course, makes the assumption that you can believe what people close to you will tell you—more specifically, it assumes that you can trust their perceptions and judgment. This poses quite a dilemma. Since you likely have difficulty trusting your partner, how in the world can you trust what he or she says about your behavior? Since you already feel that others misperceive you and misjudge your actions, how can you trust their perceptions of you? Although your partner can certainly have distorted perceptions around some issues—particularly the issues that pertain to his or her own background—when it comes to your erratic or abusive behavior, your partner's perceptions are probably closer to the truth than yours are. Unfortunately, those who have BPD frequently experience distortions in their perceptions, particularly in terms of how they view themselves in relationships. While they can be extremely sensitive and perceptive when it comes to other people, they aren't able to perceive themselves as accurately. Also, it's common for those suffering from BPD to dissociate when in a rage or when they are under a great deal of emotional stress, causing them to be unaware of their abusive behavior. Adult children can also be the source of valuable feedback.

EXERCISE

Get Feedback from Others

1. Ask your partner, child, or adult child to write a list of your behaviors that are most hurtful to him or her.

2. Ask your partner, child, or adult child to explain why each behavior is particularly hurtful.

3. Ask this person to describe the behaviors on your part that could be described as abusive or erratic and, if possible, to explain why he or she views them that way.

4. You may also wish to ask your close friends for similar feedback. Keep in mind that your friends may or may not experience the full force of your abusiveness since you may be on your good behavior with them or you may not feel threatened by them—meaning you may not fear being either abandoned by them or smothered by them. Be careful about asking family members for feedback since they are not as

likely to be objective. Also, your disorder probably stems from your family dynamics, and there is even some evidence that BPD may be at least partly genetic. This means it is likely that some members of your family also suffer from BPD and also have distorted perceptions.

Step Two: Identify Your Triggers

People who suffer from BPD or who have strong borderline tendencies tend to react similarly to certain behaviors and attitudes from others. These are called "triggers." When a person is triggered, he or she reacts spontaneously and intensely, often without realizing what caused the reaction. The following is a list of the most common triggers for those with BPD:

1. *Perceived abandonment.* Because of your fear of abandonment, you are probably acutely sensitive to any hint of perceived abandonment, and you likely react powerfully and sometimes violently to it. For example, even the slightest hint of disapproval from your partner can trigger powerful feelings of rejection.

2. *Feeling criticized.* When you feel criticized, you are likely to react very intensely. This is true for several reasons. First of all, when you are criticized, you probably become overwhelmed with shame. Shame is different from guilt, in that it makes a person feel that his or her entire being is wrong or bad, as opposed to guilt, which reminds us that committing certain acts is wrong. The second reason is closely related to the first. Those suffering from BPD tend to see things in all-or-nothing terms. When they are criticized, it makes them feel "all bad." Third, criticism feels like rejection to BPDs and can therefore trigger a fear of abandonment. It goes like this—if you don't like something I've done, it means you don't like me and that you are going to abandon me.

3. *Feeling that others are unpredictable or inconsistent.* Although borderline individuals are often unpredictable and inconsistent themselves, they have a tremendous need for consistency and

predictability, especially from those close to them. When they perceive a person as being inconsistent or a person or a situation as being unpredictable, this causes them to be fearful and anxious. This is likely due to the fact that people who suffer from BPD didn't receive the consistency they needed from their parents, especially from their mothers. In order for a child to develop a strong sense of self, he or she must have what is called "object constancy." This particular trigger can, in turn, trigger a fear of abandonment since unpredictability often goes hand in hand with rejection or abandonment.

4. *Feeling invalidated or dismissed*. Because borderline individuals have not developed a strong sense of self, they are especially sensitive to comments or attitudes that are invalidating or dismissive. Comments like "You're overreacting" or "You shouldn't feel like that" may seem as if they deny the validity of your feelings and thoughts. Even though there are many times when you may be overreacting or reacting inappropriately, these types of invalidating comments are in themselves inappropriate.

5. *Envy*. Borderline individuals are often triggered when someone else receives special recognition. They become overwhelmed with feelings of envy and may become depressed or act out in order to draw the attention to themselves. This can happen during celebrations when all the attention is focused on someone else or even during a crisis when someone else needs support.

6. *Travel or moving*. People with BPD tend to respond well to structure and predictability. When this is disrupted, they can become disoriented. Moving to a new home or town or even going on vacation can trigger feelings of insecurity and fear.

7. *Having every reaction attributed to their disorder*. If you have been diagnosed with BPD, you can be triggered when someone else attributes what you do to BPD.

Knowing your triggers can provide you with a great deal more control of your borderline tendencies. For example, if your trigger is abandonment or rejection, don't set yourself up for it by leaving plans open. When you and your partner make plans for an activity, be sure you get a clear commitment from him or her concerning both the event itself and the timing. While other people may be comfortable with "Let's wait and see how we feel" or "I'll pick you up around eight," you are not. You need to know from your partner that a plan is definite; otherwise, you set yourself up for feeling abandoned or rejected if he or she decides not to go. And you need to know exactly what time your partner will pick you up or what time you will meet so that you don't stand around waiting, feeling anxious, irritated, enraged, or, worse, abandoned. Getting clear commitments from your partner won't guarantee that you are never disappointed at last-minute changes or that you will never be kept waiting, but it will certainly help. If you have a partner who is unable to commit to a certain time or who is consistently late even when he or she does commit, it is time to make other arrangements.

Step Three: Admit Your Abusive Behavior to Your Partner and Children

It will be extremely difficult for you to admit to your abusive or erratic behavior for several reasons. First of all, because you already feel unlovable and because you fear abandonment, you don't want your partner to know there is anything wrong with you or that you've done anything wrong. Your unconscious reasoning may sound like this: "If my partner discovers I'm not perfect, he's going to reject me. Therefore, I can't admit I have a problem. It's better to make him think the problem lies with him."

Second, you probably judge yourself as harshly as you judge others. And just as you see others in all-or-nothing, black-and-white terms, you see yourself in the same way. If you admit to yourself and your partner that you have been abusive, you are likely to see yourself as "all bad" and fear that your partner will do the same.

Third, people who suffer from borderline personality disorder also tend to suffer from pervasive shame—the feeling that they are worthless, flawed, and defective. Admitting that your behavior is sometimes abusive may trigger what is commonly called a "shame attack"—an overwhelming feeling of being exposed as the defective, evil person that you feel you are at your core, and feeling isolated, empty, and alone in the world as a result of it. Nevertheless, it's still important to let your partner know that your behavior has been abusive.

Healing Your Relationship with Your Children

Although borderline parents love their children as much as other parents do, their deficits in emotional regulation and cognitive functioning can create behaviors that almost undo their love. For example, borderline mothers have difficulty loving their children with patience and consistency. Instead of loving their children unconditionally, they tend to love their children only when they behave the way the parents want them to. When there are misunderstandings and disagreements, the parents often withdraw or withhold their love as a way of punishing their children.

Borderlines also tend to hurt others, particularly their children, the way they were hurt. If they were highly criticized, they will be extremely critical of their children; if they were emotionally abandoned, they will ignore or neglect their children.

Borderline parents often accuse their children of being crazy with statements like, "There is something seriously wrong with you," or "You're out of your mind!" In reality, they are simply projecting onto their children their fears about their own sanity. Unfortunately, children often take on these parental messages (as you yourself may have done with your own borderline parent). Christina Crawford (1997) described her experience like this: "You just ease into being crazy. . . . it doesn't happen overnight. . . . You get tired of the constant battle with no victories. . . . You become exhausted hoping for the cease fire. . . . You lose your grip on the world slowly and drift into the chasm of your own hopelessness."

EXERCISE

Acknowledge the Ways You Have Harmed Your Children

- Make a list of all the ways your BPD has confused or harmed your children. Include the following if they apply: impatience, inconsistency, mixed messages, withdrawing or withholding love, being overly critical, abandoning or rejecting behaviors, neglect, projection.

- Write a letter to each of your children listing all the ways you feel that your BPD has affected your ability to be a good parent. Don't give these letters to them yet; this is just for your benefit at this time.

Tips on How to Mend Your Relationship with Your Children

The following suggestions will help you begin to heal your relationship with your children. It may take time, but with patience and consistency, you can help your children feel safer and more secure with you.

1. Explain to your children (whether they are still young or have grown) that you suffer from a personality disorder that has interfered with your ability to love them unconditionally.

2. Apologize to your children for how your emotional outbursts, inconsistent behavior, inaccurate projections, and any other emotionally abusive behavior on your part has hurt or damaged them. Refer back to the previous exercise and to your letters for help in doing this.

3. Work on developing the qualities of patience, flexibility, and tolerance. These are essential qualities for good parenting and are especially important for people with BPD to develop.

4. Work on owning your projections. Don't assume that just because you think one of your children is lying or feeling critical of you that your perceptions are accurate. In fact, before you spend any more time focusing on this, ask yourself, "Am I feeling critical of myself?" "Am I lying to myself or to anyone else?"

Step Four: Face the Truth about Your Childhood and Reach Out for Help

Although there is no absolute consensus as to the cause of BPD, most experts agree that there is definitely an environmental factor.

Most people suffering from BPD share one factor in particular—
abandonment. This abandonment can either be physical or
emotional in nature and can stem from any or all of the following
circumstances:

- An insufficient bonding experience with a primary caretaker,
  particularly the mother

- The long-term absence of one or both parents

- The loss of a parent, either through death or divorce

- An insufficient, inappropriate, or negative relationship with the
  father

- Parental neglect

- Rejection or ridicule from parents, siblings, or peers.

In addition, many, but not all, borderline individuals also experienced either emotional, physical, or sexual abuse, or all three. All
the previous experiences are extremely traumatic, and all require
that you have professional therapy in order for you to heal from
them.

Many people suffer from BPD without realizing it. Many go
their entire lives without knowing why they feel and behave as
they do, and most of them never receive any help for their problems. Others seek help for related problems, such as eating disorders, alcohol or drug abuse, compulsive shopping, or gambling.
Some seek help for depression and suicidal attempts. But few seek
help because they have the Jekyll and Hyde syndrome or because
they are emotionally abusing their partners or children. In fact,
most people who suffer from BPD believe that they are the ones
who are being abused in their relationships. By admitting that you
are, in fact, being emotionally abusive to your partner or children,
you will be exhibiting a great deal of integrity and courage. Not
only will you possibly be saving your relationship, but the help you
get will save you as well.

You've no doubt sensed for a long time that there is something
really wrong with you. After all, you've been in emotional pain
most of your life. You've experienced a constant feeling of emptiness inside that you've tried to fill up with food, alcohol, or

relationships. You've been in a constant state of either anxiety or depression.

It is especially important to reach out for help if you are experiencing chronic or severe depression. You cannot just will yourself out of depression. By its very nature, depression takes away your will and your motivation and distorts your perception. You may need medication, at least temporarily, especially if you feel suicidal. More important, you need someone to talk to, someone who is not involved personally in your life, someone who can provide an objective perspective.

You will also need the guidance of a professional to help you identify and express your emotions. The most common defense used against feelings by people who suffer from BPD or who have borderline traits is the defense called "intellectualization." When we intellectualize, we seek reasons to explain, analyze, censor, and judge our feelings. We tell ourselves that certain feelings are bad or wrong, and therefore we shouldn't feel them. Or we tell ourselves that feelings are childish and that people who express feelings openly are foolish. Yet while our emotions can sometimes be unpleasant, confusing, untimely and even disruptive, they are as natural and as necessary as any body function. You undoubtedly need help to work past your tendency to intellectualize your emotions and help to begin allowing yourself to express your emotions in constructive ways.

If You Suffer from Narcissistic Personality Disorder

You may have reason to believe that you suffer from NPD, either from reading the information on narcissism in chapter 3 or because someone, possibly your partner, may have told you that you fit the description. If this is true for you and you haven't read chapter 3, I suggest you do so now. The following questions will also help:

1. Do you feel that you are special or that you have special talents or gifts that others don't possess?

2. Do you feel entitled to special treatment or recognition?

3. Do you secretly feel that you are better than most people (for example, smarter, more attractive, more talented)?

4. Do you become easily bored with people when they talk about themselves?

5. Do you tend to think that your feelings or your opinions are more important than those of others?

6. Does it hurt you deeply if your talents, accomplishments, or physical attributes are not recognized or appreciated?

7. Do you feel deeply insulted if you are ignored or not acknowledged?

8. Have you been accused of being overly self-focused or self-centered?

9. Have you been accused of being conceited or egotistical?

10. Do you often fly off the handle or become enraged at the slightest provocation, frequently without really knowing why?

11. Do you lose respect for others when you discover that they are less intelligent, successful, powerful, or "together" emotionally than you had first thought?

12. Do you have difficulty identifying or empathizing with others, especially with their pain?

13. Do you find that you are often envious of what others have accomplished or accumulated?

14. Do you tend to focus more on what you don't have than on what you do?

15. Do you frequently feel that your efforts and accomplishments are being ignored or minimized or that you are being passed over for special recognition, promotions, awards, and so on?

16. Are you able to walk away from relationships fairly easily once someone has insulted you or hurt you?

17. Is one of your major goals in life to become successful, famous, or wealthy, or to find "perfect" love?

18. Do you feel like a failure or feel depressed because you haven't reached your goal?

19. Do you feel as if you don't really need other people all that much, that you are fairly self-sufficient?

20. Are most of your friendships based on a mutual interest or on the fact that you both have a strong desire to become successful, famous, or wealthy?

21. Do your relationships tend to be short-lived? Are you close to someone for a while but find that over time this person no longer serves a function in your life?

If you answered yes to up to five questions, you have strong narcissistic tendencies. If you answered more than five questions with a yes, especially if they were questions 10 through 21, you may actually suffer from NPD.

How Narcissistic Personality Disorder Leads to Jekyll and Hyde or Abusive Behavior

If you suffer from NPD or have strong narcissistic tendencies, your behavior and attitude toward others are often experienced as abusive even though you may not intentionally try to hurt anyone. In fact, those with NPD are often oblivious to others and to how their behavior affects other people. This doesn't make your behavior and attitude any less hurtful or damaging, however, and often it is your careless disregard toward others that hurts the most. The specific behaviors and attitudes manifested by a narcissistic individual that are most hurtful to others include:

• Negating the feelings, the ideas, and the opinions of others

• Sarcastic remarks and put-downs

• A general attitude of arrogance and condescension toward others

• A tendency to be dismissive of others, especially if one does not respect them

- Being overly critical and judgmental of others

- Unreasonable expectations—never being pleased

Although most of their abusive behavior is unconscious and unintentional, at times people suffering from NPD can be deliberately abusive. Generally speaking, the impulse to emotionally abuse is set in motion either when the relationship becomes too symbiotic or when a partner is somehow found lacking. Too much closeness terrifies narcissists, so they criticize or impose control on their partners or children to keep them at bay. By accusing her children of being too demanding or invasive, a narcissistic mother can keep them at a safe distance. By asserting control and dominance over his wife, a narcissistic husband can keep her in a dependent or one-down position. Narcissists also work at keeping their partners off-balance so they can avoid having to make the emotional commitment that they so desperately fear. The unspoken message is "I don't love you," but it remains indirect and hidden so that their partners won't leave. Neither can the partners feel safe and secure in the relationship. They are always in a state of confusion, constantly asking themselves, "Does he (or she) love me or not?"

When people suffering from narcissism experience disappointment in their partners, this can also set abuse in motion. Typical narcissistic individuals often become intensely attracted to people in a short amount of time and will tend to idealize their partners, viewing them as more beautiful, talented, popular, or giving than they actually are. When this idealization wears off, people with NPD may become so disappointed that they lose any respect they once had for their partners. This lack of respect is expressed through belittling, dismissive or sarcastic comments or put-downs, and a blatant lack of consideration. They are deliberately trying to push their partners away since the partners no longer meet their standards.

When people suffering from narcissism are faced with the inevitable ending of a relationship, either because they are unable to ignore the fact that the relationship is a failure or they are interested in someone else, they will inevitably become abusive. Unable to accept any responsibility for the failure of the relationship or for their attraction to someone else, they must make their partners responsible—in their own minds and in their partners'.

In some cases, it isn't a question of the narcissistic individual *becoming* abusive but of his or her previously hidden abusive nature being revealed. To justify his or her desire to end the relationship, the narcissistic person will force the partner to behave in unacceptable ways so that the partner can then be invalidated. In the situation where the narcissistic partner is attracted to someone else, he or she must turn the previous partner into a scapegoat and project everything bad onto that partner in order to idealize the new love object and establish a new relationship.

How You Can Begin to Change Your Jekyll and Hyde or Emotionally Abusive Behavior

The following steps will help you begin to change your Jekyll and Hyde behavior, but it will take honesty and perseverance on your part. The rewards, however, make it worth all the effort. You will not only stop abusing your loved ones, but you will begin to know and respect yourself a lot more.

Step One: Admit You Have a Problem

This will undoubtedly be very difficult. In fact, it may be the most difficult thing you will ever have to do. Believe me, I know. There came a time in my life when I had to admit to myself that I have some very clear narcissistic tendencies. Ironically, it occurred during the writing of my book *The Emotionally Abused Woman*. As I listed the symptoms of narcissism, I was amazed to find that I recognized myself in the description of the disorder.

It should have been no surprise to me because I come from a long line of narcissists. My mother and several of her brothers suffered from the disorder, as did her mother. For some reason, though, I imagined that I'd escaped our family curse. I should have known that it's not that easy to do. Having been raised as the only child of a narcissistic mother, there was no way I could escape my destiny, no matter how hard I tried. As Elan Golomb stated so eloquently in *Trapped in the Mirror*:

Each narcissistic parent in each generation repeats the crime that was perpetuated against him. The crime is non-acceptance. (The narcissist is more demanding and deforming of the child he identifies with more strongly, although all his children are pulled into his web of subjectivity). How can he accept offspring who are the product of his own unconsciously despised self? His attitude is a variant of the Groucho Marx Syndrome: "I would not join any club that would have me as its member," here transposed into "I would not love any child that would have me as its parent." The child has rejection as its birthright.

Even though it's difficult to imagine, people suffering from NPD have an even worse reputation than do those who suffer from BPD. Calling someone a narcissist is considered extremely derogatory. To be a psychotherapist with narcissistic tendencies was especially humiliating, although I have come to realize that I certainly am not alone. And neither are you. We are said to live in the age of narcissism, and because of this, few of us are entirely free of its traits. Our society worships beauty—especially beautiful bodies—as well as external things such as power, status, and money.

As difficult as it will be for you to admit your narcissistic traits, this is what you will need to do if you are going to stop your abusive behavior and possibly save your relationship. As long as you avoid admitting the truth, you will continue to be abusive, and you will continue to damage your partner and your relationship.

Step Two: Face the Truth about Your Childhood

When we look behind the self-important, self-absorbed, egotistical, "me-first" behavior of the person suffering from narcissism, we almost always discover a person whose early, *healthy* narcissistic needs (for attention, affection, and respect, as well as for food and shelter) were not met. Some of you reading this book already know the roots of your problem. You remember well the neglect or the abuse that you experienced at the hands of one or both of your parents. But others have been so good at covering up their hurt and anger that they have little or no memory of how their parents treated them. Fortunately (and unfortunately), you can almost always recognize shadows of your parents' behavior in your own. If you are domineering and tyrannical toward your partner, your children, or both, you can almost guarantee that this is the way you were treated as a child. If you are distant and aloof with your partner, you need only look to your parents for the reason.

Step Three: Begin to Let Down Your Defenses

If you are like most people with narcissistic traits, you have probably build up a fairly strong defense system to protect yourself from pain, doubt, and fear. Perhaps you learned early on in life that you couldn't depend on others, that you were essentially alone in the world. You may have had to toughen up after years of neglectful or abusive treatment from your parents or other caretakers. You may have determined early on that to reach your goals, you needed to block out all other distractions, including your own emotions. Only by looking behind these defenses will you be able to get to the roots of your problem and come to terms with your parents' abusive behavior.

To achieve success, recognition, financial gain, or adoration—prizes that people with NPD or with narcissistic tendencies value more than does the average person—you probably had to work hard. You had to keep your eye on the prize and not get distracted by other things (relationships, petty problems, your emotions, and the feelings of others). That kind of focus creates a certain kind of person, someone who doesn't give up easily, but also someone who doesn't reach out for help easily; someone who is tough, but perhaps a little too tough when it comes to his or her own feelings and the feelings of others.

Discovering that you have emotionally and possibly even psychologically damaged your partner, your children, or both, and that you have risked losing your family because of it has undoubtedly put a chink in your armor and caused you to feel more vulnerable than you are used to feeling. This crack in your facade can be the first glimpse you have to your real self. Ironically, your newly experienced vulnerability—the feeling that you are now exposed for all the world to see, that all your weaknesses are now visible—is the very thing that can save you. It is the very thing that will allow you to admit that you need help.

Step Four: Reach Out for Help

Narcissistic personality disorder is a serious psychological disorder that requires professional treatment. If you have a full-blown version of this disorder, you won't be able to recover without the help of a qualified psychotherapist. Treatment won't be easy because it will require you to admit that you have human failings like everyone else. It will require you to face the truth about how you have caused the people closest to you to suffer—namely, your partner and your children. You will also have to recognize your need for other people. At the same time you must realize that just because you need other people, it doesn't mean they will necessarily fulfill your needs. Most important, treatment will require you to once more experience the feelings of being a helpless and manipulated child who sustained considerable damage at the hands of selfish or unloving parents. You will need to begin to recognize the emptiness of a life compulsively controlled by the need for admiration and achievement.

As difficult and painful as the process is, however, the rewards are many. You will uncover your authentic self underneath your cold mask of superiority. You will gain the ability to feel compassion and empathy toward others and yourself. You will gain the ability to feel real, genuine gratitude toward others and toward life in general. And you will grow to appreciate leading an ordinary life, one with real joys and sorrows, not the false pleasures of a fantasy life filled with distorted mirrors.

My Personal Program for Overcoming Narcissistic Tendencies

It will take time to overcome your narcissistic tendencies and to reap the benefits of long-term therapy. In the meantime, you can begin to make some changes right now. The following suggestions are based on what worked for me and for many of my clients:

1. Catch yourself in the act when you begin to criticize your partner. Ask your partner to tell you each and every time he or she feels criticized, belittled, or made fun of, and then when your partner does so, thank her or him for the reminder. Realize that your need to criticize comes from either (a) your own self-hatred, (b) your need to push your partner away, or (c) your need to maintain control over your partner.

2. Instead of talking about yourself as often, start listening, really listening to your partner when he or she is talking. Ask more questions and take a real interest in what your partner has been doing. It will be difficult at first. You may find yourself bored or easily distracted. When this happens, you must will yourself to focus on what your partner is saying. You will undoubtedly slip back into monopolizing the conversation from time to time, but with continued effort you can make real changes that your partner will appreciate immensely.

3. Admit your need for people, especially your need for your partner and children. Notice how much better you feel when you and your partner are getting along and how wounded you feel when you don't feel included, acknowledged, and admired. Make the assumption that your partner and children probably feel the same way when you don't include, acknowledge, and admire them.

4. Instead of focusing only on your own needs, try focusing on the needs of others, particularly the needs of your partner and children. Think of ways to show them how much you appreciate them.

5. Ask your partner to tell you the ways that you have been abusive or hurtful, and really listen to this individual when he or she does. Ask your partner how your behavior affected him or her. Try putting yourself in your partner's place and imagine how it must have felt to be treated the way you have treated him or her.

6. Apologize to your partner for the way you have treated him or her in the past, and show your partner that you mean to make significant changes in your behavior.

7. Start appreciating the good things in your life, especially the good things your partner brings to your life. Begin to practice gratitude every day. For example, every morning, think of five things to be grateful for. Or at the end of the day, instead of keeping yourself awake by obsessing about your career or your looks, think back over the day and find at least five things to be grateful for.

PART IV

The Jekyll and Hyde within Us All

12

The Lessons of Jekyll and Hyde

Man is a little better than his reputation and a little worse.
    —Al Pacino

Evil in the human psyche comes from a failure to bring
together, to reconcile, the pieces of our experience. When
we embrace all that we are, even the evil, the evil in us is
transformed. When the diverse living energies of the
human system are harmonized, the present bloody face
of the world will be transformed into an image of the face
of God.
    —Andrew Bard Schmookler

We all have a little Jekyll and Hyde in us. We all try to partition off the parts of ourselves that we believe are unacceptable and undesirable. And we all find that the rejected and denied aspects of ourselves come back to haunt us in some way. Some of us become romantically involved with people who will act out our secret impulses and desires for us. Or we may think we can get away with leading dual lives, sneaking away to act out our more prurient interests while pretending to be pure and holy. Some of us find that our Shadows take over when we least expect it, causing us to act in ways that shock and appall even ourselves.

No matter how your personal duality has manifested itself, the way to wholeness must be a conscious effort on your part to take back those rejected, denied qualities, to embrace them and make them your own. Like little lost sheep, they must be brought back into the fold. Otherwise, you will find that your flock (your "self") will continue to diminish. For we are not full, complete human beings without our Shadows.

By owning our dark side, expressing our so-called negative emotions in constructive ways, and completing our unfinished business from the past, we can lessen the split inside us and become more integrated human beings.

If you are the victim of an abusive Jekyll and Hyde, I hope this book has given you the information you need to empower you to take better care of yourself, whether that means ending the relationship or setting firmer limits as to what you will put up with. If you are a Jekyll and Hyde, I hope you have learned enough from this book to encourage you to seek the help you need to become a more integrated person.

There are many lessons for us all in the story of Dr. Jekyll and Mr. Hyde. The primary lesson is that we need to redefine the concept of "good." For example, instead of thinking that being good means always being polite, caring, and selfless, as well as following all the rules and always thinking of others, I offer the following healthier concepts of "goodness":

- It's good to express our emotions.

- It's good to be ourselves.

- It's good to admit our imperfections.

- It's good to give up the goal of "goodness" for the goal of "wholeness."

There are many other lessons in learning to own our Shadow, including

1. There is no such thing as an "all-good" person. By coming to understand that no one is all good, we can begin to put less pressure on ourselves to be perfect. When we understand that we are all capable of committing selfish or cruel acts, we can be less judgmental of ourselves and others for making mistakes or behaving in uncharacteristic ways.

2. A rich vitality lies bottled up beneath our "acceptable" personalities, and only by finding and redeeming the wishes and traits that we chronically deny in ourselves can we move toward wholeness and healing. Exploring and owning our dark side will make us whole, transforming us not into monsters but into more empathetic, less judgmental human beings.

3. When we are detached from our dark side, we are also detached from the wonderful things our dark side offers us—passion, depth, creativity, sensuous pleasures, and a sense of humor. The dark side is a gold mine of depth, richness, substance, knowledge, creativity, insight, and power. As Carl Jung said, the dark side is 90 percent gold.

Jekyll's description of Hyde is characteristic of the human Shadow. Hyde's youthfulness suggests that as the Shadow personality of Jekyll, he contains unused energy. The human Shadow includes the unlived life, and to get in touch with the Shadow personality is to receive an infusion of new or youthful energy.

A right relationship with the Shadow offers us a great gift—it leads us back to our buried potential. Through *shadow-work*, a term Connie Zweig and Jeremiah Abrams coined to refer to the continuing effort to develop a creative relationship with the Shadow, we can

- Achieve a more genuine self-acceptance based on a more complete knowledge of who we are.

- Defuse the negative emotions that erupt unexpectedly in our daily lives.

- Feel more free of the guilt and the shame associated with our negative feelings and actions.

- Recognize the projections that color our opinions of others.

- Heal our relationships through more honest self-examination and direct communication.

- Use the creative imagination via dreams, drawing, writing, and rituals to own the disowned self.

So far, you have received merely a taste of what shadow-work can do by reading this book. I encourage you to continue exploring this powerful tool by reading some or all of the books on the Shadow that I recommend at the end of this book or by entering analysis with a Jungian psychologist or therapy with someone who has studied Jungian psychology.

I value your feedback and would appreciate hearing about how this book has affected you. I am also available for lectures and workshops. You can e-mail me at Beverly@beverlyengel.com or write to me at P.O. Box 6412, Los Osos, CA 93412-6412.

References

Unattributed quotes are from interviews conducted by the author.

Introduction

Stevenson, Robert Louis. *Dr. Jekyll and Mr. Hyde and Other Stories.* New York: Penguin, 1979.

1. What Is the Jekyll and Hyde Syndrome?

Crawford, Christina. *Mommie Dearest.* New York: W. Morrow, 1978.
Stevenson, Robert Louis. *Dr. Jekyll and Mr. Hyde and Other Stories.*

2. The Seven Types of Jekyll and Hydes

Bancroft, Lundy. *Why Does He Do That? Inside the Minds of Angry and Controlling Men.* New York: Berkley, 2002.
Lawson, Christine Ann. *Understanding the Borderline Mother: Helping Her Children Transcend the Intense, Unpredictable, and Volatile Relationship.* New York: Rowman & Littlefield Publishers, Inc., 2000.
Linehan, Marsha. *Cognitive-Behavioral Treatment of the Borderline Patient.* New York: Guilford, 1993.
Stevenson, Robert Louis. *Dr. Jekyll and Mr. Hyde and Other Stories.*

3. What Causes the Jekyll and Hyde Syndrome?

American Psychiatric Association. *Diagnostic and Statistical Manual of Mental Disorders,* 4th ed. Washington, DC: APA, 1994.
Kreisman, Jerold, and Hal Straus. *I Hate You, Don't Leave Me: Understanding the Borderline Personality.* Los Angeles: Price Stern Sloan, 1989.
Lawson, Christine Ann. *Understanding the Borderline Mother.*

Masterson, James. *The Search for the Real Self: Unmasking the Personality Disorder of Our Age*. New York: Free Press, 1988.

Stevenson, Robert Louis. *Dr. Jekyll and Mr. Hyde and Other Stories*.

Stout, Martha. *The Sociopath Next Door*. New York: Broadway, 2005.

4. How to Cope with a Jekyll and Hyde

Engel, Beverly. *The Emotionally Abusive Relationship: How to Stop Being Abused and How to Stop Abusing*. Hoboken, NJ: John Wiley & Sons, 2002.

5. Abusive or Illusive?

Engel, Beverly. *Breaking the Cycle of Abuse: How to Move beyond Your Past to Create an Abuse-Free Future*. Hoboken, NJ: John Wiley & Sons, 2005.

6. If the Jekyll and Hyde in Your Life Has a Personality Disorder

Golomb, Elan. *Trapped in the Mirror: Adult Children of Narcissists in Their Struggle for Self*. New York: W. Morrow, 1992.

Lawson, Christine Ann. *Understanding the Borderline Mother*.

Mason, R., and R. Kreger. *Stop Walking on Eggshells: When Someone You Love Has BPD*. Oakland, CA: New Harbinger, 1998.

Stout, Martha. *The Sociopath Next Door*.

8. How to Avoid Getting Involved with a Jekyll and Hyde in the Future

Golomb, Elan. *Trapped in the Mirror*.

Stout, Martha. *The Sociopath Next Door*.

Zweig, Connie, and Jeremiah Abrams. *Meeting the Shadow: The Hidden Power of the Dark Side of Human Nature*. New York: St. Martin's Press, 1991.

9. Confronting and Healing Your Jekyll and Hyde Behavior

Berendzen, Richard. *Come Here: A Man Overcomes the Tragic Aftermath of Childhood Sexual Abuse*. New York: Villard Books, 1993.

Jefferson, Margo. *On Michael Jackson*. New York: Pantheon Books, 2006.

Miller, William A. *Your Golden Shadow: Discovering and Fulfilling Your Undeveloped Self*. San Francisco: Harper & Row, 1989.

Stevenson, Robert Louis. *Dr. Jekyll and Mr. Hyde and Other Stories*.

Zweig, Connie, and Jeremiah Abrams. *Meeting the Shadow*.

10. If You Are an Abusive Jekyll and Hyde

Engel, Beverly. *Honor Your Anger: How Transforming Your Anger Style Can Change Your Life.* Hoboken, NJ: John Wiley & Sons, 2004.

Kaufman, Gershen. *Shame: The Power of Caring.* Cambridge, MA: Schenkman Publishing Co., 1980.

11. If You Have a Personality Disorder

Golomb, Elan. *Trapped in the Mirror.*

12. The Lessons of Jekyll and Hyde

Zweig, Connie, and Jeremiah Abrams. *Meeting the Shadow.*

Recommended Reading

Anger

Engel, Beverly. *Honor Your Anger: How Transforming Your Anger Style Can Change Your Life*. Hoboken, NJ: John Wiley & Sons, 2004.

Bipolar Disorder

Goodwin, F. K., and K. R. Jamison. *Manic-Depressive Illness*, New York: Oxford University Press, 1990.

Mondimore, Frank, *Bipolar Disorder: A Guide for Patients and Families*, Baltimore: Johns Hopkins University Press, 1999.

Borderline Personality Disorder

Cauwels, J. M. *Imbroglio: Rising to the Challenges of Borderline Personality Disorder*. New York: Norton, 1992.

Kreisman, Jerold, and Hal Straus. *I Hate You, Don't Leave Me: Understanding the Borderline Personality*. Los Angeles: Price Stern Sloan, 1989.

Lawson, Christine Ann. *Understanding the Borderline Mother: Helping Her Children Transcend the Intense, Unpredictable, and Volatile Relationship*. New York: Rowman and Little Publishers, Inc., 2000.

Linehan, Marsha. *Skills Training Manual for Borderline Personality Disorder*. New York: Guilford, 1993.

Mason, R., and R. Kreger. *Stop Walking on Eggshells: When Somebody You Love Has BPD*. Oakland, CA: New Harbinger, 1998.

Masterson, James. *The Search for the Real Self: Unmasking the Personality Disorders of Our Age*. New York: Free Press, 1988.

Moskovitz, R. *Lost in the Mirror: An Inside Look at Borderline Personality Disorder*. Dallas, TX: Taylor, 1996.

Tinman, Ozzie. *One Way Ticket to Kansas: Caring about Someone with Borderline Personality Disorder and Finding a Healthy You.* San Bernardino, CA: Bebes & Gregory Publications, 2005.

Boundaries

Katherine, Ann. *Boundaries: Where You End and I Begin.* New York: Hazelton, 1991.

Whitfield, Charles. *Boundaries and Relationships: Knowing, Protecting, and Enjoying the Self.* Deerfield Beach, FL: Health Communications, Inc., 1993.

Divorcing a Borderline or Narcissist

Eddy, William. *Splitting: Protecting Yourself While Divorcing a Borderline or Narcissist.* Milwaukee, WI: Eggshells Press, 2004.

Emotional Abuse

Engel, Beverly. *The Emotionally Abused Woman: Overcoming Destructive Patterns and Reclaiming Yourself.* Los Angeles: Lowell House, 1990.

———. *The Emotionally Abusive Relationship: How to Stop Being Abused and How to Stop Abusing.* Hoboken, NJ: John Wiley & Sons, 2002.

———. *Healing Your Emotional Self: A Powerful Program to Help You Raise Your Self-Esteem, Quiet Your Inner Critic, and Overcome Your Shame.* Hoboken, NJ: John Wiley & Sons, 2006.

Narcissism

Brown, Nina. *Children of the Self-Absorbed: A Grownup's Guide to Getting Over Narcissistic Parents.* Oakland, CA: New Harbinger, 2005.

Golomb, Elan. *Trapped in the Mirror: Adult Children of Narcissists in Their Struggle for Self.* New York: William Morrow, 1992.

The Shadow or Dark Side

Bly, Robert. *A Little Book of the Human Shadow.* New York: Harper & Row, 1988.

Miller, William A. *Your Golden Shadow: Discovering and Fulfilling Your Undeveloped Self.* San Francisco: Harper & Row, 1989.

Peck, M. Scott. *People of the Lie: The Hope for Healing Human Evil.* New York: Simon & Schuster, 1983.

Richo, David. *Shadow Dance: Liberating the Power and Creativity of Your Dark Side.* Boston: Shambhala, 1999.

Sanford, John A. *Evil: The Shadow Side of Reality*. New York: Crossroad, 1989.

Zweig, Connie, and Jeremiah Abrams. *Meeting the Shadow: The Hidden Power of the Dark Side of Human Nature*. Los Angeles: Tarcher, 1991.

Shame

Engel, Beverly. *Breaking the Cycle of Abuse: How to Move beyond Your Past to Create an Abuse-Free Future*. Hoboken, NJ: John Wiley & Sons, 2005.

Kaufman, Gershen. *Shame: The Power of Caring*. Cambridge, MA: Schenkman Publishing Co., 1980.

Sociopaths

Stout, Martha. *The Sociopath Next Door*. New York: Broadway, 2005.

Index